# Robert Benewick

*A Study of British Fascism*

# POLITICAL VIOLENCE & PUBLIC ORDER

Allen Lane The Penguin Press

Copyright © Robert Benewick, 1969
First published in 1969

Allen Lane The Penguin Press
Vigo Street London W1

Penquin Books Inc.
7110 Ambassador Road
Baltimore
Maryland 21207

SBN 7139 0085 7

Library of Congress Catalog
Card Number 77–81565

Designed by John Douet

Printed in Great Britain by
Latimer Trend & Co. Ltd Plymouth

# Contents

# List of Illustrations

# Acknowledgements

The idea for this book was conceived long before it was actually written. In 1955, while I was spending a year at the London School of Economics, Sir Oswald Mosley was invited to speak by one of the political societies. For two days large numbers of students turned from their more formal academic pursuits to debate whether the former British Fascist leader should be allowed a platform at the School. The issues were the right of free speech and whether someone should be granted the opportunity possibly to abuse that right. As it happened, the invitation was withdrawn. For me, it was representative of a fundamental dilemma of a stable democratic society. It also seemed important to explain why Fascism failed in Britain when it had taken its toll elsewhere. This, of course, raised questions fundamental to the political system and the political culture. To those students who posed these questions succinctly as well as dramatically, I am primarily indebted.

In my search for 'explanations' many who were active in the politics of the 1930s, as well as those who were knowledgeable about the period, kindly consented to discuss with me those issues which I considered important. These included John Beckett, Ted Bramley, Lord Brockway, A. K. Chesterton, Colin Cross, Dr Robert Forgan, Jeffrey Hamm, W. J. Leaper, the Rt Hon. Geoffrey Lloyd, Norman Mackenzie, Kingsley Martin, the late Lord Morrison of Lambeth, Sir Oswald Mosley, the late Hon. Sir Harold Nicolson, John Parker, M.P., Phil

ACKNOWLEDGEMENTS

Piratin, the late Harry Pollitt, the late Rt Hon. John Strachey and the Rt Hon. George Strauss, M.P.

I am also extremely grateful to A. H. Birch, Peter Campbell, Robert Dowse, S. E. Finer and W. J. M. Mackenzie, who have read earlier versions of this manuscript and whose comments and suggestions have proved most helpful. While much of my task has been to describe the excesses of British Fascism, Mrs Edna B. Gibson and Miss Joan Walton, of Hull University, coped admirably with the excesses of my handwriting to type the final draft of this manuscript.

I am further indebted to the following organizations and libraries whose collections and facilities were made available to me: the British Library of Political and Economic Science, the British Museum, the Board of Deputies of British Jews, the Bodleian, the Fabian Society, the Labour Party, Manchester Central Reference Library, Manchester University Library, the National Council of Civil Liberties, Odhams Press Cuttings Library, and the Wiener Library. The German Foreign Ministry provided its relevant papers and the Warden of St Antony's College, Oxford, secured those of the Italian Foreign Ministry.

Finally, to Anne Benewick, who shares with me this triumph of decency over Fascism and whose advice and comfort cannot be measured in words alone, I dedicate this book.

Sir Oswald Mosley's autobiography, *My Life*, was published after this book had gone to press. Since Mosley's work is largely an apologia, it does not alter the main themes of this volume. However, it has enabled me to make certain factual corrections.

# 1. The Political Setting

British politics in the 1930s were dominated by a world depression that led to mounting unemployment and by the growth and subsequent threat of Fascism on the European Continent. The career of Sir Oswald Mosley and the history of the British Union of Fascists focus on these two issues. It is obvious that Mosley did not have a monopoly on concern for the unemployed, but the turn to Fascism on the part of this talented politician was due in large part to the seeming inability of the British Government to deal imaginatively and effectively with the problem. Mosley's solution, the acceptance of his previously rejected proposals dressed up in a new vocabulary and enlarged upon by ideas borrowed from Fascist Italy, introduced Fascism as a serious doctrine and movement to the British political scene.

Its failure to take root in Britain is more than just a footnote in an important historical decade and more than simply an aspect of the politics of the depression for it raises questions fundamental to a democratic polity. It follows that this is not a biography of Sir Oswald Mosley, as important and fascinating as one might be, nor should it be taken as a description of a political party that failed, although the narrative must command most attention. It is a study of a political system the effectiveness of which seemed to have been declining and which was being called to account by some of its critics. Yet Britain resisted the attacks of its extreme movements, and unemployment was checked without radical economic reforms. In other words, what is involved is not just the questioning of a political system but the form that the questioning took and the response to it. Faced with conditions that contributed to crises in other Western industrialized societies, the British reaction was to explore ways of resolving the difficulties while maintaining the system, rather than to re-structure its economy and its political institutions.

The intention in this book is to describe how a movement which attempted to use political violence in an organized and systematic manner failed to emerge as a political force, and at the same time to demonstrate its considerable effect on public order and public policy. This does not deny Mosley's attempt to present a serious programme when he formed the B.U.F. nor that it was taken seriously in some quarters. He was articulating some genuine needs in a way likely to attract not only malcontents but some serious critics of British political institutions as well as of government policy. What he was up against was the same institutional and attitudinal resistance to reform that led him to Fascism in the first place.

The underlying argument then is that the introduction of Fascism was inappropriate and irrelevant in terms of British political development and that its chances for success were therefore remote. An attempt will be made to demonstrate this contention, but to provide an adequate explanation is too complex a proposition for the present undertaking. It would involve a detailed presentation of British political development and a survey of comparative political development.[1] It would also entail a study of what has begun to attract the attention of contemporary social scientists, that is, the political culture – the values, beliefs, attitudes and symbols that sustain a political system.[2] This is certainly an important variable in the political system but again it is beyond the scope of this study if only because there is little in the way of hard data to support the often acute and penetrating commentaries that exist for the period.

Given these qualifications a number of generalizations can be made in order to provide perspective. The B.U.F., unlike its Continental counterparts, attacked a political system the legitimacy of which had been established. The political forms were accepted, the political leaders respected and the political process, over time, effective. Perhaps one of the most outstanding features of the political system, and certainly of British political behaviour, has been the development of a style of politics that has been able to meet crisis, cope with stress and accommodate innovation in a relatively peaceful way. The Fascist political style, with its emphasis on revolution or counter-revolution, rather than continuity and evolution, and its search for order through political violence was alien to the traditions of British political life.

The establishment of legitimacy and the development of a distinctive national political style – what Edward Shils has called the politics of civility – interacts with and is dependent upon the beliefs and values held by most Englishmen.[3] Deference towards authority, an attitude masterfully illuminated by Bagehot, aspects of which have been substantiated empirically by recent research, is one example.[4] The relatively high value placed on trust verified by Almond and Verba is another.[5] As Shils has noted, deference is paid even when a government is distrusted. This is credited to its identification with a monarchical and aristocratic society.[6] Regardless of the emotions aroused during the abdication crises, for example, there was very little questioning of the nature of institutions. That there is a high regard for procedure and a respect for rules and the boundaries they impose for effective political action is shown by the significant support Mosley had for his criticisms of the Labour Government, particularly within the Parliamentary Labour Party, until he planned to desert the Labour movement to form another party.* A distinction can also be drawn between the legitimacy attached to the Jarrow marchers in their orderly

* There were, of course, other considerations such as loyalty to an important sub-culture, the Labour movement itself, and there were suggestions that pressure was put on some of those who were contemplating following Mosley out of the party.

procession to gain publicity for their plight and to the provocative posturings of the black-shirted B.U.F. demonstrators. It is one thing to draw attention to the shortcomings of government action and to demand reforms, or, in the case of the rise of the Labour movement, to demonstrate for the right of recognition and participation within the establishment; it is quite another to challenge a long-established form of government and the recognized procedures by which it rules.

These observations do not purport to minimize the facts that Mosley attracted a following, that the membership of the Communist Party increased during the 1930s or that there were hunger marches; but there was little evidence of a vast reservoir of people alienated from the political system from which extreme movements could recruit. At the same time, it would be wrong to underestimate the importance of a small politically active group since political activism in Britain, as distinct from electoral participation, is usually limited. Short of an institutional breakdown and the loss of governmental legitimacy, the numbers involved in extreme movements or demonstrative politics in Britain will be restricted. The quality of involvement and participation – whether it is moderate or extremist – is a test of the viability of a democratic system. This may suggest a pluralistic model of British politics.

Another preliminary consideration about the relevance of Fascism is that the British, at least up to this period, were socialized and recruited into politics on the basis of class. In other words, party loyalty was primarily, although not exclusively, based on class loyalty. One example of the ties of this loyalty is seen in the Labour Party's hold over its activists despite the disaffection of its leaders to the National Government. In that class grievances were being articulated by strong parties and, in the case of the working class by the trade unions as well, the Fascists were relegated to the periphery of political discourse. They were pre-empted from capitalizing on one of the divisive aspects of British society while their attacks on the cohesive features were not likely to cause large-scale disaffections.* If class defined much of the substance of British politics, it also contributed to the development of the confines of a political style, as witness the watered-down version of the General Strike of 1926.

The generalizations outlined above will remain just beneath the surface of the narrative. While suffering from over-simplification, they do suggest trends and factors, however tentative, working against the likelihood of a Fascist take-over. An interpretation of British politics that takes into account its political development and political culture with an emphasis on continuity and stability as basically antipathetical to Fascism can be taken as a defence of the *status quo*. It should be made clear that the *status quo* contributed to the rise of a Fascist movement, in the first place, which at the least intimidated and even tyrannized a sector of the British public.

Another question basic to a democratic polity arises: how does a government respond to extreme movements which may or may not pose a threat to the maintenance of a regime and at the same time protect its cherished liberties? This dilemma is treated at length in subsequent chapters. The concern is with street-corner politics in which the belligerents were restricted to politically conscious minority movements even if significant sectors of the general public were affected. This was in contrast to what took place in Italy and Germany where street warfare had been the prelude to political power, through constitutional channels, for both Fascists and National Socialists. The B.U.F.'s political style was tactically orientated towards violence, but Joseph Goebbels's dictum, 'Whoever conquers the street can also conquer the masses, and whoever conquers the masses thereby conquers the state', was inapplicable to Britain. Violence had, of course, played its part in British political development and it had by no means been played out, as the terrorism and brutalities that took place in Ireland just a little over a decade before testified. Moreover, although violence

* The B.U.F.'s approach was to appeal to all classes according to their assessment of the audience. In this they had a model in the Italian Fascist Party.

was deplored, there was a tacit expectation that it might occur, as indeed it does even in a civil society, but that it could be contained within the limits of public order.[7] But a deliberate and systematic effort to introduce violence into the national style of politics was out of order.

Initially the B.U.F.'s paramilitary organization, formed, in part, on the pretext of maintaining public order, was tolerated and even welcomed in some quarters. But an escalation of political violence led to public outrage, for the Blackshirts were challenging a public value. Even at the end of the 1930s, a decade marked by considerable disorder, Orwell was able to write that 'the gentleness of the English civilization is perhaps its most marked characteristic'.[8] Orwell's remark finds considerable support in the relative decorum with which political conflict was conducted in twentieth-century England as well as in the public reaction to the B.U.F.'s excesses. From the vantage point of history, further credence is given to the value of a non-violent political style when the racial difficulties of the 1950s and 1960s are considered. The Nottingham and Notting Hill riots in 1958, which compared to those in the United States during the 1960s seem trivial, were greeted by widespread public condemnation and severe penalties for the offenders. Mosley's parliamentary candidature in North Kensington in 1959, the scene of the Notting Hill riots the previous year, despite the articulation of some real grievances and the sometimes provocative behaviour of his followers, resulted in remarkably little disorder and in his losing his deposit.[9] Racialism was an issue in the General Election campaign of 1964 in at least six constituencies but was accompanied by a minimum of violence.[10]

The Government was reluctant to act in response to the B.U.F. until the limits of public toleration were exceeded. It did not legislate until the anti-Fascist opposition was mobilized to counter violence with violence – Mosley's original justification for B.U.F. tactics – thereby threatening street warfare that might cause widespread damage to persons and property. The Government's reluctance to act was presumably based on a fear of curbing political liberties and on what seems to have been a fairly accurate assessment of B.U.F. strength. It found some justification for its hesitation in that many of the former critics of government inaction were to be found among the critics of government legislation.

By the time the Public Order Act was in effect British Fascism was a spent force. The Act served to protect sectors of the public from abuse and intimidation. The political system was not at stake. It was the right of Englishmen to live decent and ordinary lives that had been threatened. The price paid to protect this right was an increase in the powers of the police – the problem was one of balance between liberty and order.

Anti-Communism and anti-Semitism were closely associated with the introduction of Fascist ideas, the creation of a para-military organization and the intentional, if not systematic, exploitation of violence. These two themes, which were often propagated in the name of patriotism – a third theme important to the B.U.F. – are singled out because the shift in emphasis from anti-Communism to anti-Semitism was not only indicative of a shift in the movement's fortunes but also followed an increase in political violence.

Sir William Hayter has commented that 'the non-Fascist right in England and Germany thought that Fascism would do their dirty work for them'.[11] Mosley, however, did not perceive his role as their agent. In so far as the Blackshirts were self-appointed protectors of the established order against the Communists, it was on their own terms. They did not intend to maintain the political system in its democratic form and they wanted to oust those who were running it who, by their identification with the system, were thereby corrupted.

Anti-Communism and anti-Socialism on the part of the British Fascists had a limited appeal to the traditional right short of an institutional breakdown. The intransigent opposition of the right to the Labour movement had been somewhat allayed by the experience of two Labour governments and the General Strike. Whatever fear of increased state power there may have been, allowing that the Conservative as well as the Labour

Party has a tradition of strong government, was as applicable to Fascism as to Socialism, and the charge of dictatorship applied to both Fascism and Communism.[12] A high price also had to be paid in that the Fascist theory of anti-Communism placed a premium on violence in order to demonstrate that a threat existed.

The B.U.F.'s adoption of an overt and militant anti-Semitic programme was the act of a desperate movement. It will be argued that there was little correlation between anti-Semitism and the loss of the B.U.F.'s upper-class and middle-class support as has been suggested elsewhere. Anti-Semitic overtones were apparent during the early stages of the movement's development so that discerning recruits and followers were warned of its possibility. More important, by the time that anti-Semitism was the dominant theme in the B.U.F. campaign, a large number of desertions had already taken place. This was mainly in reaction to the political violence which culminated at the Fascist demonstration at Olympia in June 1934.

What is crucial is that anti-Semitism failed to take root except in very limited circumstances.[13] The issue at stake is not one of discrimination or prejudice, but of organized behaviour and action. It is a matter of conjecture, however, whether the Blackshirts who succeeded in stirring up some racial hatred in East London made real converts or only prodded a latent anti-Semitism into action.[14]

A number of observations can be made which set the stage for the discussion to follow. The adoption of anti-Semitism occurred at a time when the B.U.F. could no longer be considered a serious threat or political force. The likelihood of political office and power had grown even more remote and Mosley seemed no longer interested in radical reform. His criticisms were directed less at institutions and policies and more at people. Second, Melvin Tumin, in reviewing a wealth of literature on anti-Semitism in the United States, noted the general agreement of the authors on the relationship between social conditions and anti-Semitism.[15] In Great Britain during the early 1930s, when the economic crisis had supposedly reached a peak, there was little evidence of ferment despite the presence of anti-Semitic groups. It is, however, important to recognize the peculiar nature of the depression in Britain whereby economic difficulties were experienced over a longer period so that there was never a crisis as sharp or severe as in other countries.[16] By the time that the B.U.F. concentrated its energies on an anti-Semitic campaign, economic conditions were improving. After Hitler came to power the Press devoted a great deal of space to critical accounts of the racialist aspects of the Nazi regime, which probably affected a portion of the readership.[17] Some American scholars have suggested that there is a correlation between anti-Semitism and weak democratic governments.[18] If this is the case, the relative stability of the British political system was not likely to encourage political anti-Semitism.

This study suggests two further questions in regard to anti-Semitism. There is the problem, related to the Public Order Act, of the extent to which a government should single out a minority for special protection. If an obligation does exist then it is necessary to ask what form this protection should take. This has particular relevance to the 1960s when political and electoral interests have sometimes dominated this debate rather than basic considerations of political liberty and social justice.

If ultimately the deck was stacked against a British Fascist movement, it still had a number of cards in hand. If in retrospect the economic crisis was not as severe as it was held to be at the time, distress, poverty and unemployment certainly existed and made it a time of great urgency for many political activists. Mosley and his henchmen had telling criticisms to make, no matter how erroneous their analysis or obnoxious their solutions. In Oswald Mosley the Fascists had an outstanding leader whose appeal reached charismatic dimensions. They had at their disposal reasonably sufficient resources in terms of money, talent and numbers to organize on a national basis. Thus members of the B.U.F. had ambitions as well as some expectations of obtaining political power either within the Parliamentary framework or after the collapse of the system in the event of an economic or military crisis.

An attempt has been made to suggest that the likelihood of a Fascist take-over was circumscribed, but this does not account for the actual failure of the B.U.F. nor indicate the extent of its effect on public order and public policy. In order to do so, the development of the B.U.F. will be traced. An attempt will be made to describe the interaction between changes in the economic and political setting, British Fascist ideology, the organization of the B.U.F. and its political style. Its impact will be measured by describing the effect of violence on public order, the extent to which there was organized opposition to the movement, the way in which the authorities responded and acted to prevent a breakdown in public order and the results achieved when Mosley submitted his version of Fascism to the test of the electoral process.

NOTES

1. For the development of 'conflict and consensus' in British society see Samuel H. Beer, *Modern British Politics* (1963); A. H. Birch, *Representative and Responsible Government* (1964); Stanley Rothman, 'Modernity and Tradition in Britain', *Social Research* (Autumn 1961), pp. 297–317; Bernard Crick, 'On Method and Matter', *Government and Opposition* (May 1966), pp. 414–21; for comparative political development see Reinhard Bendix, *Nation-Building and Citizenship* (1964); Barrington Moore Jr, *Social Origins of Dictatorship and Democracy* (1966).

2. See Beer, *op. cit.*; Samuel H. Beer 'The Analysis of Political Systems' in Beer and Adam H. Ulam (eds.), *Patterns of Government*, pp. 32–66; Gabriel A. Almond and Sidney Verba, *The Civic Culture* (1965 edn); Lucian W. Pye and Sidney Verba (eds.), *Political Culture and Political Development* (1965), Chapters 1, 3, 12.

3. See 'Ideology and Civility: On the Politics of the Intellectual', *Sewanee Review* (1958), pp. 450–80.

4. Walter Bagehot, *The English Constitution* (1963 edn); R. T. McKenzie and Allan Silver, 'Conservatism, Industrialism, and the Working-Class Tory in England' in Richard Rose (ed.), *Studies in British Politics* (1966), pp. 21–33; Eric Nordlinger, *The Working-Class Tories* (1967).

5. Almond and Verba, *op. cit.*, p. 213.

6. Edward A. Shils, *The Torment of Secrecy* (1956), p. 48.

7. For a discussion of gang warfare during the inter-war period which is seen as a part of a culture of poverty see T. R. Fyvel, *The Insecure Offenders* (1961), pp. 92 ff.; Sir Percy Sillitoe, *Cloak Without Dagger* (1955), Chapters VII, XIV.
8. The *Lion and the Unicorn* (1941, 1962), p. 15; see also Geoffrey Gorer, *Exploring English Character* (1955), pp. 286–7; Herbert Hyman, 'England and America: Climates of Tolerance and Intolerance' in Daniel Bell (ed.), *The Radical Right* (1964), pp. 269–306.
9. See Michael Kullmann, 'Notting Hill Hustings', *New Left Review* (January–February 1960), pp. 20–21; Keith Kyle, 'North Kensington' in David E. Butler and Richard Rose (eds.), *The British General Election of 1959* (1960), pp 173–85.
10. Nicholas Deakin (ed.), *Colour and the British Electorate* (1964).
11. Quoted by Eugen Weber in Hans Rogger and Eugen Weber (eds.), *The European Right* (1965, 1966), pp. 20–21.
12. See Beer, *op. cit.*, especially Chapter III.
13. For a cultural analysis see Howard Brotz, 'The Position of the Jews in English Society', *The Jewish Journal of Sociology* (April 1959), pp. 94–113. In summarizing his argument that anti-Semitism is relegated to the political fringes in England, Brotz writes, 'there is a remarkable wholeness to the fabric of the society which has its most visible manifestation in the public order which prevails'.
14. For a fictionalized account of East London life and the role of anti-Semitism see William Goldman, *East End My Cradle* (1940).
15. *An Inventory and Appraisal of Research on American Anti-Semitism* (1961), p. 153.
16. William Ashworth, *An Economic History of England 1870–1939* (1960), especially Chapter XVII; see also H. W. Richardson, *Economic Recovery in Britain 1932–1939* (1967).
17. See Andrew Sharf, *The British Press and Jews Under Nazi Rule* (1964); H. B. Gottlieb, *England and the Nazi Regime – Great Britain Opinion, 1933–1938* (Oxford, unpublished D.Phil. thesis, 1958).
18. Soloman A. Fineberg, 'Can Anti-Semitism be Outlawed?', *Contemporary Jewish Record* (1943), pp. 619–31; Marvin Fox, 'Three Approaches to the Jewish Problem', *Antioch Review* (March 1946), pp. 54–68; see also Tumin, *op. cit.*, p. 116.

# 2. Precursors

A few paramilitary organizations were formed in Great Britain prior to the founding of the British Union of Fascists in 1932. The British Brothers League was the first to attempt to organize on military lines in Great Britain during this century. Among the rest, the Ulster Volunteers were important, for the Blackshirts in an effort to legitimate Fascism in terms of British political experience claimed them as a forerunner to their own movement. The British Fascists were the first to use the label, while the National Fascisti was a more militant version of the British Fascists from which it broke away.

There were also numerous groups, in addition to the paramilitary organizations, that were propagating themes that were to become important in B.U.F. propaganda.[1] Militant nationalism was a sentiment of long standing and was common to all these groups as well as to the paramilitary organizations.* The British Empire Union and the National Citizens Union were typical of those groups for which anti-Communism, which was not restricted to the political right, was the predominant concern. The Britons were organized for the dissemination of anti-Semitic propaganda, while the racial anti-Semitism of

---

* Lady Houston, the wealthy, eccentric publisher of *The Saturday Review*, was an extreme example of how patriotism and the fear of Communism could lead to the support of Hitler and Mussolini. See *The Saturday Review*, 17 March 1934, 31 August 1935, 8 February 1936; see also *Chapter 9* below.

the Imperial Fascist League was more extreme than the B.U.F. brand.

These groups were interested in political propaganda rather than political power. The anti-Communist organizations were attitudinal or promotional groups in as far as they were espousing a cause, attempting to influence the Conservative Party and industry and trying to educate a sector of public opinion. They also had their spokesmen within the Conservative Party and in both Houses of Parliament. These groups, however, were the more militant and alienated elements of the Tory right in that they were preoccupied with what they regarded as a threat to stability rather than with Conservative principles and the direction in which the Conservative leaders were taking the party.

The Britons and the Ulster Volunteers were one-dimensional in their objectives. The former attempted to arouse public support for legislation to restrict immigration which the government was considering. The Ulster Volunteers were formed to resist home rule, by force if necessary. The Fascist and anti-Semitic organizations functioned in a twilight zone for they were not in a position to influence policy. Their target was the alienated sectors of public opinion. The British Fascists hoped to be utilized in the event of a general strike.

Although these bodies differed in their emphasis and approach, some of them showed characteristics which distinguished them from the B.U.F. (the Ulster Volunteers was a special case). Whereas the B.U.F. was potentially a revolutionary movement, these groups were dedicated to the preservation of the constitutional structure and, in effect, the maintenance of the *status quo*. The paramilitary organizations were willing to employ extra-parliamentary means but to defend rather than to overthrow the government. Although the B.U.F. was prepared to use parliamentary channels, it was in order to transform the political system. For the most part, these groups were not anti-democratic, although their conception of democracy was limited. Although some had legislative proposals, none was seriously interested in radical reform in the sense that

Sir Oswald Mosley was. Their membership and audiences were narrowly defined, while the B.U.F. was opportunistic in its appeals. With the exception of the Ulster Volunteers, they did not pose a threat to public order nor were they interested in the systematic application of violence. Finally their political impact was slight although the Ulster Volunteers, like the B.U.F., possessed significant potential.

What they had in common with the B.U.F. was an alertness to crisis, for these groups were operative in times of stress and strain. They shared many of the same fears and frustrations of the later movement and showed the same lack of knowledge, patience and understanding of the political system, thereby excluding themselves from the mainstream of political life. They were important in that they contributed to a climate of opinion receptive to Fascist ideas. The paramilitary organizations provided a posture of violence, while the anti-Communist and anti-Semitic groups pointed out targets.

## PARAMILITARY ORGANIZATIONS

A way in which the B.U.F. attempted to gain legitimacy was by claiming British origins and constructing a British Fascist tradition. W. E. D. Allen, the former Conservative m.p. for Belfast West and one of Mosley's early lieutenants, undertook the task and, given his background, seized upon the Ulster Volunteers. Writing under the name of James Drennan he assigned to Sir Edward Carson the role of leader of the first Fascist movement in Europe.[2] This was not a particularly new notion. Lenin, for example, in 1914, had labelled the Volunteers 'aristocrats' behaving like revolutionaries of the right.[3] Interestingly enough, however, the Blackshirts made no mention of the Irish Volunteers who formed in opposition to the Ulster Volunteer Force and were modelled on it.

Allen argued that the Ulster Volunteers, although psychologically restricted and limited in objectives, 'would have developed, had not the war intervened, into a definite revolt against the whole theory and system of democracy in Britain'.[4]

Sir Edward Carson and the Ulster Volunteers were thereafter raised onto a Fascist pedestal and Allen's argument was reprinted in various forms.[5] William Joyce compared Carson with Mosley as being the only other man in twentieth-century British politics to be regarded as a hero and proclaimed as such by his followers. Carson was described as a Fascist in 'bearing, will, act and thought', and the Ulster Volunteer movement was more than a precursor to Fascism in Europe. 'It was,' according to Joyce, 'the first real tangible resistance that Liberal Plutocracy had to encounter in Britain. . . .'[6]

This was twisting the facts to fit the interpretation. The Ulster Volunteers were a paramilitary organization formed to intimidate the government and to defy it, by force if necessary, in the event of home rule. However unjustifiable or unconstitutional the methods, its purpose was not to transform a political system into a dictatorship.* The fact that the Ulster Volunteers were organized on a military basis did not make them Fascist. The difficulty of such a definition was that it labelled all rebels Fascist and all rebellions Fascistic. What the Ulster Volunteers did represent was a 'national' movement *par excellence*, which the British right had traditionally claimed to be.[7]

The B.U.F. historians failed to discover the British Brothers League, which was founded in 1902. Its activities were confined to East London, where waves of immigrants from Eastern Europe, a large number of whom were Jewish, had arrived after 1880 and aroused enough resentment to become a political issue of some importance.[8] In 1888 the House of Commons appointed a Select Committee on Immigration and in 1894 the Marquis of Salisbury, Leader of the Opposition in the House of Lords, introduced restrictive legislation, part of which was passed by the House of Lords in 1898, but was not introduced into the House of Commons. In 1902 a Royal Commission was appointed, and by 1905 an Aliens Act was in effect.

---

* An anomaly in the law permitted two Justices of the Peace to authorize drilling within the area of their jurisdiction to maintain the British constitution and to protect its guarantee of rights and liberties. A. T. Q. Stewart, *The Ulster Crisis* (1967), p. 69 *passim*.

In January 1902, Major W. Evans-Gordon, the Conservative M.P. for Stepney, moved an amendment to the Address, calling for legislation to restrict the immigration of destitute aliens. During the same month, the British Brothers League was founded by a Captain William Stanley Shaw, and there was close cooperation between the League and Major Gordon. The League appealed for restricted immigration under the motto of 'England for the English', and Major Gordon stood for re-election in 1906 with the slogan, 'England for the English and Major Gordon for Stepney'. The League was not, at first, anti-Semitic and was only interested in the exclusion of destitute aliens. Nor did it advocate the deportation of aliens already in England. Perhaps it was inevitable that the League would broaden its attack and resort to anti-Semitism. Before the Royal Commission, the Chairman of the League assured his questioners about the limitations of their objectives.[9] Yet four days earlier, the former vice-chairman of the League blamed the Jews for most of the troubles of East London.[10]

The League's military organization was not highly developed, and its anti-Semitism only took hold after the resignation of Shaw. It maintained that it had no paid officials and that subscriptions were voluntary. Anyone who signed its manifesto was claimed a member, and the League boasted over 45,000 signatures.[11] A number of prominent people, including Members of Parliament, L.C.C. Councillors and clergy supported the League.[12] The principal honorary member was Colonel Sir Howard Vincent, the Conservative M.P. for Central Sheffield, and former Director of Criminal Investigations, Metropolitan Police. Vincent, with others, had introduced a bill in Parliament dealing with the power of excluding and deporting criminal aliens.

The League functioned as a promotional group having only one cause, but it was not alone in its cause. Indeed, many liberal and left-wing observers blamed the immigrants in general, and the Jews in particular, for what was deemed an unsatisfactory state of affairs.[13] The East End during this period was blanketed with anti-alien and anti-Semitic propaganda. If the evidence given before the Royal Commission can be taken for a guide, the propaganda had no little success in arousing the hostilities and resentment of the residents of East London. The Alien Bill was popular even outside the area, and the fact that the Jews were one of the butts of the music-hall comedians did not help matters. But East London at the turn of the century was in any case a sordid and destitute area. It had high rates of unemployment and crime, overcrowded housing conditions, and poor sanitation. An exotic and poor people had been added to these conditions.

The first organization to call itself Fascist and to acknowledge Italy as the source of its inspiration was the British Fascisti. It was founded in May 1923, by the twenty-six-year-old Miss R. L. Lintorn-Orman, the daughter of a major and the grand-daughter of a field-marshal. Later, the name was changed to the British Fascists, in order to avoid the charges that it owed loyalty to a foreign power, and that it was receiving support from abroad.

The policy of the British Fascists can be traced through three phases. During the first phase, from the organization's inception until its split over the General Strike, the British Fascists were little more than a militant version of the anti-Communist groups discussed below. In the second phase, an attempt was made to formulate a positive political programme. Solutions were offered, although not particularly radical ones, for what were felt to be the shortcomings in the economy and the government. Finally, in the 1930s, a straightforward Fascist policy modelled on Italy was adopted.

At first, the British Fascists viewed Fascism as the adult growth of the Scout movement.[14] According to their president, Brigadier-General R. B. D. Blakeney, both the Fascist and the Scout movements upheld the ideals of brotherhood, service and duty. He acknowledged Italy as the birthplace of Fascism, but maintained that the movement was world-wide with each nation interpreting it in its own way.[15] The goals of the British Fascists were to 'revive the spirit of sane and intelligent patriotism, uphold the established constitution and prevent the spread of Bolshevism and Communism'.[16] Communism was Fascism's chief enemy, followed by the 'alien menace' and 'International Finance'. Trusts and trade unions were the main weapons of the Communists but they were also infiltrating the armed services, the civil service, and the educational system. Moreover, they were working throughout the Empire to turn the coloured races against the whites. According to Blakeney, the possibility of modern inventions like the wireless and the cinema falling into 'the hands of men of alien race' presented the most sinister danger of all.[17]

The British Fascists were prepared to counter these forces to prevent them from utilizing the 'swarms from the slums'. Blakeney announced that the organization would be at the disposal of the authorities when needed. Meanwhile, its members would campaign for a ban on immigration and for a fair day's work for a fair day's pay.[18] It attempted to put its principles into practice by offering its services to the Government during the labour unrest in the winter and spring of 1924. The British Fascists wrote to the Home Secretary, Arthur Henderson, stating that, although the movement was not a strikebreaking organization, it would be willing to provide relays of 300 men to assist the authorities in the prevention of violence and intimidation.[19] The British Fascists rationalized their offer of aid to a Labour Government by announcing their willingness to support any 'loyal' government.[20]

Hence, there was little Fascist content in the original doctrine of the British Fascists. Its militancy was designed to defend the established institutions, not to overthrow them. In terms of goals and motivations, it was strikingly similar to the National Citizens' Union and, like the latter, provided a model for the Organization for the Maintenance of Supplies.

The formation of the O.M.S. not only stole the thunder of the British Fascists, but left the organization badly split. After the General Strike, the Fascists attempted to formulate a more concrete programme. Loyalties and animosities remained intact and the primary purpose was still the maintenance of a disciplined organization in the event of an emergency. But they also claimed to be, in effect, a political party seeking to elect British Fascists to public bodies to insist that there should be the strictest economy in the use of public funds. Although they still disclaimed any connection with Italian Fascism, they paid tribute to it, acknowledged its inspiration and, in fact, began to advocate some of its principles.[21] Nesta Webster, the author of several pseudo-histories obsessed with Communism, Judaism and the 'alien menace', argued that although it was not necessary for British Fascism to develop along the same lines as in Italy, if 'Heaven sent the man needed as in Italy then there would be thanksgivings'. However, it was not as essential as in Italy, for the leadership of the British Fascists was invested in a group of 'patriots'.[22] In the most militant, although perhaps not the officially adopted statement of principles during this period, the state was advocated as the centre around which all things revolved. Yet there would be no need for dictatorship, except in the event of 'absolute anarchy' or 'revolution'.[23]

The British Fascists' programme for political reform included the advocacy of a strong and efficient second chamber, raising the voting age to twenty-five, the disfranchisement of those convicted of sedition and of those in receipt of poor law relief for six consecutive months. Civil servants and parliamentary candidates would have to be of 'British birth and race'. A large part of the programme was devoted to trade-union reforms. Strikes and lock-outs were to be declared illegal. Compulsory arbitration courts were to be established and utilized in the event of a breakdown in negotiations. The Fascists proposed to outlaw trade-union alliances, substitute the secret ballot for the card vote and place employer associations on the same footing as trade unions.[24]

An outright Fascist programme was finally adopted in the 1930s. In 1931 the establishment of Fascist guilds and corporations was called for and in the summer of 1932 a twenty-four-point programme was published. The party system was to be replaced by the corporate state. Class barriers would be destroyed, and there would be a new aristocracy based on merit, character and work. Large-scale social, economic, and financial reforms would be undertaken. Jews and aliens would be barred from public posts, from voting and from 'controlling' the financial, political, industrial, and cultural interests of Great Britain. The armed forces would be increased, treaties which bound Great Britain to armed intervention on behalf of others repudiated, and British rule over the Empire and colonies firmly demonstrated.[25]

This forthright Fascist policy was less the result of the economic crisis than of the state of the British Fascists. By the summer of 1932 they had lost much of their financial and numerical support, and only a small hard core of members remained.

The British Fascists had pretensions to military organization and discipline.[26] At the apex of a hierarchy was an Executive Council, renamed the Headquarters Committee in 1924, and a larger Grand Council. Structurally the organization was then divided into three to five sections. Section I was the infantry, which was based on units of seven members or less under a leader. The units were to act on their own initiative, except in the event of an emergency. Their primary purpose was to counter the revolutionaries. In the event of it becoming necessary to man the barricades, units would be combined to form troops, companies and divisions.

The cavalry or transport section included owner-drivers, cyclists and drivers of horse-drawn vehicles. It was to maintain communications in the event of 'revolution'. The propaganda and publicity section was responsible for meetings and the publication of *The British Lion*. The purpose of the intelligence section was to inform the units of Communist activity overlooked, and counter-activity neglected. The duties of the 'Special' section were undefined and probably unperformed.

The membership was further divided into two categories: the flying squads and the reserves: the actives and the inactives. According to General Blakeney, there were 'flying squads' of young unmarried men, who were prepared to go anywhere and do anything. The reserves were composed of older men, who would garrison captured points and perform the duties of stationary guards. A second distinction was between active and inactive members, based on the monthly subscription. All members paid an initial subscription of 2s. 6d. Active members contributed 6s. a month, while inactive members were obligated to pay 1s. a month.

Geographically, the organization of the British Fascists was based on the county, which was sub-divided into district areas to which the units were attached. Reports of their activities appeared regularly in the movement's periodicals. The Camberwell District published its own bulletin in which it advertised a 'miniature rifle club', and gave the address of the local Communist Party headquarters, along with the name of the secretary, and details of their meetings.[27]

Uniforms and symbols were, at first, essentially patriotic. Meetings were decorated with Union Jacks and members wore badges, but they also gave the Italian Fascist salute. By 1927 the Blue Shirt had been adopted as the official uniform to be worn on parade. In the 1930s the beret and dark trousers or skirts were added to the Blue Shirts. *British Fascism*, the new journal, published pictures of the movement's women's units on parade in full dress.

The British Fascists made extravagant claims about the size of its membership.[28] According to the Earl of Feversham for the Home Office, the British Fascists at their inception had gained a 'fair' number of adherents. It was believed that the membership dwindled to about 300 in 1934.[29] Ten years earlier, when the organization was at its peak, its members probably numbered only a few thousand. It did not attempt to attract a mass following; it was largely a middle-class movement competing with numerous anti-Communist organizations. It was also plagued by frequent schisms and internal difficulties, which continually reduced the membership. In the autumn of 1924, the more militant elements broke away and formed the National Fascisti to pursue positive Fascism as distinct from negative anti-Communism.[30] In the spring of 1926, the top leadership left to cooperate with the Organization for the Maintenance of Supplies. In September 1927, four of the leaders, including the editor of *The British Lion*, were dismissed, and three months later twenty-two members in Birmingham were expelled for 'unreliability'. A major split occurred at the time of the formation of the B.U.F., and several members either went over to the new movement, or deserted the cause for good. Finally, the revolution never materialized. The General Strike was a failure and the Conservatives were successful in enacting the Trade Disputes Act. The second Labour Government was a cautious one, and a National Government was formed. Meanwhile, the B.U.F. was founded with greater resources and talents to exploit the economic situation.

The leaders and the prominent members of the British Fascists were retired military officers, right-wing Conservatives, obscure peers, and 'public-spirited' women. The first president was Lord Garvagh, who resigned in January 1924, for the stated reason that he lived too far from London to exercise sufficient authority.[31] Lord Garvagh was succeeded by Brigadier-General Blakeney, who was also appointed editor of the movement's original periodical, *The Fascist Week*. Blakeney had been deputy general manager of the Egyptian State Railway from 1906 to 1919 and general manager from 1919 to 1923. The Headquarters Committee included Miss Rotha Lintorn-Orman, Mrs Blanch L. Lintorn-Orman, the Earl of Glasgow, who was in charge of the Scottish Units, the Rt Hon. Arthur Hardinge, who was appointed treasurer in May 1926, Lord Ernest Hamilton, Brigadier-General Sir Ormonde Winter, who was in charge of the London area, and Colonel Sir Charles Burn. The Earl of Glasgow's anti-Communism was to take him on visits to Mussolini, Hitler and Franco. He soon became disenchanted as a result of the excesses of the first two and even entertained the exiled Emperor Haile Selassie.[32] Hardinge was a Fellow of All Souls and had been Ambassador to Spain from 1913 to 1919. He was a first cousin of Lord Hardinge of Penshurst, the first president of the O.M.S. Hamilton was the sixth son of the Duke of Abercorn and a well-known author. Winter had been Deputy Chief of Police and Director of Intelligence in Ireland from 1920 to 1922, and Director of Resettlement, Irish Office, in 1922.

Burn was the Conservative M.P. for Torquay from 1910 to 1923 and assumed the title of Forbes-Leith of Fyvie in 1925 under the terms of the will of his father-in-law, Baron Leith, a former president of the British Empire Union. The other members included two women, a lieutenant-colonel, a major, a stockbroker, an advertising and publicity agent, and a farmer. The vice-president, Rear-Admiral A. E. Armstrong, was not a member of the Committee. Two later recruits to the Committee were Nesta Webster and Paymaster Rear-Admiral W. E. R. Martin.

Local officers included Admiral Sir Reginald Tupper at Liss, Major-General T. D. Pilcher in London, Brigadier-General R. A. Carruthers at Camberley, Sir Michael Bruce, Brigadier-General S. Geoghegan and Brigadier-General J. Tyndale-Biscoe at Bournemouth, the Reverend K. L. Kempthorne at Falmouth, and Brigadier-General E. P. Sevecold at Derby. Among those claimed as early members and supporters were Sir Burton Chadwick, M.P., head of a firm of Liverpool shipowners and Parliamentary Secretary to the Board of Trade, 1924-8, the Earl Temple of Stowe, Viscount and Viscountess Downe, later of the B.U.F., Lord De Clifford, Lord Langford and Sir Gerald du Maurier. Retired Services personnel included the Hon. Sir Admiral Edmund Fremantle, who had written numerous books on naval subjects, Admiral Richard Hyde, General E. W. Appleby, General J. Spens, Major-General C. B. Knowles, Major-General Sir Francis Mulchay, and Brigadier-General G. Soady.

After the General Strike, the prominent supporters of the British Fascists tended to drift away. Nevertheless, the organization continued to attract titled recruits.

The organized public activities of the British Fascists included holding meetings – although it held only one sizeable demonstration in Trafalgar Square – publishing, and occasionally stewarding meetings for Conservative M.P.s. The organization gained a certain degree of notoriety as a result of the pranks of its members. They were a nuisance rather than a menace, although their early exploits prompted *The Manchester*

*Guardian* to comment that they were a more serious menace to public order than the Communists, whose activities had become an obsession with the Home Secretary.[33] The kidnapping of Harry Pollitt, then the general secretary of the National Minority Movement, outraged some and amused others. In March 1925, Pollitt was taken from a train on his way to Liverpool where he was to address a conference of the Minority Movement. The publicity value of the kidnapping was worth more than a dozen speeches or demonstrations to both organizations. Pollitt maintained that he had not gone directly to the police for that reason. Five British Fascists were arrested and charged with unlawfully conspiring to assault, and with unlawfully imprisoning Pollitt against his will. The five were found not guilty and discharged. The defence was simply that they had planned to take Pollitt away for a pleasant little week-end, and that they thought it would be a good joke. They also accused Pollitt of accepting £5 for expenses. Although the accuracy of the accusation was irrelevant, it had its effect. The judge's summary was admirably fair, but the jury acquitted the five defendants.[34]

The other activities of the British Fascists were even more innocuous. Some minor street clashes with the Communists took place. Threatening letters were sent to Labour leaders. One letter to A. J. Cook, the miners' leader, warned that his 'fate would be far worse than Matteotti's'.[35] In 1925, a British Fascist spoofed *The Daily Mail* with a forgery, purporting to show that the British Communist Party was arming. Some stir was created by an announcement of the alleged intention of the Liverpool authorities to enlist two or three thousand British Fascists in the event of a General Strike. The movement supported Commander Locker-Lampson, Conservative M.P. for the Handsworth constituency of Birmingham, in his 'Keep out the Reds' campaign by publicity work, the stewarding of his meetings, and by providing him with a platform on occasion. The British Fascists started a few children's clubs in an effort to counteract Communist Sunday schools. In 1932, it offered to send 500 men to the aid of the Bolivian Government in its dispute with Paraguay. This was sheer bravado for no one knew from where the men would come. The Bolivian Government politely expressed 'Its warm appreciation of this gallant offer'.[36]

The dispute, which arose over what action should be taken in the event of a General Strike, resulted in a split in the Headquarters Committee, and ended the likelihood of the British Fascists ever developing into a serious Fascist movement. General Blakeney, Rear-Admiral Armstrong, and four other members of the Committee resigned and formed the Loyalists.

The immediate issue was whether to cooperate with the Organization for the Maintenance of Supplies. Since the O.M.S. had repeatedly asserted that it was non-political, the Fascists would have had to change their name and register under the O.M.S. It was also claimed that they had received an offer of financial assistance if they changed their name, abandoned their military structure and altered their manifesto.[37] According to Miss Lintorn-Orman, the Grand Council defeated the proposal by a vote of forty to thirty-two.[38] Blakeney and Armstrong denied this.[39] In a broadsheet addressed to the British Fascists, they claimed that the membership of the Fascists was insufficient to obtain the desired ends and that the Conservative victory in the General Election had sapped their strength. Moreover, the name 'Fascist', and their exploits, along with those of the National Fascisti were insuperable barriers to the further solicitation of funds. Finally, they maintained that it was necessary to cooperate with other patriotic bodies to meet the 'coming crisis', and the O.M.S. was acceptable to the authorities.[40] In a statement issued to the Press Blakeney and Armstrong dealt directly with the split in opinion within the British Fascists and the attitude of the authorities, namely the Home Secretary. The 'moderates', they claimed, objected to the militants' use of military titles, and to the willingness to resort to unconstitutional action.[41]

At the same time as Blakeney and Armstrong formed the Loyalists, which were incorporated into the O.M.S. and utilized during the General Strike, the Earl of Glasgow reorganized the Scottish Units under the title of the Scottish Loyalists. One month later the women's units of the British Fascists in Scotland were reorganized under the title of the Scottish Women's Loyalists by a former vice-president of the women's units. The formation of the Loyalists by the moderate elements within the British Fascists dealt the decisive blow. Individual members of the British Fascists helped during the General Strike, but the organization was moribund, although it formally survived until 1935. The company's registration showed that subscriptions and contributions decreased from £6,848 in 1925 to £604 in 1928, and averaged approximately £330 a year over the following five years.[42]

Negotiations between the British Fascists and Mosley's supporters took place prior to the formation of the B.U.F. The negotiations failed, but the effective membership of the British Fascists did go over to the B.U.F. These included three members of the Headquarters Committee: Lieutenant-Colonel H. W. Johnson, who had been in charge of the men's units; E. G. Mandeville Roe, a young schoolmaster and advocate of the Corporate State; and Neil Francis-Hawkins, who became the Director-General of Organization of the B.U.F.

The short-lived National Fascisti were more obscure, although they did attract a certain degree of publicity.* The movement was not large in numbers, and for the most part its activities were restricted to London. Even during the General Strike, it had only a few hundred members.[43] In some ways, however, it had greater pretensions towards being a Fascist movement. The black shirt was adopted at its inception and the National Fascisti, utilizing the prevalent Fascist myths and symbols, adopted the fasces and axe as an emblem. There was even some evidence of military drilling. Moreover, the membership, limited as it was, had a broader base than the anti-Communist groups and the British Fascists, in that it included a thuggish element.

According to the first president, L. A. Howard, the split with

* In 1925, probably as a result of financial difficulties, they were reconstituted the British National Fascisti under the leadership of Lieutenant-Colonel H. Rippon-Seymour. See *John Bull*, 5 March 1927.

the British Fascists was inevitable because the National Fascisti wanted deeds instead of words.[22] Its motto was, 'Hats off to the Past – Coats off to the Future'. During its more violent moments it issued such statements as:

We are anti-Socialist, anti-Communist, and anti-Jewish. . . .
Ours is a broad, national policy of country before self. . . .
We are out to smash the reds and the pinks.[45]

While a 'Fascist Guard' told a reporter:

We keep up boxing practice to be fit for meeting the Communists. We are sworn to tear down the Red Flag wherever we see it.[46]

The programme of the Fascisti was vague and undefined, and contained many of the myths associated with Fascism.[47] Communist and Socialist agitators were to be eliminated from factories, although it was never explained how this would be done. The National Fascisti advocated the suppression of 'revolutionary' speakers and 'seditious papers'. The revision of the Alien Act and the naturalization laws was demanded. Trade licences for aliens and the establishment of an alien-tribunal were considered necessary.[48] It was more outspoken in its anti-Semitism than the parent organization. According to its conspiracy theory, the Socialist Party and the Communist Party were 'Jew-inspired' and financed by Jewish capitalists.

The National Fascisti stood for the maintenance of the monarchy, and the preservation of the Empire with closer ties and greater preferences. Individual enterprise was to be encouraged and developed. But for the most part its economic and social policy was never clarified, and remained indistinguishable from the policies of the anti-Communist groups. Its goal was the development of a 'truly national spirit'. The National Fascisti denied any intention to substitute a dictatorship in place of Parliament. Instead, it sought to establish a government of experts and a governing executive of men of British birth and breeding with the will and power to govern.

Like its parent movement, pranks dominated the activities of the National Fascisti. A minor incident of hooliganism attracted public attention as a result of the Government's handling of the court case. Four members of the National Fascisti 'captured' a *Daily Herald* delivery van in October 1925, and crashed it into the railings of a London church. They were eventually arrested and charged with larceny, but the Public Prosecutor reduced the charge in court to committing a breach of the peace, on the grounds of insufficient evidence to sustain the original charge. The magistrate, in binding the defendants over to keep the peace in the sum of £100 each, commented that the Public Prosecutor had been extremely lenient in the matter. The Public Prosecutor had stated that 'All of them appreciated that their conduct was not what it should have been, however meritorious it might have been from another point of view'.[49] This occurred against the background of the trial of the twelve Communist leaders, who had been charged under the Incitement to Mutiny Act of 1797, for seditious libel and incitement to mutiny. Angry protests broke out in the Labour and Liberal Press asking what would have happened if it had been a *Morning Post* van. George Bernard Shaw caustically commented:

It seems to me that a mere withdrawal of the charge against these gentlemen was, after all, a very poor acknowledgement of their services to the Government; I think they might at least be given the O.B.E. at the first opportunity. . . .[50]

Oswald Mosley, a recent convert to the Labour Party, called it a public scandal and one of the most shameful acts of injustice that the country had ever known.[51] A brief storm arose in the House of Commons, where the Attorney-General had to defend the action. It was learned that the Public Prosecutor had consulted him on withdrawing the charges.[52]

The influence of the British Fascists and the National Fascisti on public order, policy and opinion, was negligible. The public, for the most part, was unaware of their existence, and those who did know of their activities ignored them. The political forces on neither the right nor the left took them seriously. The public authorities regarded them as a nuisance. The Assistant Commissioner of the Metropolitan Police described them as an 'intolerable nuisance' and not only valueless, but a menace to the country. He condemned them for taking the law into their own hands in the 'sacred name of patriotism'.[53]

## ANTI-COMMUNISM

The British Empire Union was an outgrowth of the Anti-German Union founded in 1915. Its primary purpose was to counter Communist propaganda, and to counter the extremists in the Socialist and Labour movements, which by its definition were revolutionary and Communist. The remarks of the vice-chairman, Sir Ernest Wild, Conservative M.P. for Upton, who chaired the 1920 conference, were typical. In announcing the decision of Sir Edward Carson to accept the presidency of the British Empire Union, he stated:

. . . and now that the British Empire Union had got him as their President they would go on from strength to strength in their fight against anarchy and Bolshevism and all pernicious forms of Internationalism.[54]

The British Empire Union formed an industrial peace department to carry out propaganda in industrial areas. It sought the assistance of employers and their organizations to cooperate with 'Labour' in the removal of grievances by promoting profit-sharing schemes, encouraging high wages based on production, and in other ways as in the United States.[55] It advocated that employers should interest workers in the affairs of their trade unions, and that businessmen should take an active interest in the lives of their employees. Businessmen, however, should work for revision of the Trade Disputes Act of 1906, the abolition of 'terrorism and despotism', and of the 'so-called peaceful picketing'.[56]

The Union's anti-alien attitude seems to have been a hangover from the Anti-German Union era. Its publications were headed by the inscription, 'The British Empire Union for British Influences, British Labour, British Goods – Britain for the British'. Traces of anti-Semitism were to be found, but were incidental rather than deliberate.[57]

39

The membership of the British Empire Union was formidable. The Presidents from 1919 to 1922 were Lord Leith of Fyvie, Sir Edward Carson, the Earl of Derby, and Stanley Machin. Carson resigned when appointed Lord of Appeal. In 1920, its members included J. C. Gould, M.P., chairman; Sir J. S. Harmood-Banner, M.P., treasurer; Lord Morris of St Johns, the Duke of Somerset, the Duke of Northumberland, the Earl of Bradford, the Earl of Harewood, the Earl of Plymouth, Lord Dunleath, Lord Iveagh, Sir John Hewitt, Viscount Astor, Viscount Midleton, Brigadier-General Henry Page Croft, M.P., J. H. Havelock-Wilson, M.P., and over 100 other M.P.S.

The Empire Union continued to wage an anti-Communist campaign during the 1930s and also attacked Fascism which it identified with Communism. For a short period the British Empire Union along with the National Citizens Union and other right-wing organizations cooperated with Captain A. H. M. Ramsey, M.P., who was later detained under Defence Regulations, to present a united front against Communism. Ramsey, however, attacked their publication, *Empire Record*, as being anti-German, and in turn the Union refused to tolerate his anti-Semitism.[58] The Empire Union also flirted with the B.U.F. According to the *Empire Record*, the Union agreed with much in Mosley's policy, especially as applied to the Throne and the Empire, but rejected the proposal to abolish parliamentary institutions. It did not oppose the Fascists, however. The Black-shirt speakers, on the other hand, abused the British Empire Union from the platform. A meeting was arranged between the two organizations, where two officers of the B.U.F. promised to correct the situation. The attacks continued.[59]

The Middle Classes' Union was founded in 1919 and later became the National Citizens' Union. In one respect it was a rival of the Organization for the Maintenance of Supplies. It was not opposed to strikes as such, but declared the 'right of self-preservation', and was organized to maintain essential public services in case of an emergency. By 1923 it claimed 300 to 350 branches.[60] In the early 1920s the Union was mainly concerned with combating Socialist and Communist activities, especially the 'red' Sunday schools. It eventually developed a more far-reaching, but essentially right-wing programme.

In 1923, the National Citizens' Union gave Nesta Webster a platform. On this occasion she spoke on 'Socialism and Secret Societies'. The audience was instructed to tell the workers that aliens were behind the Socialist movement, and that the influence of aliens and Jews predominated in secret societies. The real purpose behind the movement was to subvert all Britain's moral and religious ideas and to produce moral chaos. The only way to make the National Citizens' Union a real movement was to eliminate all aliens.[61]

Among the leading members of the National Citizens' Union during the first years of its existence were Lord and Lady Askwith, Colonel H. D. Lawrence, Gervais Rentoul, M.P., the Reverend Prebendary Gough, Brigadier-General A. E. F. Cavendish, and Colonel Sir Charles Burn who was to sit on the executive of the British Fascists. By 1925, the vice-presidents included the Home Secretary, Sir Kingsley Wood; the Earl of Malmesbury and Esmond Harmworth, M.P. Sir Philip Cunliffe-Lister, the President of the Board of Trade, addressed the annual conference that year. At the fifth annual conference of the National Citizens' Union in 1924, Sir J. R. Pretyman Newman, Unionist M.P. for Finchley, who was one of the founders and a vice-president, remarked that he was a Fascist, and stated that he was sorry that the Fascist movement had come into existence because it had stolen part of the thunder of the National Citizens' Union.[62] The 'stolen thunder' was not Fascist in content but anti-Communist, and included the idea of organizing in the event of a public emergency caused by a general strike.

These two examples should suffice, although others could be found. Their formation or re-organization, as the case may be, was during a period of social and political unrest. They were motivated by anxiety at the Russian Revolution, Britain's troubles in India and more particularly in Ireland, the formation of the Triple Alliance, the rise of the Labour Party, and the

Government's alarmed preparations for a general strike in 1921. An examination of the reports and conferences of the National Union of Manufacturers or the Association of British Chambers of Commerce would reveal pronouncements in a similar vein. Whereas these groups had multiple objectives, the British Empire Union and the National Citizens' Union emphasized one. They could also be distinguished by the interests they represented. In a sense, they were insecure and unsophisticated versions of today's propagandist groups for private enterprise.[63] The Economic League, for example, was founded in 1919 for 'the preservation of personal freedom and free enterprise' and 'actively to oppose all subversive forces whatever their origin or inspiration, that seek to undermine the security of Britain in general and of British industry in particular'.[64]

## ANTI-SEMITISM

The organized dissemination of anti-Semitic propaganda was introduced into twentieth-century England by Henry Beamish and the Britons. His father was an admiral who had been A. D. C. to Queen Victoria. Beamish fought in the Boer War, after which he settled in South Africa. According to Beamish, it was when he discovered that all the industries in South Africa were controlled by Jews that he began his anti-Jewish crusade.[65] He founded the Britons in London in 1918 and became involved in the Silver Badge Party of Ex-Servicemen, founded by Lieutenant-Commander E. M. Frazer. The objectives of the party were to put ex-servicemen into political life, to try and clear England of aliens, and to root out 'jiggery-pokery' generally.[66] It was not anti-Semitic.

It was Beamish's association with Frazer that led to a libel case involving Sir Alfred Mond and to Beamish's decision to leave England. Beamish and Frazer, who had once been thrown out of the Albert Hall for calling Lord Robert Cecil a traitor, produced a poster in March 1919; Sir Alfred Mond, who was then Commissioner of Works, was called a traitor, and it was claimed that he had allotted shares to the 'Huns' during the war.

Mond brought suit and won £5,000 damages, and Beamish disappeared without paying.[67]

Beamish then went around the world preaching the existence of an international Jewish conspiracy. He appeared in Germany and later claimed to have taught Hitler.[68] He eventually settled in Southern Rhodesia where he became an Independent Member of Parliament, being interned in 1940. Meanwhile, he continued as president of the Britons until his death in 1946. The chairman and vice-president of this anti-Semitic organization from its inception until 1931 was Dr John Henry Clarke, who was chief consulting physician to the Homeopathic Hospital. He was supposedly the contact man between the organization and right-wing Conservatives, who were unwilling to identify openly with the Britons.[69] Walter Crick, a Northampton boot-manufacturer, was a vice-president from 1925 to 1946. One prominent writer and lecturer for the Britons was Arthur Kitson, responsible for the 'Kitson Light' and some 500 other inventions. Brigadier-General R. B. D. Blakeney, the president of the British Fascists, held a membership as he did in the Imperial Fascist League and the B.U.F.

The Britons sought to eliminate alien influence from British industry and politics. All aliens were Jews, and it claimed to have no programme other than to get rid of them by forcing their return to Palestine.[70] Membership was restricted to those who could prove 'their parents and grandparents were of English blood'.[71] Activities were limited to publishing ventures, and in 1930 it was reconstituted as the Britons Publishing Company. The Britons' first journal, published in 1918, was *Jewry Uber Alles*. The *British Guardian* was published later, and in 1937 *The Investigator* was produced. The latter publication was adorned with a swastika and the motto 'For Crown and Country, Blood and Soil'. In addition, a number of books, including Lord Sydenham of Coombe's *The Jewish World Problem*, were published. The most important publishing venture, however, was the Victor Marsden translation of the *Protocols of the Learned Elders of Zion*, which was taken over when Eyre & Spottiswoode ceased to publish it in 1922. This famous forgery purported to show that there was a Jewish plot to dominate the world by undermining Western institutions by the use of liberalism, communism, and high finance.[72]

Prior to Mosley's political anti-Semitism and distinct from the Britons was the racial anti-Semitism of Arnold Leese. The B.U.F. viewed the Imperial Fascist League as its closest competitor, but it was no competitor at all. Like the majority of Fascist organizations operating in England during the period, the I.F.L. was dominated by one man.

Arnold Leese joined the British Fascists in 1924, at the age of forty-five. He was a veterinary surgeon who had worked in India and Africa for twenty years, and had published a book on the diseases of camels. After serving in the First World War, he set up a private practice in Stamford. Leese and a fellow-Fascist, Henry Simpson, successfully contested the municipal elections in Stamford in 1924. Simpson was re-elected in 1927. By this time, however, they had broken with the British Fascists and formed their own splinter group. According to Leese, British Fascism 'got its impulse' from Italy and Mussolini, although there was little in his early programme that resembled the Italian model. He defended individual initiative and the right to accumulate private property. He desired government abstention from the affairs of the economy and the society in general. He advocated 'true democracy', which he described as a government elected by a restricted electorate. His conception of Fascism emphasized nationalism, and the furthering of the 'splendid qualities' of the British Race. The enemy was Socialism.[73]

Leese retired and moved to London. There, he gathered a handful of supporters and founded the I.F.L., which began publishing *The Fascist* in the spring of 1929. Financed largely out of Leese's own pocket, the I.F.L. never gathered strength. The Press, which estimated the membership at 800 to 1,000, was generous.[74] Leese admitted a limited membership, defending it on the grounds that 'I could have more, but I want them to represent an aristocracy of character'.[75] There was little in the way of organization. Leese was Director-General, and Leslie H.

Sherrard was Commandant-General of the Fascist Legions. The Legions, who never numbered more than three dozen, wore black shirts and breeches. Like the B.U.F., the League at first adopted the fasces as the emblem. But when Hitler gained prominence, the I.F.L. switched to the swastika superimposed on the Union Jack as a patriotic gesture, whereas the B.U.F. adopted its own symbol of the 'flash in the pan'. Activities were limited to selling papers and to the occasional public meeting. If an indoor meeting was planned, it was announced that 'in the interests of good order Jews and other undesirable persons will not be admitted'.[76] Hence, the I.F.L. received little publicity from disorder and, in fact, held few meetings as local authorities were not inclined to accept these conditions.[77] Brigadier-General Blakeney, a Major C. Draper, and a Mr E. H. Cole were among the speakers for the League. A Lady Dalton held 'at homes' for the members, a function she also performed for the B.U.F.

The I.F.L. defined Fascism as the 'patriotic revolt against democracy and a return to statesmanship'. It planned to impose a corporate state on England. The economy would be left in private hands, but Parliament would be reformed to consist of a lower industrial house based on occupational representation, and an appointed upper house of eminent members of the community. Executive authority was to be vested in a Fascist Grand Council, from which the monarch would select the prime minister, who would in turn appoint his ministers from the same body. Lists of candidates would have to be approved by the Fascist Grand Council, and the electorate was restricted to those members of the confederations represented in Parliament, who paid an unspecified minimum in rates and taxes. National monetary reform was proposed and Jews were banned from citizenship.[78]

Before long, Jew-baiting had become central to the policy and activities of the I.F.L. The League's enemies were Free-masonry, Communism, Mosley and the Jews; and Leese attempted to show that the first three were dominated by the latter. Leese had visited Julius Streicher, for whom he expressed great admiration, in Germany, and *The Fascist* was now modelled on *Der Stürmer*. The League's programme was re-named the Racial Fascist Corporate State. The superiority of the 'noble Aryan Race', and the need to preserve and protect its purity lest it become polluted by 'ignoble Jewish money power' was preached.[79]

In a fashion similar to Mosley's, Leese had embraced the Italian Corporate State and had later turned to anti-Semitism, but unlike Mosley he had a racial theory. Leese even used anti-Semitism to denounce Mosley, whose movement he had refused to join. Mosley's Fascism was referred to as 'Kosher Fascism', and Leese advertised the League as having 'absolutely no con-nection with the pro-Jewish so-called "Fascism of Sir Oswald Mosley" '.[80] Meanwhile, Mosley during the formative period in the development of the B.U.F. had made some efforts to sup-press the latent anti-Semitism in his followers. Hence, the President of the Oxford Union Jewish Society wrote to *The Jewish Chronicle* stating, 'Our greatest supporters in our fight against the Imperial Fascists are the Mosley Fascists them-selves'.[81] Leese's taunts at Mosley finally reached the stage where Mosley sought revenge, and the Blackshirts broke up one of Leese's meetings in a central London hall in November 1933.

Leese's rantings against the Jews reached such outrageous proportions that in 1936 the Crown brought charges of sedi-tious libel against him. Several articles in *The Fascist* were mentioned, but two were referred to in particular. In the first, Leese wrote that the Jews were not wanted anywhere on earth, but that they were in England destroying everything good and decent by their contaminating influence. The I.F.L. solution was to segregate them at their own expense. In the second article, Leese accused the Jews of ritual murder.[82] Leese con-ducted his own defence, and argued that his intentions had been purely political, and that this was not a criminal prosecution, but a political prosecution in favour of the Jews. Although the court dismissed the libel action, he was convicted for conspiring to create a public mischief.[83]

When Leese was released from prison, he continued his

propaganda against the Jews until he was interned under Defence Regulation 18B. After a serious operation in 1944, he was released from detention. He set up a 'Jewish Interest Information Bureau' and published a new anti-Semitic paper called *Gothic Ripples*. In 1947, he was sent to prison for one year for conspiring with seven others, all of whom were former members of the I.F.L., to aid escaped German prisoners of war.[84] He died in 1956 at the age of seventy-six.

## NOTES

1. The concern here is with organized group activity rather than with the intellectual journalism of the Chesterton–Belloc circle, anti-democratic writers such as T. S. Eliot and Wyndham Lewis, and publicists like the Duke of Northumberland and Dame Lucy Houston. But see Hilaire Belloc, *The Servile State* (1911); Hilaire Belloc and Cecil Chesterton, *The Party System* (1911); C. E. Chesterton, *Party and People* (1910); G. K. Chesterton, 'The Patriotic Idea' in Lucian Oldershaw (ed.), *England: A Nation* (1904); John R. Harrison, *The Reactionaries: Yeats, Lewis, Pound, Eliot, Lawrence: A Study of the Anti-Democratic Intelligentsia* (*1967*); the Duke of Northumberland's weekly *The Patriot*, 1922–4, which was subsequently published by Lady Houston; Lady Houston's other ventures included *The Saturday Review*, 1932–6 and the Boswell Publishing Co.; see Warner Allen, *One of the Few. A Memoir* (1947); J. Wentworth Day, *Lady Houston* (1958).
2. James Drennan (W. E. D. Allen), *BUF, Oswald Mosley and British Fascism* (1934), pp. 290–91.
3. V. I. Lenin, 'Constitutional Crisis in Great Britain' (1914), reprinted in V. I. Lenin, *On Britain* (1959), pp. 197–200.
4. Drennan, *op. cit.*, pp. 290–91.
5. W. E. D. Allen, *Fascism in Relation to British History and Character* (1936?); 'The Fascist Idea in Britain', *Quarterly Review* (October 1933), pp. 223–38.
6. William Joyce, 'Obituary of Edward Carson', *Fascist Quarterly* (January 1936), pp. 27–9.
7. J. R. Jones, 'England', in Hans Rogger and Eugen Weber (eds.), *The European Right* (1965, 1966), p. 53.
8. See Lloyd P. Gartner, *The Jewish Immigrant in England 1870–1914* (1960).
9. Royal Commission on Alien Immigration, 1903, *Minutes of Evidence* (Cmd 1742), Vol. II, paragraphs 8553–614, 8710–28.
10. *East London Advertiser*, 18 January 1902.
11. Royal Commission on Alien Immigration 1903, *op. cit.*, paragraph 8612.

12. James H. Robb, *Working Class Anti-Semite* (1954), p. 203; Royal Commission on Alien Immigration, 1903, *op. cit.*, paragraph 9699.
13. Robb, *op. cit.*, p. 202; Royal Commission on Alien Immigration, 1903, *op. cit.*; see also Beatrice Potter, 'The Jewish Community', in Charles Booth (ed.), *Life and Labour of the People in London*, Vol. III, *Blocks of Buildings, Schools and Immigration* (1892), pp. 185–92. For a discussion of anti-Semitism and anti-Semites active during this period see Gartner, *op. cit.*
14. R. B. D. Blakeney, 'British Fascism', *The Nineteenth Century* (January 1925), pp. 132–41.
15. *ibid.*
16. *Memorandum of Association*, as registered 17 May 1924.
17. Blakeney, 'British Fascism', *loc. cit.*
18. Blakeney, article in *Referee*, 15 February 1925.
19. *The Daily Herald*, 28 March 1924.
20. *ibid.*, 17 March 1924.
21. 'Provisional Policy', *The British Lion*, 9 October 1926. 'The British Fascist Manifesto', *The British Lion*, October, November 1927.
22. Nesta Webster, *The Need for Fascism in Great Britain* (1926), p. 11.
23. Phoenix, 'Fascism for Freedom, Being an Account of the Origin, Principles and Policy of the British Fascists', *The British Lion* (1928).
24. 'Provisional Policy', *The British Lion*, 9 October 1926. 'The British Fascist Manifesto', *The British Lion*, October, November 1927.
25. 'Summary of Policy and Practice', *British Fascism*, 1931; *British Fascism*, summer, 1932.
26. *The Daily Herald*, 30 August 1923. *The Evening News*, 4 October 1923; Labour Defence Council, *Memorandum Concerning the Development of Fascism in Great Britain* (Mimeograph), (1924?); R. B. D. Blakeney, 'British Fascism', *loc. cit.*; *Memorandum of Association*, *loc. cit.*
27. *The Daily Herald*, 8 October 1924.
28. *ibid.*, 1 February 1924; 18 January 1934; *The Daily Express*, 13 February 1924; *The Daily Telegraph*, 25 April 1933.
29. 90 *H. L. Deb.* 5s. (28 February 1934), col. 1018.
30. George E. G. Catlin, 'Fascist Stirrings in Britain', *Current History* (February 1934), p. 542.
31. *The Daily Herald*, 31 January 1924.
32. Obituary, *The Times*, 16 December 1963.
33. *The Manchester Guardian*, 24 June 1925.
34. *The Times*, 24 April 1925; *The Daily Herald*, 24 April 1925.
35. *The Daily Herald*, 23 October 1926; Giacomo Matteotti was a Socialist member of the Italian Chamber of Deputies and an outspoken critic of the Italian Fascist government. He was murdered in 1924. For a detailed account of the incident see Sir Ivone Kirkpatrick, *Mussolini – Study of a Demagogue* (1964), pp. 20–34.
36. *The Manchester Guardian*, 9 August 1932.
37. R. L. Lintorn-Orman, *Memorandum*, 31 March 1926.

38. *The Daily Herald*, 26 April 1926; see also *The Fascist Bulletin*, 1 May 1926.
39. *The Times*, 28 April 1926.
40. *The Loyalists* (broadsheet), 28 April 1926.
41. *The Times*, 28 April 1926.
42. *ibid.*, 20 July 1935.
43. Major-General Sir Wyndham Childs, *Episodes and Reflections* (1930), pp. 223–4.
44. *The Evening News*, 30 July 1925.
45. Quoted in *The Daily Herald*, 31 July 1925.
46. *The Evening News*, 30 July 1925.
47. Unless noted, the policy of the National Fascisti is summarized from their periodicals, *The Fascist* and *The Tribune*, 1925–6.
48. *The Evening News*, 30 July 1925.
49. *The Manchester Guardian*, 4 November 1925.
50. *The Daily Herald*, 7 November 1925.
51. *ibid.*, 9 November 1925.
52. 188 *H.C. Deb. 5s.* (17 November 1925), col. 191.
53. Childs, *op. cit.*, pp. 215–16, 223–4.
54. *The Morning Post*, 29 July 1920.
55. British Empire Union, *Industrial Unrest* (1920).
56. British Empire Union, *Our Campaign of 1921* (*January–June*) (1921).
57. *The Morning Post*, 29 July 1920.
58. British Empire Union, *Empire Record*, February and May 1939; 11 June 1940.
59. *ibid.*, February 1938 (?).
60. *The Morning Post*, 12 February 1923; 3 April 1924; *The Times*, 3 February 1923.
61. *The Morning Post*, 13 December 1923.
62. *ibid.*, 14 June 1924.
63. See S. E. Finer, *Anonymous Empire* (1958), especially Chapter VII.
64. Quoted by S. E. Finer, 'The Political Power of Private Capital', Part II, *Sociological Review* (July 1956), p. 11.
65. *The Times*, 6 December 1919.
66. *ibid.*, 5 December 1919.
67. *ibid.*, 6 December 1919, 13 January 1920.
68. Lewis W. Bondy, *Racketeers of Hatred* (1946), p. 132.
69. *The Britons* (1952).
70. The Britons, *Leaflet* (n.d.).
71. *ibid.*
72. *ibid.*
73. A. S. Leese, *Fascism* (n.d.).
74. *The Daily Express*, 12 February 1934; *Sunday Referee*, 11 October 1936.
75. Quoted in Frederick Mullally, *Fascism Inside England* (1946), p. 21.
76. *The Daily Herald*, 10 February 1934.
77. *Daily Despatch* (Manchester), 7 April 1934.
78. Imperial Fascist League, *The Government of the Future – Fascism* (n.d.).

79. Bondy, *op. cit.*, pp. 125–7.
80. Imperial Fascist League, *Kosher Fascism in Britain* (n.d.); A. S. Leese, *Disraeli, the Destroyer* (n.d.).
81. *The Jewish Chronicle*, 29 September 1933.
82. *The Times*, 19 September 1936.
83. *ibid.*
84. *ibid.*, 25 February 1947; 4 April 1947.

# 3. Portrait of a Leader

Neither the paramilitary organizations, the anti-Communist nor anti-Semitic groups planted the Fascist idea in Britain, nor were any of them seriously interested in doing so. It must be traced directly to the rise of Mussolini in Italy. Although Fascism did not gain its formal expression in Britain until Sir Oswald Mosley founded the British Union of Fascists, there had always been those who admired the way Mussolini crushed the Communists and contained the Socialists. Anti-democrats, fed up or restless with the parliamentary system and fearing the rising power of the Labour Party, also looked to Italy. A few thought that they saw in Fascism a method of preserving a disintegrating Empire, if not of forging an imperial renaissance. Still others saw a state dedicated to authority, discipline and action. And there were those who were intrigued by the concept of the corporate state and, in so far as the doctrine was digested, it was seen as a system of preservation by reform.

In tracing Mosley's intellectual development it is important to realize that, whatever frustrations he encountered in the political system, he was not excluded from it. He rejected the system. Like Mussolini, Mosley was a man of energy, ambition and intellect, as well as an attractive public figure.[1] The combination of slow promotion, unsettled beliefs, personality conflicts and the ponderous parliamentary system of government, along with the hierarchical nature of the political parties, sent him scurrying from one party to another until he founded the

B.U.F. Up to a point, it is easy to understand Mosley's impatience with a political system that has at times failed to recognize talent or to utilize skill. But the crucial factor was Mosley's own character, which prevented his coming to terms with the system except on his own conditions and made Fascism a suitable alternative for him.

Mosley was born in 1896, the heir to the fifth baronet. Educated at Winchester and Sandhurst, he distinguished himself as a boxer and a fencer, rather than as a scholar. In 1914, he was gazetted to the 16th Lancers and later joined the Royal Flying Corps. His leg was injured twice, leaving him with a permanent limp.

It is most striking that Mosley grew up and was educated in a non-political environment. He embarked upon a parliamentary career without the benefit of an emotional, let alone a practical, political apprenticeship. If this produced a mind uncluttered by party indoctrination and unaffected by party tradition and loyalties, it also resulted in a poor sense of political judgement.

When the future Fascist leader was five years old, his parents separated, and he was brought up alternately by his mother and his grandfather. Pro-Mosley writers stressed the influence that the latter had over the young Mosley.[2] As the subject of a famous John Bull cartoon he was seen as the embodiment of true British characteristics.* It may have been more pertinent that a portion of the fourth baronet's estate was left directly to the young Mosley.[3]

Despite infrequent contact, relations between father and son were good although strained. After the younger Mosley had joined the Labour Party, a rude public exchange took place. When reports appeared in the Press in 1926 that his son and daughter-in-law desired to relinquish their titles, the elder

---

* The fourth baronet, in fact, was identified as the Victorian symbol of John Bull not so much for his 'British' characteristics as for his 'British' figure, which was used to popularize wholemeal bread. See 'Sir Oswald Mosley, Bart., John Bull', *Vanity Fair*, 1 September 1898; Obituary, *The Times*, 15 October 1915 and 12 February 1916; *Action*, 16 July 1938.

Mosley wrote a letter stating that they would be of more service to the country if, instead of achieving cheap publicity over relinquishing titles, they relinquished some of their wealth.[4] Shortly thereafter, he launched a further attack against his son, who was standing as a Labour candidate in a by-election in Smethwick. According to the fifth baronet, his son had been born with a gold spoon in his mouth; he had never done a day's work in his life, and while he claimed to do one thing or another he lived in the height of luxury.[5] The younger Mosley re-affirmed his intention of giving up his title, and maintained that the only contribution that his father had made to his education and upbringing was in the form of alimony, which he had been compelled to contribute by the court.[6]

Mosley's Parliamentary career began in 1918 when he was returned as the Conservative Member for Harrow with a majority of over 10,000. He was never at ease as a supporter of the Coalition. His questions and interjections in the House of Commons were usually to harass the Government.[7] At twenty-three, he was the youngest member of the House of Commons and, as in the General Election, he was constantly taunted with this fact. Parliament, as if instinctively, resented new and young recruits, and the experiment of a New Members Association with Mosley as secretary failed. On entering the House, he devoted special attention to the problems of ex-servicemen.[8] He later concentrated on the League of Nations, of which he was an outspoken supporter, and on the Government's Irish policy, of which he was an outspoken critic. He crossed the floor over the latter issue in November 1920, after arousing the hostility of the Government benches by his bitter criticisms.[9]

Mosley did not officially leave the Conservative Party until 1922. In July of that year, with a General Election approaching, his constituency organization demanded a firm commitment on Mosley's part that, in the event of a Conservative Government, he would not depart from the Whip without consulting his constituents. He replied that 'a gramophone would be more suitable to these requirements than a human being', and that he held himself absolutely free to deal with new issues as they arose.[10] Mosley, standing as an Independent Conservative, was returned with a majority of over 7,000 after an abusive campaign. He was again re-elected in 1923 with a reduced majority of 4,646 over his Conservative opponent. On this occasion, Mosley stood as an Independent rather than an Independent Conservative.

Although Mosley broke with the Conservative Party, he did not join the Labour Party until April 1924, three months after the latter had formed the Government. It was generally felt at the time that the Labour Party had gained an important recruit, and Mosley rose rapidly within the Party hierarchy. Mosley's background was considered at the time to be a handicap, however, as was his marriage to Cynthia Curzon, the second daughter of the Marquis Curzon of Kedleston. He had married the daughter of the then Foreign Secretary, in 1920, at the Chapel Royal, in the presence of the King and Queen. Fortunately for Mosley, Lady Cynthia became universally respected throughout the Labour Movement. She was adopted as a prospective Parliamentary candidate for Stoke-on-Trent in 1925 and was returned to the House of Commons as a Labour Member in 1929. Her Parliamentary career was undistinguished but, possessing the tact her husband lacked, Lady Cynthia proved invaluable as his aide. Despite her reservations about Mosley's turn to Fascism, she remained loyal until her death in 1933.

Mosley made an immediate impact upon joining the Labour Party by his courage and radicalism, although his radicalism aroused suspicion in certain quarters as to the 'intentions' of the former Conservative who had become more 'Socialist' than most of the Socialists. In fact, even though Mosley's induction into the Labour Party was through the Independent Labour Party, it would probably have been more correct to have described him as a radical rather than a Socialist. He devoted his energies to economic matters especially financial and currency reforms. His programme, known as the 'Birmingham proposals', was first outlined at the I.L.P. Annual Conference in 1925.* Shortly thereafter, Mosley advanced a more elaborate scheme at an I.L.P. summer school, which was published in a pamphlet form, *Revolution by Reason*, and expanded into a book under the same title by John Strachey.

The Birmingham proposals were the result of Mosley's collaboration with Strachey and Allen Young who were influential in shaping much of Mosley's economic thinking, until they broke with him during the New Party era.[11] Shortly after leaving Oxford, Strachey contested the Aston Manor division of Birmingham. This was in 1924, when Mosley was contesting a neighbouring division, Ladywood. Strachey was elected to Parliament in 1929, and Mosley appointed him his Parliamentary Private Secretary. Young was appointed political organizer for the Birmingham Borough Labour Party in 1924, a post which he later resigned to become Mosley's personal secretary. On the formation of the New Party he became its general secretary and a Parliamentary candidate. Shortly after his break with the Party, Young became private secretary to Harold Macmillan. He helped the future Prime Minister in writing *The Middle Way*, in which a programme for 'planned capitalism' with an economic council to control the conditions to which industries respond, was advocated.[12]

In the Birmingham proposals, Mosley called for public control of the supply of credit and currency through the nationalization of the banking system and the issuing of consumer credits to the unemployed. The extension of credit would create a demand. According to Mosley, this would not be inflationary because an increase in the amount of money in circulation would mean an increase in the supply of goods. The money would be repaid from the excess profits collected from industry during the boom periods created by the extension of credit.[13] Mosley in his pamphlet *Revolution by Reason* suggested an economic council as the planning and controlling mechanism

* The name, 'Birmingham proposals', was a title of convenience, although they were endorsed by the Birmingham Labour Party and the Birmingham I.L.P. Federation. John Strachey, 'Revolution by Reason: The Author's Reply to a Criticism', *The Labour Magazine* (March 1926), pp. 510–11.

and advocated an alternative method for the increase in purchasing power. Instead of issuing consumer credits to the unemployed, the economic council would control wages and establish minimums; increases would be financed by overdrafts from state banks. At the same time, unemployment benefits would be increased.[14] The economic council would also be responsible for contracting bulk purchases of basic food stuffs and raw materials.[15] Moreover Mosley, in his pamphlet, argued for the need to take over the more prosperous industries, especially the monopolies, rather than the inefficient ones.[16] Strachey suggested 'national corporations' for basic industries.[17]

Several constituency Labour parties desired Mosley for their Parliamentary candidate. Given Mosley's personality and background, it was not surprising that he chose to contest the Ladywood Division of Birmingham, a stronghold of the Chamberlain family for over fifty years. If Mosley could defeat Neville Chamberlain, he would have enhanced his prestige within the Labour Movement and throughout the country for, despite the fuss that the Labour Party made over its new recruit, he did not have a national reputation. On the other hand, if he lost, he anticipated little trouble in being adopted as a candidate at a by-election. This proved to be the case.

Although the Labour Party increased its vote substantially in the second General Election of 1924, the Conservatives gained a majority in Parliament. At Ladywood, Mosley lost by seventy-seven votes after two recounts. But the Chamberlains' hold on Birmingham was broken. Neville Chamberlain abandoned Ladywood, and the Labour Party won the seat by eleven votes in 1929. In the neighbouring constituency of West Birmingham, Austin Chamberlain survived by a few dozen votes in 1929. The President of Birmingham Borough Labour Party credited Mosley with being largely responsible for the change in the political complexion of the city.[18]

Mosley was returned to Parliament at a by-election at Smethwick in 1926, after a campaign that was punctuated by considerable disorder. The Tories announced that 'offers have been received from the members of a local organization to attend

Conservative meetings and preserve order' to which Mosley replied that his opponents were bringing in 'the black-shirted, wretched imitators of the ice-cream merchants of another country, but entirely devoid of their genius'.[19] The Mosleys were also the target of personal abuse because of their social position and what was described as the 'dirtiest by-election in recent years' culminated with Mosley's father publicly attacking him.[20] Mosley emerged from the abuse and disorders with a handsome majority of 6,582, a substantial increase over the Labour majority of 1,253 at the previous election.

Mosley's role as an opposition back-bencher was undistinguished. He was active enough in his first year as a Labour M.P. He criticized the Government's Trade Disputes Bill with great agility.[21] He took an interest in miners' problems, which were being championed by the I.L.P. in general, and Strachey in particular, in his role as editor of *The Miner*.[22] He bitterly attacked the restoration of the gold standard, and on this issue was in conflict with Philip Snowden.[23] But he was constantly heckled from the Conservative benches. Hence his own contributions were characterized by invective.[24] Interestingly enough, a frequent charge levelled against the Government by Mosley was that they were Fascists. In criticizing the Government for what he claimed to be their hidden intentions behind the Trade Disputes Bill, Mosley declared: 'The fact is that the Government would like to be Fascists but have not the courage; they have not the courage to wear their black shirts.'[25] During a debate on foreign affairs he described Mussolini as 'the friend and ally' of the Conservative Party.[26] According to Mosley, the main indictment of British foreign policy was the impression that Fascist Italy was being used as an instrument to overthrow Russia.[27] Outside Parliament, at an I.L.P. summer school, Mosley warned that Fascist Italy and its alliance with Britain was the greatest danger to peace in Europe. His evidence was that members of the Government, particularly Churchill, had given special praise to Fascism, which showed what they were thinking.[28]

Illness and trips abroad kept Mosley from the House of

Commons for most of 1928. On his return in November, he focused his attentions on the problems of unemployment. This was partially motivated by a proposed Government scheme for relocating unemployed workers from distressed areas to more prosperous areas, which would have included Birmingham.[29] His solution for unemployment differed little from what the Labour Party was committed to in principle in their programme, *Labour and the Nation*, and from those proposals later set out in the election manifesto for 1929. In fact, Mosley was a member of the drafting committees for both statements and, along with Ellen Wilkinson, Sir Charles Trevelyan and George Lansbury, submitted a separate statement, more militant than *Labour and the Nation*.[30] As in the Birmingham proposals, Mosley recommended the qualitative and quantitative control and direction of credit, through reform of the banking system. He called for the removal of the aged and the young from the employment market by pensions and by raising the school-leaving age. Mosley advocated an emergency programme of public works, as well as long-term plans for public ownership and control of industry. He stressed the necessity for a state board to control imports and to facilitate bulk purchases from the dominions.[31]

Meanwhile, Mosley tried to consolidate his position within the Labour Party. He was elected as a constituency representative to the National Executive at the annual conference in 1927 and 1928.* He also stood for the Parliamentary Committee in 1928, but finished twenty-third out of twenty-four contestants for twelve places.[32] Mosley was not elected to the National Executive in 1929, probably due to a change in the voting procedure.[33] But, when re-elected in 1930, he was the idol of the rank and file, and his election was a personal triumph, for he had resigned from the Government and had been defeated at the conference on the issue of his unemployment manifesto.

Mosley also used his income to enhance his prestige within the Labour Movement. Although his contributions to the

* In 1927 he replaced Hugh Dalton who claimed that this was a result of Mosley's attack on him in *The New Leader*. Dalton, *Call Back Yesterday, 1887–1931* (1953), p. 171.

I.L.P. were meagre, he made large donations to the Labour Party when he was negotiating for a Parliamentary constituency.[34] Once he had been selected as a prospective Parliamentary candidate for Ladywood, it was widely reported that he had used his private income to build up the Labour Party in Birmingham and the West Midlands, and in the General Election of 1929 the so-called Mosley group had considerable success.[35] Finally, although Mosley identified himself politically with the left-wing elements of the Labour Party, his social position was useful in maintaining and strengthening his contacts with the leadership. For example, Philip Snowden wrote that 'an intimate social relationship was established such as never existed between Mr MacDonald and the plebeian members of the Labour Party'.[36] It was, however, difficult to determine whether Mosley was courting MacDonald, or vice versa. In any case, Mosley was rewarded politically with an office in the Labour Government of 1929. Nevertheless, the leadership of the Labour Movement remained ambivalent towards him.

The sequence of events leading to Mosley's resignation from the Labour Government and his battle to win acceptance for his proposals within the Labour Party are disputed.[37] It is important, however, to follow his course, at least in outline, for it had an important influence on his intellectual development. The Labour Party was returned to power at the General Election of 1929 and Mosley was re-elected at Smethwick with a slightly increased majority in a larger poll. It was rumoured that MacDonald considered Mosley for the post of either Foreign Secretary or First Lord of the Admiralty.[38] He was, in fact, appointed Chancellor of the Duchy of Lancaster without cabinet rank, but to assist the Lord Privy Seal, J. H. Thomas, with developing employment schemes. This was a more suitable selection in terms of Mosley's interests and considering the others with prior claims to higher political office. A committee of ministerial rank was formed, with Thomas as chairman, George Lansbury, the Commissioner of Works, Thomas Johnston, the Under-Secretary of State for Scotland, and Mosley as Thomas's chief deputy.

The number of unemployed decreased immediately after the Labour Government took office in June 1929. But by the end of the year, the numbers were again increasing. During 1930, the unemployment problem became alarming and by December there were over two-and-a-half million reported unemployed. Even though unemployment in Great Britain was a reflection of world conditions no government could afford simply to wait for international recovery. At first Thomas met the challenge with initiative.[39] But the magnitude of the problem soon left him bewildered and the committee did not function effectively. Thomas's efforts fell far short of halting the swelling tide of unemployment. This in turn led to mounting dissatisfaction and criticism not only from the opposition, but from within his own party. The adherence of Philip Snowden, the Chancellor of the Exchequer, to orthodox financial policies meant that the committee's proposals would not be guaranteed a favourable reception. Although Thomas worked cooperatively with Snowden, the two of them did not get on well with the other members of the committee. Snowden wrote that the relations between Thomas and the three ministers were never harmonious, and that Thomas wanted to keep things in his own hands.[40] Arthur Henderson, then Foreign Secretary, told Beatrice Webb that Thomas was in such a state of panic that he was bordering on lunacy, an opinion shared by MacDonald. Henderson suggested to the Prime Minister that a new committee be formed, and that Thomas should be removed and Mosley installed in his place.[41] Finally the committee's work was frustrated by the cautious weight of officialdom and bureaucracy. Mosley complained to the House of Commons that the committee met on only nine occasions. Neither Lansbury, Johnston nor Mosley had been invited to the first two meetings where Thomas and the department heads made the major decisions with the result that the initiative was placed in the hands of the civil servants.[42]

On 23 January 1930, Mosley submitted a series of proposals to the Prime Minister. Not only was the memorandum Mosley's inspiration, but he seems to have been the sole author, although J. M. Keynes was consulted and Lansbury and Johnston con-

curred on the final draft.[43] Thomas claimed to have been by-
passed, yet Mosley in his covering letter to MacDonald stated
that he had also sent a copy to the Lord Privy Seal.[44] In any
event, it was apparent that there had been an almost complete
breakdown of communication. The incident reached a climax
for Thomas when, according to his account, the document had
not only been distributed to other members of the Cabinet, but
left lying openly in the House of Commons by Strachey.[45] There
can be little doubt that there was a leak, for *The Manchester
Guardian* published the substance of the proposals.[46] Consequently, Thomas submitted his resignation to MacDonald, who
refused it.

This was on 21 February by which time a Cabinet sub-
committee had already been appointed with Snowden as chairman. Mosley now had to wait over two months for a decision.
A Cabinet rejection was highly likely in terms of the costs of the
schemes and Snowden's crucial position and financial ortho-
doxy. Indeed *The Daily Herald* reported that after two meetings
between the Cabinet and the sub-committee it was rejected on
the grounds that 'the mere spending of money will not cure
unemployment'.[47] Yet taking into account the Cabinet's work-
load, the time lag suggests that the memorandum was given
serious consideration, or at least that alternatives were discussed, and in any event there were strategic issues involved.*
If this was the case Mosley had achieved a minor tactical
triumph.

Mosley's proposals were more impressive for their scale than
their originality. He drew upon his earlier pronouncements and
many of his ideas were in tune with *Labour and the Nation*, the
election manifesto, *Socialism in Our Time* and the I.L.P.'s
*Socialism Now*. It is clear that others were thinking along similar
lines, as shown by the Liberal Party's election manifesto and

---

* The Cabinet sub-committee met with Mosley, Johnston and Lansbury
and they were present at what seems to have been the decisive Cabinet
meeting of 19 May. *The Manchester Guardian*, 10 April 1930; 21 May 1930;
Robert Skidelsky refers to a meeting with the Prime Minister and others
on 20 May: *Politicians and the Slump* (1967), p. 184.

'We can Conquer Unemployment', Ernest Bevin's submissions to the Mond–Turner Conference and *Industry and State* by three young Conservatives, Harold Macmillan, Robert Boothby and Oliver Stanley. Within the Government, specific recommendations had been mooted by members of the Thomas committee and suggestions for the committee's reform submitted by the British representative to the International Labour Organization, H. B. Butler, were incorporated into the memorandum.[48] That the proposals were Keynesian and post-Keynesian in tone is undoubted, but what was important was that the memorandum represented a serious attempt to deal with a serious problem and that it formed, at least initially, much of the substance of Mosley's British Fascism.[49]

Mosley's short-term programme included proposals to expand the public works programme under national direction and the acceleration of works projects already in operation or approved. In particular, he advocated a £100,000,000 road scheme to be concentrated into a three-year period. He recommended emergency pensions for those who had reached the age of sixty by a certain date and advocated raising the school-leaving age. To finance the public works projects Mosley proposed a loan of £200,000,000, not including estimates for slum clearance and land drainage. The long-term programme stressed the development of home markets and agriculture in particular. A policy of insulation would be achieved by instituting import control boards and by a more constructive tariff policy based on the premise that outright protection was as outdated as free trade. Emphasis was also placed on the rationalization of industry. The key instrument would be a government-controlled development company which would overcome the stultifying effect of the banks. Finally, he strongly recommended a co-ordinated transport policy.

In order to administer these schemes, Mosley suggested a central organization served by an adequate research and economic advisory department. At its apex would be an executive composed of the Prime Minister and his senior economic ministers. This executive would coordinate the work of a number of policy committees as well as advisory committees which would enlist the services of experts from outside Whitehall. The civil service would provide a secretariat of senior officials under the control of the head of the Treasury. The development bank would be closely linked to this *apparat*.[50]

Following the rejection of the memorandum in May 1930, after an adverse report by the Cabinet sub-committee and after further attempts to convince the Prime Minister and his colleagues, Mosley resigned from the Government despite reported efforts to dissuade him.[51] Nor was he prepared to let the matter rest. Taking great care to observe the proprieties of party loyalty he used a number of channels to present his views. He corresponded with the Prime Minister;[52] his resignation speech was a devastating attack on the Government's unemployment policy;[53] and he took his case to the country, criticizing the Government for its lack of initiative.[54] The audiences and the Press reactions were sympathetic rather than enthusiastic.[55]

The first of two crucial tests took place immediately on Mosley's resignation at two meetings of the Parliamentary Labour Party. Although his resolution, calling for an unemployment policy more in keeping with the Party's election pledges, was defeated, by 210 to twenty-nine, most accounts state that he received a favourable hearing.[56] It seems that he placed himself in a strategically awkward position by allowing the resolution to be interpreted as a vote of censure and then pressing for a division. Whether he miscalculated or was outmanoeuvred, the effect was the same.* Faced with a showdown, many M.P.s rallied to the leadership.[57] Yet soon afterwards some sixty members joined in demanding Thomas's resignation, and there were one hundred signatures to a resolution for a meeting of the Parliamentary Labour Party to consider a re-statement of the Government's unemployment policy.[58] The Annual Conference at Llandudno in October 1930 provided a second critical

* Mosley maintains that he 'decided after deep reflection, coldly and deliberately in advance of the meeting, to bring the party to a decision or eventually to leave'. *My Life* (1968), p. 260.

test. The Government's unemployment policy was the subject of radical criticism from a number of sources. The General and Municipal Workers' Union moved a resolution which called for the application of definite Socialist principles. James Maxton for the I.L.P. then moved an even more forceful amendment chastising the Government for applying capitalist methods instead of Socialist solutions. Although Ernest Bevin regretted that a motion of censure had been introduced, he too attacked the Government. The I.L.P. amendment was soundly defeated, but the Conference passed the General and Municipal Workers' resolution. With this condemnation of the Government, the stage was set for a debate on the Mosley Memorandum.[59]

The Doncaster Labour Party moved a resolution calling for the Parliamentary Party to consider the Mosley Memorandum, and instructing the National Executive to examine the proposals and issue a report. Mosley followed with a brief and pungent speech summarizing the criticisms and proposals that he had made in the House of Commons in May. He made it quite clear that his policy was in direct conflict with the policy advocated by the Chancellor of the Exchequer.[60] Fenner Brockway described the scene: 'As Mosley ended, the delegates rose *en masse* cheering for minutes on end. I have never seen or heard such an ovation at a Labour Party Conference.'[61]

George Lansbury replied for the National Executive. It was seemingly a strategic choice, but proved ineffectual. After a half-hearted attempt to defend the Government and to criticize Mosley's proposals, he concluded by asking the Party to close its ranks.[62] The result was that Mosley almost won the day. The resolution was defeated by a narrow margin, 1,251,000 to 1,046,000. Had A. J. Cook, the general secretary of the Miners' Federation who was unavoidably delayed, arrived on time, and had he been able to persuade his union to support Mosley, the National Executive would have been defeated. On the following day, Mosley was returned to the National Executive in fourth place on the ballot for the Constituency and Central Labour Parties. Thomas, who had been third on the ballot for the thirteen places allotted to the National Societies on the National Executive the previous year, was not re-elected.

Mosley's position was considerably strengthened by the reception he had received at the Conference and by the fact that criticism of the Government's unemployment policy was not confined to a particular wing of the Labour Movement. Moreover, where Mosley's methods at the Parliamentary Labour Party Meeting had alienated potential support, he made no strategic errors at Llandudno.[63] This tactical correctness proved to be short-lived, however.

Mosley was faced with decisions as to how to consolidate his gains and re-state his proposals in the most effective manner. Initially he made some use of the public platform. Whether motivated by his apparent success or by a growing impatience with the parliamentary process, he made his views on the political system more explicit.

Addressing an audience in his wife's constituency, Stoke-on-Trent, he argued that it was impossible to meet the needs of the present economic system with the present economic machinery and that Britain required strong executive government.[64] This was followed by a speech before the Association of British Manufacturers for the Printing and Allied Trades, in which he said that he was not suggesting dictatorship on the Continental method, but that Britain would have to transform a 'nineteenth-century debating chamber into a twentieth-century business assembly'. The country should get a government that they believed would carry out the task and give them the opportunity to get on with the job. According to the future Fascist leader, the government should not be encumbered by parliamentary machinery and debate, although it would be necessary to retain parliamentary control over the Executive.[65]

It was soon clear that Mosley had no intention of becoming a spokesman for lost causes on the Government back-benches. He began to canvass support within the Parliamentary Labour Party and to enlist the collaboration of a number of colleagues in drafting an alternative programme based on the Memorandum. Mosley's cause would be strengthened by the weight of the other signatories, while the Party would be confronted with the threat of an organized opposition within its ranks as well as the ultimate possibility of the splinter movement. It must have seemed a sound enough approach in view of the conference and the fact that a minority government could be placed in a precarious position.

It proved a miscalculation. Mosley overestimated his own position and underestimated the strength of the leadership. His performance at Llandudno was impressive, but the leadership was not routed. MacDonald, no matter how muddled in his thinking, retained his oratorical and manipulative skills and was master of the Conference. In addition, the formation of a group within the Party which presented an organized challenge to Government policy was bound to arouse hostility. Nor were Mosley's intentions clear. There is little doubt that he was contemplating the formation of another party, but it was not certain when and under what conditions this would take place and to what extent his collaborators on a policy statement would be committed.[66] Further, if more than a working alliance with the I.L.P. was envisaged, it never materialized.[67] Finally, in a party that values loyalty, dynamism is no substitute and Mosley was unable to shed the stigma of an adventurer.[68] As a result the Cabinet ignored the proposals, the rank and file ignored the rebels and the public was not aroused.[69]

Approximately fifty M.P.s were meeting regularly with Mosley in the autumn of 1930, but when it came to signing the new draft of the Memorandum for public consumption only seventeen members, and A. J. Cook, did so. The Mosley Manifesto was released in December, a second version appeared in January and *A National Policy*, upon which the New Party was founded, to campaign for its adoption, was published the following month. The signatories were mainly drawn from constituencies in the Midlands and had been associated with Mosley at least since the General Election. Only three were from the I.L.P. Of the nine that eventually left the Labour Party only Strachey and Dr Robert Forgan remained with the Mosleys in the New Party. W. J. Brown and Oliver Baldwin became independents, although the latter rejoined the Labour Party after six months. J. Lovat-Frazer and Frank Markham joined the National Labour Party and John McGovern left with the I.L.P. Aneurin Bevan was probably representative of those who remained, in that he thought it was possible to convince the Labour Party to adopt the proposals.*

The *Manifesto* included what was already known about the contents of the *Memorandum* with additional proposals for the development of Commonwealth trade and the suspension, at least temporarily, of war debts.[70] The main departure, however, was in the prominence given to the need to reorganize the political and economic systems in order to implement the programmes. The Cabinet was to be retained for consultation and direction of routine matters. Real power was to be vested in a super cabinet of five ministers without portfolio, who would be in office for 'a stated period' to carry out the 'emergency' programme. These ministers would be permitted to make decisions without the consultation or approval of Parliament, although they would be ultimately responsible to it, in that Parliament could censure and dismiss them.[71] Commodity boards composed of the producers and users in each industry would be established to employ either licences or tariffs for the control of imports. A public utility organization would direct the public works programme, and a National Planning Organization would supervise and plan rationalization and industrial development. The relationship of these bodies and boards to the Government was not worked out.

In as far as the Manifesto attracted attention, it was received with expressions of agreement and sympathy rather than commitments of support. It was, of course, difficult to know what was the next move. *The Times* and *The Manchester Guardian*

* *The Manchester Guardian*, 2 March 1931. Bevan was also upset by a 'leak' to the Press that Mosley intended to form another party and had grave reservations about Mosley personally. He helped to dissuade several I.L.P.-ers who were contemplating leaving the Labour Party with Mosley. Michael Foot, *Aneurin Bevan*, Vol. I (1962), pp. 130–32. Forgan claimed that MacDonald offered him a minor post in the Government in an attempt to hold off his disaffection. *Interview*, 13 December 1960.

published the full text. The Sunday papers gave it wide coverage and J. L. Garvin in *The Observer* challenged those who disagreed with the contents to produce an alternative.[72] L. S. Amery, Walter Elliot and Lieutenant-Colonel John Moore-Brabazon praised it, while Sir William Morris, later Lord Nuffield, lent his qualified support.[73] Yet its impact was slight and Strachey, at least, understood the implications and wrote, 'Maybe we have committed political suicide. Who knows, and who cares?'[74]

Consequently *A National Policy* was more than just an elaboration and refinement of the proposals set forth in the *Memorandum* and the *Manifesto* and it was no longer an alternative programme for the Labour Government. Written by Strachey, Brown, Bevan and Allen Young, it provided a policy for the founding of another party.[75] As such the number of Labour M.P.s in the Mosley group dwindled from seventeen to six.

It was a radical rather than a socialist programme appealing to Conservatives and Socialists to unite to meet the economic crisis. Nationalization was not mentioned nor were Mosley's earlier proposals for currency reform and welfare measures. The emphasis on institutional reform remained. A super-cabinet was essential and Parliament would have the right to interrogate the government and to debate general principles of policy, as well as the right to censure and dismiss the government. A National Planning Council, apparently distinct from the National Planning Organization, would coordinate the activities of the Commodity Boards and bring into consultation representatives of the large industrial corporations. Under Fascism, Mosley saw the Commodity Boards comprised of employers and workers forming the industrial corporations.[76] But while the National Council was to be an executive body, the National Corporation under Fascism was conceived as an industrial parliament. The chief instrument of the National Planning Council would be a National Investment Board, which would facilitate and control the utilization of capital resources.

Mosley was now seeking support along a broad political front.[77] In fact, he carried on negotiations with several young members of the Conservative Party as well as a few Liberals right up to the public announcement of the formation of the New Party.[78] According to Strachey, Mosley conceived the New Party as a 'centre ginger group'.[79] Although Brown claimed that it was a breakaway to the left, C. E. M. Joad, an early member of the New Party, maintained that the New Party had come into being not to introduce Utopia, but to prevent collapse.[80]

## NOTES

1. For testimonials on his personal attributes during this period see *Oswald Mosley, The Facts* (1957), pp. 21-9.
2. A. K. Chesterton, *Oswald Mosley: Portrait of a Leader* (1937), pp. 11-12.
3. Frederick Mullally, *Fascism Inside England* (1946), pp. 15-18.
4. *The Daily Mail*, 4 April 1926.
5. *ibid.*, 12 April 1926.
6. *ibid.*, 13 April 1926; Chesterton, *op. cit.*, pp. 64-5.
7. For example, see 123 *H.C. Deb. ss*, (15 December 1919), cols. 110-23.
8. For example, see 123 *H.C. Deb. ss.* (23 December 1919), cols. 1277-8.
9. For example, see 133 *H.C. Deb. ss.* (20 October 1920), cols. 1008-13.
10. *Westminster Gazette*, 22 July 1922.
11. John Strachey, *Interview*, 7 April 1960; see also Fenner Brockway, *Inside the Left* (1942), p. 209.
12. Harold Macmillan, *Winds of Change 1914-1939* (1966), p. 339; see also Hugh Massingham, 'Mac v. Rab', *The Sunday Telegraph*, 21 August 1966; Harold Macmillan, *The Middle Way* (1938).
13. *The Manchester Guardian*, 15 April 1925.
14. Oswald Mosley, *Revolution by Reason* (1925), pp. 14-15, 18-19.
15. John Strachey, *Revolution By Reason* (1925), pp. 132-51.
16. Mosley, *Revolution By Reason, op. cit.*, p. 20.
17. Strachey, *Revolution By Reason, op. cit.*, p. 144.
18. J. Johnson, 'Birmingham Labour and The New Party', *The Labour Magazine* (April 1931), p. 534.
19. Christopher Farman, 'The Day Smethwick Voted for Mosley', *The Guardian*, 9 April 1966.
20. *John Bull*, 1 January 1927; see above, pp. 52-3.
21. 206 *H.C. Deb. ss.* (17 May 1927), cols. 1113-18; 207 *H.C. Deb. ss.* (20 June 1927), cols. 1558-67.
22. 205 *H.C. Deb. ss.* (11 April 1927), cols. 103-11; see also 222 *H.C. Deb. ss.* (8 November 1928), cols. 291-305; 226 *H.C. Deb. ss.* (25 March 1929), cols. 2125-39.
23. *ibid.*; *The Financial Times*, 23 December 1926.
24. See 206 *H.C. Deb. ss.* (24 May 1927), cols. 1942-3; 207 *H.C. Deb. ss.* (13 June 1927), col. 739; (22 June 1927), cols. 1981-2.

25. 206 *H.C. Deb. ss.* (17 May 1927), col. 1117.
26. 208 *H.C. Deb. ss.* (11 July 1927), col. 1810.
27. *ibid.*, col. 1813.
28. *The Daily Herald*, 1 August 1927.
29. 222 *H.C. Deb. ss.* (8 November 1928), col. 293.
30. Hugh Dalton, *Call Back Yesterday, 1887–1931* (1953), p. 172.
31. 222 *H.C. Deb. ss.*, *op. cit.*, cols. 291–305; 226 *H.C. Deb. ss.* (25 March 1929), cols. 2125–39; see also Oswald Mosley, *Industrial Problems and the Socialists* (1929).
32. Mosley, *op. cit.*, p. 180.
33. See Egon Wertheimer, *Portrait of the Labour Party* (1930), pp. 245–8.
34. Brockway, *op. cit.*, p. 210.
35. For example see Dean E. McHenry, *The Labour Party In Transition, 1931–38* (1938), p. 234.
36. Philip Snowden, *An Autobiography*, Vol. II, (1934), p. 776. See also Mary Agnes Hamilton, *Arthur Henderson* (1938), pp. 262, 350–2; L. MacNeil Weir, *The Tragedy of Ramsay MacDonald* (1938), pp. 165, 234; Margaret Cole (ed.), *Beatrice Webb's Diaries, 1924–1932* (1956), pp. 67, 221; John Scanlon, *Decline and Fall of the Labour Party* (1932), pp. 183–4.
37. The most convincing account is provided by Robert Skidelsky who has had access to the Keynes, Lansbury and, particularly, the Mosley papers for the period. *Politicians and the Slump* (1967), Chapter 8; for a complete summary of the published sources see W. F. Mandle, 'Sir Oswald Mosley's Resignation from the Labour Government', *Historical Studies* (1961), pp. 493–510; for Mosley's own account, see *My Life, op. cit.*, Chapters 13–15.
38. Kingsley Martin, *Harold Laski* (1953), p. 171; Snowden, *op. cit.*, p. 766; Brockway, *op. cit.*, p. 210; John Paton, *Left Turn* (1936), p. 338; according to Hugh Dalton, MacDonald informed Walter Citrine that he was thinking of Mosley as a possible successor. Citrine replied that it was out of the question. Dalton, *op. cit.*, p. 293; *Action*, 30 May 1940. Mosley maintains that he was unaware of the controversy, *My Life, op. cit.*, p. 219.
39. See 229 *H.C. Deb. ss.* (3 July 1929), cols. 91–110.
40. Snowden, *op. cit.*, p. 775; see also pp. 875–6.
41. Margaret Cole (ed.), *op. cit.*, p. 230; see also Brockway, *op. cit.*, p. 209; W. J. Brown, *So Far* (1943), pp. 156–7; J. Lee, *To-morrow is a New Day* (1939), pp. 148–9; Snowden, *op. cit.*, p. 775; Thomas Johnston, *Memories* (1952), p. 103.
42. 239 *H.C. Deb. ss.* (28 May 1930), col. 1349; see also Thomas Johnston, *op. cit.*, pp. 103–6; Mosley, *My Life, op. cit.*, pp. 231–4, 237.
43. Skidelsky, *op. cit.*, pp. 169–70; for conflicting views see Mandle, *op. cit.*, p. 501; Raymond Postgate, *George Lansbury* (1951), p. 256; Johnston, *op. cit.*, p. 106; Brockway, *op. cit.*, p. 209; G. D. H. Cole, *A History of the Labour Party from 1914* (1948), p. 238; R. Basset, *1931, Political Crisis* (1958), p. 38; George Lansbury, 'Address to the 30th

Annual Conference of the Labour Party', *The Labour Party, Report of the Thirtieth Annual Conference* (1930), p. 203; Colin Cross, *Philip Snowden* (1966), pp. 245–7.

44. Letter from O. E. Mosley to the Prime Minister dated 23 January 1930, in Skidelsky, *op. cit.*, p. 404.

45. J. H. Thomas, *My Story* (1937), pp. 169–73.

46. *The Manchester Guardian*, 7 February 1930.

47. Mandle, *op. cit.*, p. 502; see also Snowden, *op. cit.*, p. 875; G. D. H. Cole, *op. cit.*, pp. 237–8; Martin, *op. cit.*, p. 72; Alan Bullock, *The Life and Times of Ernest Bevin*, Vol. I (1960), p. 450.

48. Skidelsky, *op. cit.*, pp. 134, 178.

49. See Sir Oswald Mosley, 'Lost Lib-Lab Opportunity in the 1929 Parliament', *New Outlook* (May 1966), p. 15.

50. The Mosley Memorandum as cited by Skidelsky, *op. cit.*, pp. 171–82. The gist of Mosley's proposals were also described in his resignation speech and at the Labour Party Annual Conference. 239 *H.C. Deb. 5s.* (28 May 1930), cols. 1348–72; *Labour Party, Report of the 30th Annual Conference, op. cit.*, pp. 201–3; see also *The Manchester Guardian*, 19 March 1930.

51. *The Times*, 22 May 1930; *The Manchester Guardian*, 21 May 1930; Skidelsky, *op. cit.*, pp. 184, 407–8.

52. Colin Cross, *The Fascists in Britain* (1961), p. 37.

53. 239 *H.C. Deb. 5s.* (28 May 1930), cols. 1348–72.

54. *The Times*, 9 June 1930.

55. *ibid.*, 29 May 1930; *The Manchester Guardian*, 29 May 1930; *The Observer*, 1 June 1930.

56. See, especially, Baroness Ravensdale, *In Many Rhythms* (1953), p. 193; see also Snowden, *op. cit.*, p. 877; Brown, *op. cit.*, p. 157.

57. Again Skidelsky provides the best account emphasizing Henderson's superb tactics, *op. cit.*, pp. 184–9.

58. Michael Foot, *Aneurin Bevan*, Vol. I (1962), pp. 122–3.

59. *The Labour Party, The Report of the Thirtieth Annual Conference* (1930), p. 200.

60. *ibid.*, pp. 200–3.

61. Brockway, *op. cit.*, p. 211.

62. *The Labour Party, The Report of the Thirtieth Annual Conference* (1930), pp. 203–4.

63. For expressions of trade-union dissatisfaction with Government policy at the meeting of the Parliamentary Labour Party on 22 May, see W. F. Mandle, *op. cit.*, pp. 505–6.

64. *The Times*, 20 October 1930.

65. *ibid.*, 30 October 1930.

66. See Nigel Nicolson (ed.), *Harold Nicolson, Diaries and Letters 1930–1939* (1966), pp. 59, 61; W. J. Brown, *op. cit.*, p. 158; James Drennan, *BUF, Oswald Mosley, and British Fascism* (1934), p. 157.

67. See Cross, *op. cit.*, p. 42; Brockway, *op. cit.*, pp. 212–13.

68. Mosley's route through the Labour Party was lined with the sus-

picious from among the leadership to the I.L.P. See Margaret Cole (ed.), *op. cit.*, pp. 138, 243; Herbert Morrison, *An Autobiography by Lord Morrison of Lambeth* (1960), p. 321; Paton, *op. cit.*, p. 179.

69. *Annual Register*, 1930, p. 48; the value placed on loyalty gains credence when the number of desertions to the National Labour Party is taken into account.

70. For the full text see *The Times*, 8 December 1930.

71. Speech at the Manchester Engineering Council, *ibid.*, 10 December 1930.

72. *The Observer*, 6 December 1930.

73. *The Times*, 11, 17 December 1930; Cross, *op. cit.*, p. 44; Robert Boothby, Harold Macmillan and Oliver Stanley also expressed approval. George E. G. Catlin, 'Fascist Stirrings in Britain', *Current History* (February 1934), p. 544.

74. 'The Mosley Manifesto: Why We Have Issued It', *The Spectator*, 13 December 1940, pp. 629–30.

75. Allen Young, John Strachey, W. J. Brown and Aneurin Bevan, *A National Policy* (1931).

76. Oswald Mosley, *The Greater Britain* (1932 edn), p. 98.

77. Robert Boothby, *I Fight to Live* (1947), p. 91.

78. *The Observer*, 8 March 1931; see Sir Oswald Mosley in *New Outlook*, October 1966; Skidelsky, *op. cit.*, pp. 277, 280; Mosley, *My Life, op. cit.*, pp. 273–7.

79. John Strachey, *Interview*, 6 April 1960.

80. Brown, *op. cit.*, p. 159; C. E. M. Joad, *The Case for the New Party* (1931), p. 13.

# 4. The New Party

The formation of the New Party was announced at the beginning of March 1931, following still another attempt by Sir Oswald Mosley to convert the Labour Party to his views at a meeting of the Parliamentary Party on 27 January. It was to be a party of 'action' based on 'youth' and would mobilize 'energy, vitality and manhood to save and rebuild the nation'.[1]

John Strachey, Dr Robert Forgan, W. J. Brown, Oliver Baldwin and Cynthia Mosley resigned from the Labour Party, which later performed the ritual of expelling them, as did W. E. D. Allen, Unionist M.P. for West Belfast, from the Conservative Party.[2] Baldwin and Brown, however, soon dissociated themselves from the New Party with Brown claiming that Mosley had permitted *The Observer* to publish an interview which gave the party a quasi-Fascist complexion without consulting his colleagues.[3] Instead of resigning, Mosley was expelled. He had been stricken with pneumonia, although this should not necessarily have prevented his secretary or colleagues from drafting the letter of resignation. It suggests that, given his career and a sense of history, he wanted to place the onus of the final break on the Labour Party. It is also possible that he was using the resignations of his colleagues to blackmail the Party into a reconciliation.

Whatever his motivations, Mosley's expulsion added credence to Beatrice Webb's assessment that 'the New Party will never get born alive; it will be a political abortion'.[4] Certainly there were few defections to the Mosley group from outside the Parliamentary Party despite the criticism of the Government's unemployment policy within the Labour Movement. G. D. H. Cole attributed this to the adroit handling of Mosley's expulsion by the National Executive, particularly on Arthur Henderson's part.[5] There were stories that Mosley was trying to bribe candidates and agents away from the Labour Party. A statement by the Chairman of the Birmingham Labour Party to this effect was given publicity in the national Press and in Labour publications. This was denied, although it was admitted that Strachey's agent had been offered a position.[6] The assent accorded his criticisms and the appeal of his personality seem to have been neutralized by what many felt to be repulsive tactics, and these feelings extended beyond Labour Party circles. John Maynard Keynes told Harold Nicolson that he thought the programme was 'more sound and certainly more daring than that which any other party can advance'.[7] This was followed by a discussion with Keynes and Garvin who objected to Mosley's methods although they were sympathetic to his programme.[8]

The first public rally of the New Party was held on 6 March in Memorial Hall, Farrington Street, London, the premises from which the Labour Party had been launched thirty-one years earlier. Mosley was still ill, leaving Strachey, Forgan and Cynthia Mosley to deputize for him. Keen interest or curiosity was evident, for both the hall and an overflow room were full. The New Party was not without advantages, for its leader had been the only Minister to resign on behalf of the unemployed. It was also a non-Communist movement primarily devoted to removing the evil of unemployment. But ideals and grandiose schemes were easier to formulate than concrete proposals for election purposes. It was one thing to attract adherents by what Strachey described as 'an entirely utopian appeal for social compromise' and quite another to find common agreement as to the remedies.[9] Moreover, Mosley's schemes were bound to appeal to middle-class radicals and young idealists, rather than to the public at large. As originally conceived, there was little in the New Party programme to attract a mass following.

The New Party attracted a mixed bag of supporters: Liberals, Conservatives, Socialists, and intellectuals with varying shades of opinion joined. The former Liberals included: Sir J. W. Pratt, who had been Parliamentary Under-Secretary of Health for Scotland, 1919–22; Major C. R. Dudgeon, an ex-M.P. for Galloway; Selick Davies, who had contested Evesham in 1929, became a New Party candidate; and another former Liberal Party candidate, James McDougall, was appointed organizer for the London area. F. M. Box, who had worked for the Liberal Party and the Conservative Party for twenty-five years, was recruited from Conservative Party Headquarters to become Chief Agent of the New Party. A Mr W. Lowell, who had been 'active' in Unionist politics, and M. F. Woodroffe, a former 'supporter' of Beaverbrook's Empire crusade, were selected as Parliamentary candidates. From the Labour Party came John Stuart Barr, the former Parliamentary candidate for Tynemouth, and Arthur Reade, who had contested the Abingdon Division of Buckinghamshire. W. J. Leaper, L. J. Cumings, and Wilfred Risdon were formerly associated with the I.L.P. Cumings was eventually appointed Assistant Director of the New Party. Leaper was a Parliamentary candidate, who later joined the B.U.F. along with Risdon, a former organizer in the Midlands for the I.L.P.

The intellectuals included Osbert Sitwell, Harold Nicolson, and C. E. M. Joad, who was appointed Director of Propaganda. Prior to the publication of the Mosley Manifesto, Joad had written a sympathetic warning about Mosley's appeal to the young, stating that this particular brand of Socialism might develop into Fascism.[10] Evidently, Joad's doubts were never sufficiently appeased, for he left the New Party shortly after Strachey and Allen Young resigned. Nicolson was the editor of the short-lived New Party weekly, *Action*. A close friend of the Mosleys for several years, he was responsible for the relatively high literary quality of the paper. He modelled it on *John o' London's Weekly* and attracted a number of prominent young writers.[11] Regular contributors included Gerald Heard, Raymond Mortimer, V. Sackville-West, Peter Quennell and Peter

Cheyney, whose articles were the most aggressive and violent. Among the occasional contributors were Cecil Melville, Christopher Isherwood, Eric Partridge, and E. Arnot Robertson. It began with a sale of 160,000 in October 1931, but this was reduced to about 15,000 for its final issue at the end of the year and it incurred a weekly loss of £340.[12]

The organizational structure of the New Party was never formalized. There was a council responsible for policy and strategy which included Mosley, Strachey, Young, Forgan and Nicolson. Young, as secretary of the party, was in charge of organization until his resignation when he was succeeded by Box and Cumings. Forgan served as the New Party Whip in the House of Commons. But real power remained in Mosley's hands for he had the reputation, contacts and money and he would act unilaterally and autocratically.[13]

The New Party gradually developed, in terms of both policy and organization, into a near-Fascist movement. This can be traced through four phases: the National Policy campaign culminating in the Ashton-under-Lyne by-election; the formation of a youth movement, which alienated some of Mosley's left-wing supporters; the electoral failure of the New Party at the General Election in 1931; and, finally, the transformation of the New Party into the B.U.F.

During the early weeks of the New Party, the speakers continued to propagate *A National Policy*. Mosley was given an opportunity to set forth his plans for the reform of the political system when he was invited as leader of the New Party to submit testimony to the Select Committee on Procedure of Public Business. His written statement was largely a repetition of his earlier proposals. The government would request extraordinary powers to deal with the economic crisis. He was more precise than previously about the role of Parliament. Although it would have the power to accept or reject an order, to question and dismiss a government, and to deal with budget and supply under a strict guillotine procedure, Parliament would meet less frequently and ministers would not have to sit in the House. One of his stated objectives was to introduce men into the government who were not necessarily or primarily 'politicians'. On the other hand, Mosley was evasive about the extent of power that would be vested in his super-cabinet. It would supposedly be responsible for economic matters, while the larger cabinet would be responsible for the other spheres of government as he had previously outlined. Under close questioning, however, he admitted that the definition of an economic measure would be broadly interpreted, subject to the limits of existing analogies and precedents.[14]

While these aspects of the New Party programme were being re-stated, a by-election was announced at Ashton-under-Lyne as a result of the death of the Labour member. The constituency held some promise of success since forty-six per cent of the insured population was unemployed.[15] At the very least, Labour's majority was threatened. The seat had been held in 1929 with just over 13,000 votes against the Conservatives' 9,700 votes and 7,000 votes for the Liberals. Moreover, the Liberal candidate had gone over to the Labour Party and the Liberals had not had time to select a new one. For its first electoral contest, the New Party chose Allen Young as its candidate without consulting its Manchester branch which claimed jurisdiction and thereby resigned *en bloc*.[16]

The New Party marshalled its resources for the campaign. Mosley returned to the public platform telling his audiences that the New Party stood for 'Action! Action here and now!'[17] Cynthia Mosley, Strachey, and W. E. D. Allen also campaigned for Young. Other speakers included Strachey's American wife, Wyndham Portal, the G.W.R. magnate and two ex-Communists.[18] They spoke on the problems of unemployment and expounded the New Party proposals for economic and political reform at well-attended meetings. The local Press reported that it was one of the keenest elections ever experienced by the constituency.[19] The Labour Party was worried that Mosley might split the vote giving the Conservatives a victory and it was impossible to predict which way the Liberal vote would go, or who would gain the large Catholic vote. Hence, MacDonald, Tom Johnston and Arthur Greenwood appeared for the

Labour Party. The Conservatives overturned the Labour majority of 3,407 to win by 1,415 votes while Young polled 4,472 votes, enough to save his deposit.

The bitterness engendered was evident at the declaration of the poll. The crowd booed, jeered, and drowned the cheers of Mosley's supporters. Mosley, Cynthia Mosley, and Young could not get a hearing. They received the same treatment when they returned to the party offices.[20] Strachey later claimed that British Fascism was born that evening. Mosley, surveying the scene, had commented to him: 'That is the crowd that has prevented anyone doing anything in England since the War.'[21]

It is doubtful that this incident turned Mosley to Fascism as such. But the by-election may have raised serious doubts as to the prospects of the New Party. It had devoted all its energies to the campaign and the results were disappointing. It was apparent that the New Party needed different appeals and gimmicks, if it was to have more than a negative political impact. Two such appeals were to 'action' and 'youth', and they were complementary. Mosley had been drumming for action for some time and, provoked by Joad or impressed by Mussolini, he may have realized the possibility of rallying a following from among young people. At the same time, there had been disturbances at New Party meetings throughout the country, and two of Cynthia Mosley's meetings had actually been broken up. The New Party could hope to win additional supporters and attract attention by the formation of a youth movement. In addition, a corps of stewards could be formed from the youth movement to protect meetings and symbolize 'action' for the New Party. The first step would be taken towards the systematic use of political violence.

The party council debated the question for some time, and then in May 1931 reports began to circulate about the formation of a youth corps to be instructed in gymnastics and boxing.[22] Mosley announced that they were organizing an active force of their young male supporters to defend the right of free speech and to meet violence by appropriate measures. According to Mosley: 'The only methods we shall employ will be English methods. We shall rely on the good old English fist.'[23] In June it was reported that Mosley had sent Leslie Cumings and a Major Thompson of Rugby to Germany to study the methods of Hitler.[24]

Sir William Morris contributed substantially to the 'clubs' and 'Institutes', but only a limited number were established.[25] In any case, the New Party attracted enough young recruits to form a body of trained and provocative stewards – the 'active forces' or pioneers. Several of Mosley's meetings, particularly two in Glasgow and one in Birmingham, were broken up during the autumn of 1931.[26] Mosley described the meeting at the Birmingham Rag Market as the finest he had ever addressed in Birmingham.[27] Fist fights had broken out throughout the meeting and chairs were smashed. Peter Howard, then a prominent rugby player and New Party worker, suffered a lacerated temple.[28] Mosley was attacked by an opponent with a raised chair and was forced to leave the platform to defend himself. Charges of assault with a truncheon were later brought against Mosley, but his plea of self-defence was accepted.[29] Political violence was providing Mosley with his cherished publicity and, on occasions at least, breaking the apparent Press boycott on the New Party.[30]

Meanwhile, tensions arose within the New Party which led to the resignations of Strachey and Young and, later, Joad. The principal cause of their resignations was the formation of the youth movement, which was viewed as an outward manifestation of the direction in which Mosley's thoughts had turned. According to Strachey, Mosley had been flirting with Fascist ideas before the Ashton-under-Lyne by-election, but it was not until the summer of 1931 that he had made up his mind to turn the New Party into a Fascist-type organization.[31] Strachey and Young issued a statement on resigning from the New Party, in which they claimed to quote from the office short-hand report of one of Mosley's speeches. Mosley was alleged to have praised the 'modern movement' as it had developed in Italy and other countries and to have spoken of the necessity of forming such an organization in Britain to meet the Communist challenge

79

when it came. This organization would require an 'Iron Core' which would be the youth movement.[32]

Other causes of dissension were Mosley's attitude towards unemployment insurance, and India. The dispute over unemployment reached a climax in June 1931, when the New Party M.P.s crossed the floor in protest against the Government's proposals to abolish 'anomalies', thereby reducing the cost of the unemployment benefit. As for India, Strachey and Young charged that Mosley's attitude was 'indistinguishable from Churchillism'.[33] The immediate cause of their resignation in July 1931 was the rejection of Strachey's policy statement advocating trade with Russia. Mosley's reaction to their resignations was indicative of his new position: 'We have purged the party of all associations with Socialism.'[34]

The General Election held on 27 October 1931 spelled disaster for the New Party, which had had less than eight months to build a national organization. By September of that year, it had modified its original hope of contesting 400 seats by half and, in fact, only twenty-four candidates stood. Negotiations took place with the Conservatives, and although they did not seem profitable the New Party concentrated its resources in twenty constituencies held by the Labour Party and in two others that had been won in 1929, but lost at by-elections.[35] It discreetly avoided contesting the Midlands constituencies of Mosley's former allies.

Mosley engineered an 'about-face' in policy for election purposes. During the summer, he had hinted at his interest in the corporate state. The New Party committed itself to the corporate state early in October, conveniently dropped the idea for the General Election, and then re-adopted the idea after its defeat. The first issue of *Action* appeared on 8 October, two days after the Prime Minister had informed the House of Commons that the King had acceded to his request for an immediate dissolution. It was too late to stop the presses. An editorial announced that the New Party was ready to study the ideals of all creeds and take from them what was most efficient and effective. The central doctrine of the New Party was to be

British, 'framed to accord with the character and high experience of this race'. Fascism was condemned for its violence, but the editorial went on to state that, 'within the framework of the Corporate State, we wish to give the fullest possible expansion to individual development and enjoyment'. The watch-words were to be order, discipline, and self-control. Finally, it was announced that the New Party planned to form a special defence corps.[36]

Yet when the election manifesto was issued on 7 October, it was based on *A National Policy* and omitted any reference to the corporate state. During the campaign, Mosley stated that he had no use for Fascism or any other imported doctrine.[37] Harold Nicolson was less opportunistic for in his election address he warned of the possibility of a 'proletarian revolt' and the need for 'the Corporate, the Organic, State' to avert it.[38]

The results conclusively indicated the electorate's reaction to the new intruder on the political scene for the New Party polled only two per cent of the total vote. Twenty-two of the twenty-four candidates finished at the bottom of the poll. These included Mosley, although he polled 10,534 votes in his wife's former constituency of Stoke-on-Trent; Forgan who polled 1,304 votes in West Renfrew; Nicolson who received 461 votes in contesting the Combined English Universities seat; and Kid Lewis, a former middleweight boxing champion who was in charge of Mosley's personal stewards, with 421 votes in Whitechapel. The four seats formerly held by the New Party, although Cynthia Mosley and W. E. D. Allen did not stand, were won by Conservatives and at Ashton-under-Lyne the New Party candidate polled 424 votes. With a total vote of 36,777 and twenty-two deposits lost, the New Party's record was worse than the Communists'.

The electoral failure of the New Party had not completely discredited Mosley as a politician. Although he had earned the reputation of an adventurer, he had proved himself to be a man of considerable ability and energy and since he was only in his middle thirties the possibility of a political career remained open, if he chose to re-enter parliamentary politics. There were overtures from both the Conservative and Labour Parties and at the time Lord Rothermere expressed a willingness to back his ventures in the Harmsworth Press.[39] Yet this seemed to reinforce Mosley's determination, and his decision to propagate Fascism must be interpreted as something other than opportunism. Thus in a discussion with Nicolson in April 1932, Mosley reasoned that to return to the older parties 'would place himself in a strait-jacket' and that he did not want power on those terms. He was convinced of an approaching emergency and felt that he could accomplish more as a Fascist leader than as a party back-bencher and was willing to risk failure.[40]

The New Party was not abandoned, but if there were any doubts about the direction in which Mosley was moving they were now dispelled. He wrote of the need for a movement greater than class or party. This 'modern movement' would be inspired by completely new ideas of economic and political organization, particularly that of the corporate state. According to Mosley, the corporate state was not only the opposite reality to Communism, but was probably more suited to Great Britain than to any other country in the world. Mosley denied that he intended to import Italian Fascism, but he wanted to do for England what Mussolini had done for Italy. He reasoned that the New Party, through its advocacy of planning boards, councils, and similar conceptions, had evolved the germ of the corporate state long before it was suggested that they were imitating Italy.[41] Hence, Italy was seen as the primary, but not the exclusive, source of the new faith. An editorial in *Action* favourably commented on Hitler's 'achievement' in Germany.[42]

*Action* ceased publication after thirteen issues through lack of funds with the announcement that Mosley and Nicolson along with other members of the New Party were off on a trip to Italy, Germany, and possibly Russia 'to collect information'.[43] Mosley had to postpone the German trip but met Mussolini, whom he found 'affable but unimpressive', and who advised him against forming a paramilitary organization.[44] On his return to England, however, he wrote a glowing account of Fascist

Italy and called for the creation of a modern movement which would be 'natural to the British character'.[45]

Mosley set to work to create a 'Union of Fascists' based on the remnants of the New Party's Youth movement. In doing so, he alienated more of his colleagues, particularly Harold Nicolson. He began to draft a new programme, *The Greater Britain*, and negotiations were opened with the existing Fascist organizations. In a circular to prospective recruits, he wrote, 'Our object is no less than the winning of power for Fascism, which we believe is the only salvation for our country'.

## NOTES

1. *The Daily Telegraph*, 3 March 1931.
2. See Oswald Mosley (ed.), *Why We Left the Old Parties* (1931).
3. W. J. Brown, *So Far* (1943), p. 159; for Mosley's interpretation, see *My Life* (1968), p. 283.
4. Margaret Cole (ed.), *Beatrice Webb's Diaries, 1924–1932* (1956), p. 268.
5. G. D. H. Cole, *A History of the Labour Party from 1914* (1948), p. 243; The Labour Party, 'Correspondence from Arthur Henderson to Oswald Mosley, March 5th and March 10th, 1931', *Annual Report, 1931*, p. 31.
6. See J. Johnson, 'Birmingham Labour and the New Party', *The Labour Magazine* (April 1931), pp. 534–6; *Forward*, 14 March 1931; *The Manchester Guardian*, 7 March 1931.
7. Nigel Nicolson (ed.), *Harold Nicolson, Diaries and Letters, 1930–1939* (1966), p. 72.
8. *ibid.*, p. 74; Harold Macmillan was 'tempted to work with the New Party, but felt that the traditional parties were "too strongly entrenched" ': *Winds of Change 1914–1939* (1966), p. 247.
9. John Strachey, *The Menace of Fascism* (1933), p. 159.
10. C. E. M. Joad, 'Prolegomena to Fascism', *The Political Quarterly* (January 1931), pp. 82–99.
11. Sir Harold Nicolson, *Interview*, 15 December 1960.
12. *Action*, 31 December 1931; Nicolson, *op. cit.*, pp. 86, 99.
13. Nicolson, *op. cit.*, pp. 81–2.
14. *Special Report from the Select Committees On Procedure of Public Business, 1931* (4 June 1931), pp. 311–17; see also John Strachey and C. E. M. Joad, 'Parliamentary Reform: the New Party's Proposals', *The Political Quarterly* (July 1931), pp. 319–36; Mosley, of course, was not alone in advocating radical reforms for Parliament. See G. D. H. Cole, 'Socialist Control of Industry', in Christopher Addison, *et al., Problems of a Socialist Government* (1933), p. 173; A. H. Hanson, 'The Purpose of Parliament', *Parliamentary Affairs* (summer 1964), p. 280.

15. W. F. Mandle, 'The New Party', *Historical Studies* (October 1966), p. 246.
16. *Ashton-under-Lyne Reporter*, 25 April 1931; *The Manchester Guardian*, 20 April 1931.
17. *The Manchester Guardian*, 23 April 1931.
18. Mandle, *op. cit.*, p. 347.
19. *Ashton-under-Lyne Reporter*, 25 April 1931.
20. *ibid.*, 2 May 1931.
21. Strachey, *op. cit.*, p. 161.
22. John Strachey, 'Fascism – It Leads to Terror', *The Sunday Dispatch*, 23 July 1933; *The Daily Express*, 15 May 1931.
23. *The Manchester Guardian*, 16 May 1931.
24. *The Daily Herald*, 6 June 1931.
25. Communications with the late Lord Nuffield, 14 April 1961; Mosley sets the figure at £50,000, *My Life, op. cit.*, p. 345.
26. For Glasgow, see Colin Cross, *The Fascists in Britain* (1961), p. 49; Nicolson, *op. cit.*, p. 91.
27. *The Times*, 19 October 1931.
28. *ibid.*
29. *The Daily Herald*, 29 August 1931.
30. See letter from Lord Beaverbrook to Harold Nicolson, 25 June 1931, in Nicolson, *op. cit.*, pp. 79–80.
31. Strachey, *The Menace of Fascism, op. cit.*, p. 169.
32. *The Daily Herald*, 29 August 1931.
33. *ibid.*
34. *The Sunday Chronicle*, 26 July 1931.
35. Nicolson, *op. cit.*, p. 93.
36. *Action*, 8 October 1931.
37. *The Times*, 19 October 1931.
38. Nicolson, *op. cit.*, p. 94.
39. *ibid.*, pp. 98, 108, 112, 115; Cross has written that MacDonald approached Mosley about becoming a supporter of the National Government, but does not give the source, *op. cit.*, p. 53.
40. Nicolson, *op. cit.*, p. 115.
41. *Action*, 26 November, 24 December, 31 December 1931.
42. *ibid.*, 10 December 1931.
43. *ibid.*, 31 December 1931.
44. Nicolson, *op. cit.*, p. 107; this differs from the account given to Cross, *op. cit.*, p. 56, and to this author, 15 December 1960.
45. *The Daily Mail*, 1 February 1932.

# 5. From Party to Movement

In October 1932 those who had remained loyal to Mosley along with those who had been privately recruited to his new cause put on black shirts. It seemed like a singularly opportune moment for a movement with a radical cause. Britain was sharing in a depression affecting the older industrial nations and seemed on the verge of crisis. Unemployment rose from 1·5 million, or 10·4 per cent of insured males, in January 1929 to approximately three million, or twenty-three per cent, in 1933.[1] The Government response was one of orthodox policies and piecemeal legislation, while economic planning had gained acceptance elsewhere. In Italy Fascism had triumphed and Hitler had been moving towards power in Germany.

The Fascists, however, were deprived of their crisis. Great Britain had not experienced the economic boom of the previous decade so that the crash was neither sharp nor sudden. The bottom was reached at the beginning of 1933 but thereafter Britain experienced recovery sooner than other nations. Unemployment declined and by 1937 it had dropped to 10·8 per cent of the insured male population.[2] Production and foreign trade rose.[3] Wages remained stable and real income for the period was 17·7 per cent higher than for the previous decade, so that those who were employed more than held their own. A breakdown of the statistics reveals the regional, local and industry-centred basis of unemployment. While the percentage of registered unemployed in the peak year of 1932 averaged 13·7 for London and the South, it was 27·1 in the North and 36·5 in Wales. In 1937, unemployment dropped to 6·4 per cent for London and the South and 13·8 per cent in the North, but 22·3 per cent remained unemployed in Wales.[4] Workers in ship-building, textiles and coal were among the hardest hit and in 1934 in Jarrow and Maryport, 67·8 and 57·0 per cent, re-spectively, were reported unemployed.[5] Thus, although there was severe distress and deprivation, it tended to be confined to certain occupations and localities, and, as A. J. P. Taylor has observed, it was remote from London, the political centre.[6]

Despite economic recovery, the Government could not be credited with a bold, imaginative policy. It remained, along with the whole parliamentary system, an object for criticism stemming from both the left and the right. But despite the protests, the pamphleteering and the demonstrations, most people remained off the streets and where the Fascists predicted gains, i.e. in the areas of unemployment, they made little pro-gress. In other words, Mosley's crisis did not materialize, and even where there was economic depression the Fascist move-ment did not benefit.

Another source of potential support was the traditional right, especially anti-Communists, anti-Socialists, anti-Democrats and those who were critical of Conservative leadership and policies. There were several expressions of these moods; in 1934 after the B.U.F. had been receiving a bad press, Stanley Baldwin still found it necessary to appeal to his supporters not to break away.[7] Baroness Ravensdale has written that at the time many eminent Conservatives had toyed with the idea of joining her brother-in-law while Viscount Wolmer, Unionist M.P. for Aldershot, claimed that many young men were going over to the Blackshirts because the Conservatives had lost their former enthusiasm.[8]

The pronouncements of the Socialist League and its leading figure, Sir Stafford Cripps, aroused resentment in the Labour Party and the Conservative Party, let alone the traditional right.[9] The League demanded that a Socialist Government upon obtaining office should be given emergency powers approximating to those of a dictatorship. In January 1934 Cripps, in a speech before the University Labour Federation, stated that it was a requirement for a Socialist Government to deal with the House of Lords and the influence of the City and that the opposition of Buckingham Palace and other places would have to be overcome.[10] Despite repeated denials these remarks were interpreted as an attack on the Crown and they apparently prompted Sir William Wayland, Conservative M.P. for Canterbury, to say, 'If we had a Socialist Government in power . . . I very much doubt whether I should not become a Fascist myself'.[11]

Antipathy towards democratic practices which were often interpreted as being synonymous with Socialism was expressed in the House of Lords during a debate on a bill to alter its composition and extend its power. Lord Salisbury, who moved the second reading, expressed his fears of Socialism and eulogized the merits of a hereditary governing class.[12] What was, perhaps, the most memorable speech of the debate was made by Lord Monkswell:

The organized wastrels are overawing the House of Commons, partly by the voting power of the masses and even more by the threat of revolutionary violence. . . . When organized revolutionary force, dependent either on voting or on rioting, can be met by greater force supported by the intelligence and patriotism of the best elements in the country, then will peace and prosperity be at hand.[13]

The traditional right, for the most part, however, remained loyal to the Conservative Party. Baldwin's fears of large-scale defections were never realized. If the vote of the Communist Party substantially increased, the B.U.F. may have gained some significant support. But Communist and Fascist success were contingent on the same factors.

The formation of the British Union of Fascists proceeded at a deliberate but cautious pace and it was some time before the movement gained national attention. Yet it would be unwise to underestimate the arrangements necessary for launching such a venture. In a relatively short time, meetings were planned, publishing ventures were organized, funds were solicited and future colleagues were recruited. Dr Robert Forgan recalled the excitement of those days when his office was literally his home and his life was the movement.[14]

Fifteen days after the announcement of the B.U.F.'s formation, Mosley addressed the movement's first public meeting in Trafalgar Square. Towards the end of October, the Blackshirts held their first indoor meeting and parade in London.[15] At a meeting in Kentish Town in November there were disturbances and one or two Blackshirts were treated for injuries.

In February 1933, the *Blackshirt* was launched and the *Fascist Week* appeared the following February only to be incorporated with the former after five months. The *Blackshirt*, until the appearance of *Action* in 1936, was the main propaganda organ of the B.U.F. In the spring of 1933 Mosley, accompanied by a contingent of uniformed Blackshirts, made his second visit to Rome on the occasion of the Fascist festival celebrating the 'Birth of Rome', Italian Labour Day, and the founding of Fascism. He was photographed taking the salute with Mussolini. On his return, he denied that the B.U.F. took orders from Mussolini, stating that they were not affiliated or subordinate to any other Fascist movement, although close relations were maintained.[16]

Before his journey, however, the first of the major disturbances that were to become the hallmark of B.U.F. meetings occurred at Manchester's Free Trade Hall. Mosley stood alone on the platform and called attention to an estimated 140 black- and grey-shirted stewards on duty throughout the hall. He announced that they did not want violence, but that they were going to insist on the right of free speech, and that this was the reason for the Defence Force being present. Later in the meeting an argument broke out between a member of the audience and a steward. Mosley was heard telling the steward to leave the man alone, but evidently the steward did not hear and the dispute ended in a scuffle.

The audience was soon in an uproar, and several incidents

occurred throughout the hall. The *Manchester Guardian* reporter claimed that some men could be seen using what looked like rubber truncheons. The police entered the hall and ushered the stewards into the lobbies. A number of the Blackshirts were indignant, but Mosley could be heard shouting from the platform not to resist arrest. Meanwhile, the Union Jack had been torn from the platform box, and the audience was divided between singing the 'Red Flag' and 'God Save the King'. The stewards reappeared on the platform, and Mosley requested the police to restore order so that he could speak. The police insisted that the Blackshirts leave, and order was restored.[17]

In an interview with *The Manchester Evening News* Mosley maintained that the meeting did not get out of control until the police took over, and that under their protection the Communist Party had been able to break up the meeting. Mosley claimed that this was the first Fascist meeting to end in disorder, and that there had been disturbances at only two per cent of 300 to 400 meetings in the last year.[18]

The meeting was important in a number of ways. It set the pattern for future B.U.F. meetings in that Mosley went out of his way to display and mention the Defence Force. They were uniformed, intimidating, and apparently beyond his control. Moreover, *The Manchester Guardian* reported, 'It was apparent that they were not, in the main, Manchester members of the Union'.[19] This was in reference to the paid National Defence Force which accompanied Mosley and stewarded his meetings throughout the country. The stewards, however, were not always or exclusively drawn from London.[20] In this instance, at least, there was undisputed evidence that weapons were used by the Blackshirts. Mosley testified under oath three years later, in connection with a libel suit, that twenty-four out of 140 stewards carried lengths of rubber hose at the meeting, although this was forbidden thereafter.[21] Although the B.U.F. tactics were provocative, there were members of the audience who were waiting to be provoked. It was difficult to tell how organized they were at this particular meeting although they became well organized later. The police entered the meeting apparently unsolicited. They acted with a high degree of efficiency and with little show of favouritism. This was significant, for the behaviour of the police at Mosley meetings throughout the 1930s was frequently charged with favouritism towards the Fascists. Finally, Mosley blamed the Communists for breaking up the meeting and for challenging the constitutional right of free speech. This line was pursued by the Blackshirts throughout 1933.[22]

Two other meetings addressed by Mosley in the autumn also resulted in disorder. The Blackshirts held a rally at Belle Vue, in Manchester, in October. It was reported that between 2,000 and 2,500 Blackshirts were on hand. A contingent of over 400 travelled in a special train from London while some 900 were from Manchester. For the most part, the meeting was orderly, but when there was a scuffle, spotlights deliberately switched from Mosley to focus on the scenes of disturbance where the defence corps had converged – a tactic that was to be repeated at Mosley's future meetings. After the meeting, the Fascists formed ranks and marched away. *En route* they were attacked by about sixty people, in what Mosley described as a 'Communist ambush'.[23] Approximately two weeks later, Mosley faced an audience composed mostly of undergraduates at the Oxford Town Hall. About 100 Blackshirt stewards were present. The meeting proceeded peacefully until Mosley began to comment on Oxford pacifism and the famous resolution, 'This House will in no circumstances fight for its King and Country', which had been passed by the Oxford Union the previous February. A number of interruptions followed. Ejections followed the interruptions and fists and chairs followed the ejections.[24]

The Blackshirts were now receiving their share of publicity. They capitalized on the tithe disputes which were taking place in Suffolk. On three occasions, beginning in the summer of 1933, they appointed themselves the defenders of the downtrodden against the established forces. In one incident the Blackshirts took over a farm near Wortham, Suffolk, without the owner's consent and despite police warnings. They dug trenches, erected barricades, and raised the Fascist flag. Richard Plathen, the National Political Officer of the B.U.F., stated that the Fascists did not ask permission: 'We suit our actions to the needs of the moment.'[25] They remained there for sixteen days, until fifty policemen arrested nineteen of about fifty Blackshirts present. They eventually pleaded guilty before the High Court to conspiring to effect a public mischief, but were bound over and ordered to pay the costs of the prosecution.

Of the nineteen arrested, eleven were from London, which suggested that the episode was not a local uprising. Only two gave their occupations as farmers. Five of the nineteen were over forty years old, four were over thirty, three were in their late twenties, six were between the ages of twenty and twenty-four, and one was eighteen. Yet, both the Attorney-General, Sir Thomas Inskip, and the defending counsel, Sir Patrick Hastings, tried to emphasize their youth. The Attorney-General may have been correct in that the accused did not belong to the criminal classes (nor were they farmers, a point neglected), but the adjectives 'young and headstrong' implied men younger than was in fact the case.[26]

The B.U.F. had gained momentum by 1934 and meetings and demonstrations were held throughout the country with dozens of speakers parroting Mosley. The leader appeared on the grand occasions. On 22 April, he spoke for an hour and a half without interruption at the Albert Hall. The emphasis of his speech was on coming to power peacefully, and exercising power constitutionally within the framework of the corporate state. The speech, for the most part, was moderate and suggested the influence of Lord Rothermere, a recent convert.[27] Sir Thomas Moore, M.P., was so pleased with Mosley's performance that he wrote in *The Daily Mail* that there was little, if any, of Mosley's policy that could not be accepted by the most loyal Conservative. He stressed that the true parents of the Blackshirts were the Conservatives and that the two were bound together by loyalty to the throne and love of country. He concluded by calling for closer cooperation.[28]

A Mosley demonstration was also conceived to be a spectacle, and by the Albert Hall meeting it had been perfected as such. Mosley stood alone on the platform with the spotlights focused on him. He had been preceded in his long march down the length of the hall by Fascist standard-bearers and was greeted with the Fascist salute and 'Hail Mosley'. Fascist songs had been sung before his arrival including '*Giovinezza*' and the '*Horst Wessel Lied*'. Uniformed Blackshirt stewards occupied the aisle seats in each row or stood at the sides. The audience included a wide cross-section and one reporter noticed many women, and commented on the absence of young men.[29] The meeting was relatively free from disturbances, but the anti-Fascists also had their day. A number of members from the Surrey Federation of Youth in black shirts distributed some 3,000 free programmes outside the hall in competition with the official programmes at 6*d*. The free programme was an anti-Fascist pamphlet, 'British Fascism Explained'.[30]

Spectacle, however, was reserved for those occasions addressed by the leader. Most meetings, both indoors and outdoors, were modest.[31] But whether demonstrations in large urban centres or street-corner orations in provincial towns, they were frequently accompanied by violence. In the Metropolitan Police District alone, the Commissioner of Police reported that disturbances attributed to the wearing of political uniforms doubled from eleven in the first six months of 1933 to twenty-two in the last six months of the year.[32] Commander Oliver Locker-Lampson, Unionist M.P. for Handsworth, introduced a bill, under the ten-minute rule, in May 1934, to prohibit political uniforms, but without success or support. The Bill was opposed because of the difficulties involved in defining a political uniform and on the grounds that it would interfere with the right of all political demonstrations and martyr Mosley.[33]

During the first two months of 1934 Blackshirt meetings were orderly, but violence increased in the spring. The B.U.F. held a meeting at the Dome in Brighton early in March where Walter Faulkner, who was a member of the Labour Party and chairman of the Brighton branch of the National Unemployed Workers Movement, was invited to debate. According to Faulkner, when the National Anthem was sung he stood up, but before the end, when he bent down to pick up his little daughter, he was set upon and badly bruised. Three Blackshirts were subsequently charged with assault; two were found guilty, one of a technical offence, and the charges against the third were dropped.[34] Just to balance the books, a Blackshirt was beaten up by two anti-Fascists and was detained in hospital for five days, although his injuries were not serious. One of his two assailants was given six weeks in jail, and the other was bound over.[35]

In Bristol, a scuffle after a B.U.F. meeting led to an exchange of letters between Mosley and the Home Secretary, Sir John Gilmour. Mosley had addressed a crowd of some 2,000 at the Empire Theatre, and at the conclusion of his speech 400 to 500 Blackshirts assembled and marched away. They were attacked *en route* and several incidents resulted, but the police prevented any serious disorder. Gilmour stated in the House of Commons:

I think there is no doubt that this disorder was largely due to the adoption of semi-military evolutions by the Fascists, their marching in formation, and their general behaviour, which was regarded by the crowd as provocation.[36]

Mosley replied that he was unaware of any disorder, except that of two Negroes, one with a raised knife, who attempted to attack him and were knocked down by Fascists. He did not feel that to defend oneself from being knifed by Negroes in the streets of an English city was provocative. He denied that marching in columns of three as distinct from columns of four was a semi-military evolution and illegal, and argued that this was the best way to prevent disorder in the circumstances of Red terrorism which prevailed in Bristol. Mosley concluded that:

If men who were well known to be Fascists, whether wearing the black shirt or not, had left the hall in small parties they would certainly have been attacked by bands of highly organized roughs and a series of fights would have taken place resulting in considerable disorder.[37]

Gilmour answered that he had not said that marching in

formation was illegal, but that the semi-military evolutions invoked in marching, and the general behaviour of the Fascists were considered provocative by the crowd. As for the two Negroes, one was a 'half-caste Communist', who had been protesting to the Fascists about the way they had treated some of his colleagues. The police had not observed a raised knife. The Home Secretary suggested that if his followers had not been wearing black shirts they would not be well known to be Fascists.[38] Mosley had the last public word by repeating a request for the Home Secretary to state precisely what semi-military evolutions were. He argued that Gilmour had implied that anyone who wore a badge that indicated political affiliations other than socialism was liable to attack.[39]

While the national campaign was gaining in tempo, private functions and dinners were arranged by Forgan to enlist the support and cooperation of business and professional men. Mosley and Major-General J. F. C. Fuller were often the speakers, but Forgan spoke to these gatherings on the majority of occasions. Forgan, operating in the background, was also able to control the January Club, which was formed under the chairmanship of Sir John Squire to discuss the problems of Fascism. Both Squire and the B.U.F. claimed that the Club, which was founded on New Year's Day in 1934, and hence its name, was not a Fascist organization, although Fascists were members.[40] Squire stated that most of the other members were in sympathy, and that although Fascism would not come to Britain as it had to Germany and Italy, it was inevitable.[41] The objects of the Club as announced in its first notice were:

(a) to bring together men who are interested in modern methods of government;
(b) to provide a platform for leaders of Fascist and Corporate State thought. The club, however, will not formulate any policy of its own;
(c) to enable those who are propagating Fascism to hear the views of those who, while sympathizing with and students of twentieth-century political thought, are not themselves Fascists.[42]

The January Club claimed over 120 members.[43] In addition

to Squire, who was then the editor of the *London Mercury*, those responsible for the organization of the Club included Forgan, a Captain H. W. Luttman-Johnson, who acted as the Honorary Secretary and was later detained under Defence Regulation 18B, and Francis Yeats-Brown, author of *Lives of a Bengal Lancer*, who as editor of *Everyman* had used the magazine to publicize the corporate state.[44] Lord Midleton had put his London flat at their disposal as a headquarters.[45]

The Club's methods were to hold a number of dinners for members and guests, where they would be addressed by both Fascist and anti-Fascist speakers. At one meeting, the speakers included Miss Muriel Currie, co-author of *The Working of the Corporate State*, Commandant Mary Allen, who publicly joined the B.U.F. in 1940 and was duly detained under 18B, Air-Commodore J. A. Chamier, who spoke on air defence, Major H. L. Nathan, a Jewish Liberal M.P. for North-East Bethnal Green, who spoke against the Mosley movement, as well as Forgan and Alexander Raven Thomson for the B.U.F.[46] Among those in regular attendance at meetings were Sir Donald Makgill, until he quit in July 1934, Wing-Commander Sir Louis Greig, who was Gentleman Usher to the King and was identified by *Fascist Week* as a member of the Club, Colonel Norman Thwaites, Ward Price of the Rothermere Press, and Sir Henry Fairfax-Lucy.[47] The Club dropped out of the news at the end of June after the B.U.F. meeting at Olympia and the Hitler purge, but was reported to be functioning one year later under the chairmanship of Colonel Thwaites, who later became a director of the Right Club.[48]

The Fascists' paramilitary organization also attracted its share of attention. Mosley created an authoritarian movement. He saw himself as standing above the party at the head of the movement which would transform the state. It was his personal instrument for he created it and could destroy it at his will. His task was two-fold. First, he had to mould conflicting interests into a radical and disciplined body. Second, he had to construct the image of himself as leader and, having done so, promote, preserve and protect this image. The military provided a natural model for integrating dissimilar elements of a society and establishing the authority of the leader. The present headquarters was unsuitable for this undertaking and that Mosley had more grandiose plans in mind was evident by the Press reports that he was negotiating for the Wellington Barracks. In any event, he was successful in leasing the sprawling quarters of the former Whitelands Teachers Training College in Chelsea. Black House as it was known, housed the nest of Fascist administrative offices, provided dormitories for the paid Defence Force and was complete with gymnasium, grounds for drilling, canteen and recreational facilities, all of which were at the disposal of the membership.

The size of the professional Defence Force has been variously estimated as a few dozen to 300 to 400 Blackshirts.[49] According to former Blackshirts, they received free lodging at Black House and free or subsidized food at the canteen.* In addition they were given a spending allowance, probably a maximum of £1 a week, and they probably collected relief benefits. In return for their keep, the larger proportion of the clerical and custodial personnel was drawn from their ranks, while others acted as guards and messengers. At night they served as stewards and paper-sellers. The *Blackshirt* published glowing accounts of the benefits of military discipline and the 'glories' of military life, while the anti-Fascists 'exposed' the 'sinister' military preparations and denounced their scandalous existence. B.U.F. propaganda described the virtues of their day: reveille, inspection, physical exercise, drill, meals, duties, discipline, recreation, and stewarding. These activities were not restricted to the Chelsea Black House nor to the paid National Defence Force. In Birmingham, the Union Jack was lowered and 'Retreat' sounded at the Fascist headquarters every evening.[50] The anti-Fascists were not convinced about these virtues, nor were they reassured by the pictures in B.U.F. publications of Blackshirts standing at attention for inspection, Blackshirts at drill, or by the two

---

* Mosley maintains that they paid for their keep and that the barracks was almost self-supporting. *My Life* (1968), pp. 303-4.

Blackshirts posed with an Alsatian and a bulldog, simply captioned 'Good Pals at Fascist Headquarters'.[51]

A former B.U.F. official tells the story about a Press conference that he held to reassure the Press that the movement's military regimentation was a secondary factor in the activities of the B.U.F. At one point during the conference a bugle sounded. As he proceeded the bugle calls grew louder until the bugler burst into the room accompanied by two Blackshirts and announced the approach of the Chief of Staff on his daily tour of inspection.

The formation of a Fascist 'motor corps' and 'air force' attracted further notoriety. Most of the vehicles in the motor corps were privately owned and in part-time use. The purchase of four vans, however, raised more than eyebrows. The Home Secretary, Sir John Gilmour, in answer to a question in the House of Commons, admitted the purchase of 'specially constructed motor vans for the conveyance of speakers to and from the meetings', but he went on to state, 'As far as I am aware, there is no question of armoured cars in the sense of carrying arms'.[52] In 1934, a Gloucestershire branch of the B.U.F., which had organized a flying club, held a meeting at a disused airfield attended by about 250 Blackshirts. There were five planes, and instruction was given by a qualified pilot. Fascist Commander Godman stated that the object of the meeting was to give any member who intended to qualify for a pilot's certificate a chance of becoming acquainted with airplanes.[53]

The plan to build a disciplined movement was vitiated by the opportunistic nature of the B.U.F.'s recruitment policy which in effect admitted everyone who bothered to apply. This not only led to a high turn-over in membership but created organizational difficulties. The Defence Force both at the National Headquarters and in the provinces tended to attract a bad lot. This was realized and even rationalized on the grounds that, while during good times people resented it, in bad times they wanted a show of toughness. Nevertheless, expulsions ranged from six to ten weekly.[54] There were also reports of funds being stolen, of infiltration and of perversions. It eventually became necessary to reorganize a number of branches and by 1935 the National Headquarters had to order the closing of all social clubs which had replaced many of the branches in all but name.[55] A provision was inserted in the 1936 constitution that the district office was to be 'an office not a social club'.[56] A number of adventurers tried to damage the prestige of the movement. They sold what information they could get to the Press or to other bidders, because they were embittered at not making the Fascist grade or simply because they needed the money.[57] *The News Chronicle* and *The Daily Herald* were the primary outlets for this information.

For example, in February 1934, three members of the B.U.F. were charged with 'being concerned in unlawfully and maliciously inflicting certain grievous bodily harm on George Stanley Richardson'. Richardson had joined the B.U.F. early in January. Shortly thereafter, he sold a letter to *The News Chronicle* for £1, which formed the basis of an article entitled 'Fascist Fiction', and alleged the existence of a Fascist secret service. Richardson claimed that Ian Hope Dundas, the chief of staff, had called him a 'crawling rat', and had accused him of writing to A. J. Cummings of *The News Chronicle*. He was then dismissed, and his membership badge and papers were taken from him. Subsequently he was taken to the Defence Force room where he was struck, seized, and pinned to the floor by five Blackshirts. He alleged that half a pint of castor oil was forced down his throat. The resident medical officer at Westminster Hospital said that, when his stomach was washed out, the contents contained a small quantity of oily material, which would have been compatible with his having taken castor oil. He was unable to determine the quantity. One of the defendants admitted striking Richardson but only in self-defence. Otherwise, the whole incident was denied. The magistrate acquitted the defendants, on the grounds that the evidence was not strong enough to convict for causing bodily harm.[58]

The B.U.F. gained its most formidable recruit at the beginning of 1934 when it enlisted the support of Lord Rothermere who used *The Daily Mail, The Evening News, The Sunday Dispatch* and *The Sunday Pictorial* to promote the British Fascist cause. Rothermere had offered his services to the New Party and, if it had shown some chance of succeeding, an agreement would probably have been reached.[59] There were rumours that nego-tiations had been resumed in 1933, and they proved to be correct when the publisher's article, 'Hurrah for the Black-shirts', appeared in *The Daily Mail* on 15 January 1934.[60] Rothermere informed his two and a half million readers that the B.U.F. was purely British and had nothing to do with Italian Fascism. Yet Germany and Italy under Fascism were the best governed nations in Europe and there were no other countries where 'the people feel such confidence and pride in their rulers'. At the next election the survival of Britain as a great power would depend on the existence of a well-organized 'Party of the Right with the same directness of purpose and energy of method as Hitler and Mussolini have displayed'.

It was apparent from the outset that Mosley and Rothermere differed in their conceptions of the purpose of British Fascism. Politically, Rothermere was more interested in Conservatism and anti-Communism and anti-Socialism than he was in Fascism. As for Mosley, it seems that Rothermere hoped either to catch the Fascist leader for the Conservative Party or to use him as the prototype of leadership he thought the Party ought to have. The B.U.F. was seen as the armed wing of the Con-servative Party and attempts were made to demonstrate their compatability.

A report of Mosley's meeting at the Albert Hall in April 1934 referred to the B.U.F.'s policy as a British policy: 'the sort of policy that the Conservative Party ought to stand for but does not, owing to sentimental and weak-kneed leadership'.[61] A leading article in *The Daily Mail* in June affirmed:

Sir Oswald Mosley at his meetings has only expressed with one or two exceptions − views that are identical with those of the robuster minds in the Conservative Party. Like them, he stands for law, order, free speech and English methods.[62]

The Rothermere Press avoided referring to the B.U.F. as a

99

Fascist movement and never described its adherents as Fascists. For Rothermere, British Fascism was always the 'Blackshirt' movement, 'Blackshirt' policy and the 'Blackshirts'. Although the accomplishments of Italy and Germany were praised, the corporate state was not supported and it was made clear on several occasions that a dictatorship was not being advocated.[63] The Press baron shared with the Fascists a hatred of Communism and Socialism. As late as 1939 he wrote: 'The destiny which both Hitler and Signor Mussolini know themselves to be fulfilling is that of defenders of Europe against Communism.'[64] At home, Sir Stafford Cripps and his 'predatory Communists' and 'revolutionary socialists' were singled out and disturbances and violence were blamed solely on the Communists.[65]

Rothermere attacked international finance only occasionally and the City not at all. He did not feel persecuted nor did he see any conspiracies. Yet his position on the Jews was somewhat ambivalent. On the formation of the Mosley–Rothermere alliance, the Press baron announced that the Blackshirts had never attacked anyone for his race or creed, for this was not in keeping with the British character.[66] This was analogous to the B.U.F.'s subsequent position that, 'we attack the Jews not for what they are but for what they do', but it can be assumed that Rothermere accepted it at face value, for the containment of the movement's anti-Semitic tendencies from December 1933 until spring 1934 must be credited to his influence.[67] On withdrawing support from the B.U.F., Rothermere gave his dislike of anti-Semitism as one of the reasons and two leading articles praising British Jewry were published in *The Daily Mail*. But where Mosley at first had not made up his mind on Hitler's persecution of the Jews, Rothermere excused Hitler. He informed his readers that 'The Jews do not dominate certain professions in Britain as they do in Germany'.[68] Rothermere's position had not changed in its essentials in 1939. He wrote that the 'Jewish citizens' in certain European countries seem to have 'emerged' stronger and wealthier at the expense of the 'native race'. This did not excuse the Nazis, but explained them.[69]

Rothermere and Mosley were closest in agreement on Empire

policy and air defence, but where these were the primary considerations for the former, they were only aspects of wider or more basic policy for the latter. Rothermere was at odds with the Government for 'giving India away' and for allowing 'Ceylon to be handed over to a crazy system of rule by coloured democracy',[70] Mosley saw the Empire as part of his national self-sufficiency doctrine and therefore advocated a strong hand in India.[71] Air defence was a part of overall defence, which was only a minor point of the B.U.F. foreign policy. For Rothermere, it was most essential: *'The Daily Mail* has consistently advocated a programme of building at least 5,000 first-line machines without delay.'[72] Mosley's speeches and articles on this topic were given particular prominence.[73]

Rothermere's initial enthusiasm for the Blackshirts faded by the middle of February, although his support lingered on until July. He was quoted in February as having denied that his support for Mosley was a 'crusade'. He labelled it only an 'incident'.[74] Although the pace of the campaign slowed, it by no means came to a halt. The Rothermere Press continued to publish articles by Mosley, gave biased accounts of his meetings, and ran large publicity campaigns to advertise B.U.F. demonstrations. Full reports of the meetings were printed, and Rothermere utilized his best reporters. For example, Randolph Churchill wrote of Mosley at Leeds:

Sir Oswald's peroration was one of the most magnificent feats of oratory I have ever heard. The audience which had listened with close attention to his reasoned arguments were swept away in spontaneous reiterated bursts of applause.[75]

The final break was precipitated by the public outrage which greeted the political violence employed at the B.U.F.'s meeting at Olympia in June 1934 and the reaction to Hitler's purges, 'the night of the long knives', later that month. In a public exchange of letters Rothermere based his disagreements with Mosley on four counts. First, he thought that a movement calling itself Fascist would never succeed in Great Britain. Second, he could never support any movement with an anti-

Semitic bias. Third, he disagreed with the conception of dictatorship. Finally, he objected to the idea of substituting the corporate state for the parliamentary institutions of Great Britain. He went on to say that he had given Mosley assistance in the hope of allying him with the 'Conservative forces' to defeat Socialism at the next election. He hoped it would be possible for them still to come together, but stressed that he never thought that the political situation in Britain resembled that in Germany or Italy.[76] Mosley's reply was a courteous defence of the principles that Rothermere disputed. He argued that Rothermere was a Conservative interested in a revived Conservative Party. He was in agreement with several aspects of B.U.F. policy, such as the maintenance of a strong Empire and the building of a strong air force. The B.U.F., however, would not give up those aspects of its policy which were obnoxious to Rothermere. Accordingly, the B.U.F. could not abandon the creed of Fascism or the label 'Fascism', for they meant everything in the world to the movement.[77]

The Fascists later attributed Rothermere's withdrawal of support to pressures exerted by his Jewish advertisers.* In fact, the advertising revenue of the Rothermere Press was the highest in four years.[78] Average circulation declined, but it had been declining and continued to do so after the Blackshirts were dropped.[79] This can be credited to the circulation war being waged by the popular Press.

This had not been Rothermere's first venture on what he must have viewed as the fringes of the Conservative Party. He founded an Anti-Waste Party in 1921 and nine years later he joined with Lord Beaverbrook in an 'Empire Crusade' in the United Empire Party. Moreover, admiration for strong leaders and personalities including Hitler and Mussolini pre-dated and post-dated his support for the B.U.F. For example, he had previously championed the cause of Lloyd George, Lord Beaverbrook and M. Poincaré. In 1933, Rothermere stated that

* According to Mosley, 'he [Rothermere] was quite frank in explaining that he pulled out on account of his advertisers, and the firms in question were under Jewish influence.' *My Life, op. cit.,* p. 343.

Hitler had saved Germany from the ineffectual leadership of half-hearted politicians, and in 1939 Nazi atrocities were excused as necessary counter-measures to 'Bolshevist-financed terrorism'. Such methods were described as 'means' to prevent the alternative of 'failure' and 'destruction'.[80]

Rothermere seems to have realized fairly soon after joining forces with Mosley that he had become involved in another lost cause. Mosley may still have been received in important circles but he was not influential.[81] Nor was the alliance received favourably in the Press. Beaverbrook was not content to ignore the alliance and went out of his way to repudiate Fascism. In an article in *The Daily Express* on 17 January, he wrote: 'Empire ever. Nazi-ism never.' The two were described as incompatible, for the continuance of the Empire depended upon the maintenance of democratic principles for which he looked to the Conservative Party. 'Sentinel' in *The Morning Post* defended the Fascists from Rothermere. He wrote that the chief danger to its healthy growth as a group of patriots with a policy of compromise between socialism and nationalism was the recently received patronage of a portion of the syndicated Press.[82] *The Economist* described British Fascism as a subject for the cartoonist rather than the political philosopher and *The Spectator* correctly predicted the course of the B.U.F.'s most eventful years: 'There is little sign of the British Fascists becoming a danger, but they may well become a nuisance.'[83] While *The Spectator* was telling Rothermere that the average *Daily Mail* reader was a potential 'ready made' Blackshirt, George Bernard Shaw rejoiced in *The News Chronicle*, 'As a red hot Communist, I am in favour of Fascism'.[84]

The Blackshirts also proved an embarrassment. Following Rothermere's initial article in support of the B.U.F., *The Daily Mail* printed a series of letters all favourable to the campaign. The letters, however, had been inspired, not by *Daily Mail* readers, but by Blackshirts, and were exposed as such.[85]

It was clear that the alliance had been an unlikely one in the first place. Rothermere's suspicions were confirmed by the events of June 1934 which discredited British Fascism. The violence at Olympia was denounced in all quarters and there were proposals to increase police powers and ban paramilitary organizations. Rothermere may have been able to rationalize the 'night of the long knives' and the B.U.F.'s defence of it, but it was doubtful that public opinion would.[86] If Rothermere still hoped to exert an influence on the Conservative Party, it was apparent that he was not going to do so through the Blackshirt movement.

The Rothermere Press and the B.U.F. remained on friendly terms after the exchange of letters. The B.U.F. received fairly wide and complete coverage, until the autumn of 1935. Although the reports were less partial, articles by Mosley were still published, and the Blackshirts' anti-Communist fight was emphasized.[87] The Rothermere Press remained sympathetic towards Germany until the outbreak of the Second World War. The Blackshirts blamed Rothermere's defection on his misunderstanding of Fascism and on advertising pressures, but lauded his patriotism.[88]

## NOTES

1. *Twenty-Second Abstract of Labour Statistics of the U.K., 1922–1936* (Cmd 5576, 1937), pp. 50–51, 58.
2. William Ashworth, *An Economic History of England 1870–1939* (1960), p. 411; according to Ashworth the non-insured were less subject to unemployment than the insured so that it is possible that unemployment in general was two per cent less, p. 416.
3. C. L. Mowat, *Britain Between the Wars, 1918–1940* (1955), p. 432.
4. *ibid.*, p. 464.
5. *ibid.*, p. 465; Ashworth, *op. cit.*, pp. 420–21.
6. A. J. P. Taylor, *English History 1914–1945* (1965), p. 285.
7. *The Daily Herald,* 18 June 1934; see also *The Morning Post,* 5 March 1934; *The Evening Standard,* 23 April 1934.
8. Baroness Ravensdale, *In Many Rhythms* (1953), p. 143; *The Daily Herald,* 18 June 1934.
9. Patricia Strauss Cripps, *Advocate and Rebel* (1943), pp. 67–8; for examples of keen attacks in the House of Lords see Marquis of Salisbury, 90 *H. L. Deb. 5s.* (19 September 1933), cols. 607–8 and the debate on the second reading of the House of Lords Reform Bill, 129 *H. L. Debs. 5s.* (9–10 May 1934), cols. 179, 192, 236; see also *The Manchester Guardian,* 8 January 1934; *The Times,* 25 January 1934.

10. *The Times*, 8 January 1934.
11. *The Daily Herald*, 20 February 1934.
12. 129 *H. L. Deb. 5s.* (8–10 May 1934), cols. 67–296; see 8 May, cols. 67–8 for Lord Salisbury's remarks.
13. *ibid.* (10 May 1934), cols. 231–2.
14. Dr Robert Forgan, *Interview*, 13 December 1960.
15. See Chapter 7.
16. *The Morning Post*, 26 April 1933.
17. *The Manchester Guardian*, 13 March 1933.
18. *The Manchester Evening News*, 14 March 1933; *Blackshirt*, 18 March 1933.
19. *The Manchester Guardian*, 13 March 1933.
20. For example, see *Fascist Week*, 15 December 1933.
21. 'Mosley *v.* Marchbanks', *The Times* (*Law Reports*), 5 February 1936; see also 'Mosley *v.* Daily News Ltd', *The Times* (*Law Reports*), 6 November 1934.
22. *The Manchester Guardian*, 13 March 1933.
23. *ibid.*, 16 October 1933; *The Times*, 16 October 1933.
24. *The Times*, 3 November 1933.
25. *The News Chronicle*, 14 February 1934.
26. *The Times*, 19, 21, 22, 27, 28 February 1934; *The Manchester Guardian*, 19 February 1934.
27. *The Daily Mail*, 23 April 1934.
28. *ibid.*, 25 April 1934.
29. *The Manchester Guardian*, 23 April 1934.
30. *Labour* (May 1934), p. 203.
31. For example, see J. B. Priestley, *English Journey* (1934), p. 29; *Maidenhead Advertiser*, 31 January 1934.
32. 286 *H. C. Deb. 5s.* (20 February 1934), cols. 173–4.
33. 289 *H. C. Deb. 5s.* (16 May 1934), cols. 1765–72.
34. *Evening Argus* (Brighton), 14 March 1934, 9 April 1934.
35. *The Times*, 9 March 1934.
36. 288 *H. C. Deb. 5s.* (9 April 1934), cols. 14–15.
37. *The Daily Telegraph*, 11 April 1934.
38. *The Sunday Times*, 25 April 1934.
39. *The Daily Telegraph*, 25 April 1934.
40. *The Times*, 22 March 1934.
41. *Fascist Week*, 30 March–5 April 1934; *The Times*, loc. cit.
42. *The Week*, 5 June 1940.
43. *Fascist Week*, loc. cit.
44. *ibid.*, 16–22 February 1934.
45. *The Times*, 22 March 1934.
46. *Fascist Week*, 30 March–5 April 1934; see also *Fascist Week*, 25–31 May 1934; 16–24 February 1934; 4–10 May 1934; 2–9 July 1934.
47. *ibid.*, 16–24 February 1934; 30 March–5 April 1934; 4–10 May 1934; *The News Chronicle*, 3 July 1934.
48. Frederick Mullally, *Fascism Inside England* (1946), p. 63.

49. Dr Robert Forgan, *Interview*, 13 December 1960, a few dozen; Wilfred Risdon, *Interview*, 7 November 1960 (courtesy of Colin Cross, by permission of Wilfred Risdon), 100 to 150; John Beckett, *Interview*, 14 December 1960, 300 to 400.
50. 291 *H. C. Deb. 5s.* (27 June 1937), col. 1122.
51. *Fascist Week*, 16 March 1934; see also British Union, *Pictorial Record*, 1932–7 (1938).
52. 285 *H. C. Deb. 5s.* (31 January 1934), cols. 360–61. The Secretary of State later qualified his answer. They were ordinary commercial vans with wire protection at the windows; 290 *H. C. Deb. 5s.* (11 June 1934), col. 1341.
53. 290 *H. C. Deb. 5s.* (14 June 1934), cols. 1875–6.
54. *The Manchester Guardian*, 3 March 1934.
55. *Blackshirt*, 11 October 1935.
56. B.U.F., *Constitution and Regulations* (1936).
57. See 'Mosley *v.* Marchbanks', *The Times* (*Law Reports*), 4–8 February 1934.
58. *The Times*, *The Manchester Guardian*, *The News Chronicle*, 26 February 1934, 3, 12 March 1934.
59. Nigel Nicolson (ed.), *Harold Nicolson, Diaries and Letters 1930–1939* (1966), pp. 98, 108.
60. *The Week* (privately circulated), 6 December 1933; according to Mosley, Rothermere's decision was quite sudden. *My Life* (1968), pp. 343–4.
61. *The Sunday Dispatch*, 22 April 1934.
62. *The Daily Mail*, 14 June 1934.
63. *ibid.*, 19, 26, 31 January 1934; 20 February 1934; 2 May 1934; 7 June 1934; 3 July 1934.
64. Viscount Rothermere, *Predictions and Warnings* (1939), pp. 144–5.
65. *The Daily Mail*, 29 January 1934; 14 June 1934.
66. *ibid.*, 20 January 1934.
67. Colin Cross records a rumour that Rothermere did warn Mosley. *The Fascists in Britain* (1961), p. 102.
68. *The Daily Mail*, 22 January 1934.
69. Rothermere, *op. cit.*, pp. 148–9.
70. *The Daily Mail*, 15 February 1934.
71. Oswald Mosley, *The Greater Britain* (1934 edn), pp. 140–45.
72. *The Daily Mail*, 29 January 1934.
73. *ibid.*, 23 March 1934.
74. *The Yorkshire Post*, 23 February 1934; *The Times*, 24 February 1934.
75. *The Daily Mail*, 27 April 1934.
76. *ibid.*, 19 July 1934.
77. *ibid.*
78. *The Newspaper Press Directory* (1935), p. 49.
79. *Willing's Press Guide* (1931–40); P.E.P., *Report on the British Press* (1938), p. 84; see also Kingsley Martin, 'Fascism and *The Daily Mail*', *Political Quarterly* (April 1934), p. 276.

80. *The Manchester Guardian*, 11 July 1933; Rothermere, *op. cit.*, pp. 134, 169.
81. *The Week*, 29 November 1933.
82. *The Morning Post*, 27 January 1934.
83. *The Economist*, 20 January 1934, p. 109; *The Spectator*, 19 January 1934, p. 74.
84. *The Spectator*, 19 January 1934, p. 74; *The News Chronicle*, 17 January 1934.
85. *The Daily Mail*, 20 January 1934; *The News Chronicle*, 20 January 1934.
86. *The Daily Mail*'s German coverage was straight-forward news reporting. Andrew Sharf, *The British Press and Jews under Nazi Rule* (1964), p. 20.
87. *The Daily Mail*, 1 November 1934; 19 December 1934; 4 January 1935; 19 December 1934.
88. A. K. Chesterton, *Fascism and the Press* (n.d.), p. 2.

# 6. Leaders and Followers

During the period of the Mosley–Rothermere alliance, the B.U.F. reached a peak in terms of membership and scale of activities and there remained the likelihood of its developing into a political force. Curiously enough, it was not until the summer of 1934, when it achieved notoriety, that the B.U.F. became of political consequence. Its impact was less the result of the worthiness of its policy or the novelty of its approach than of the use of political violence. It is possible to gain an impression of some of the people who were recruited to British Fascism, but it is more difficult to determine what attracted them. Both the Fascist leadership and the membership in general were characterized by a high rate of turn-over which suggests a distinction between those who found in Fascism a serious cause and those who were attracted by anti-Semitism and violence. This distinction gains in credibility when the decline in membership beginning in the summer of 1934 is taken into account.

The nature of the leadership can be indicated through a number of personal histories. Any such survey inevitably suffers from the limited and fragmentary nature of the available data. As well as two sample surveys, use will be made where relevant of a briefer survey by Colin Cross.[1] Despite their apparent defects, the three samples tend to substantiate each other and taken together provide at least a basis for a rudimentary analysis. W. F. Mandle has quantified data for 103 B.U.F.

leaders including the top echelon of the movement, prospective Parliamentary candidates, volunteer as well as paid officials and 'prestige' members.[2] The second survey deals exclusively with eighty-three prospective Parliamentary candidates, while Cross includes eighty candidates in his sample, although his categories are more limited.* The more restrictive samples provide useful supplements in that they describe a stratum of the Fascist *élite* during 1936–7, and include women prominent in the movement whom Mandle excludes from his sample.

Recruitment to the B.U.F. was essentially opportunistic. No rigid commitment was adhered to in practice and hence all who were willing were welcome. The original terms of membership stipulated that a prospective member pledge loyalty to the King and Empire and to the Leader; accept the discipline of the movement and promise not to associate with other political organizations; pay a minimum subscription of 1*s.* a month, or, if unemployed, 4*d.* a month.[3] A member had no obligation to commit himself publicly to the B.U.F., or to wear a uniform, and there was no way of telling whether a man maintained his former political allegiances.[4] A distinction was later drawn between political members and Blackshirt members. The latter were awarded the right to wear the uniform based on service to the movement. This was formalized in the B.U.F.'s first Constitution drafted in 1936 where a further division among uniformed Blackshirts was set forth which according to Mosley corresponded to the German model of black guards and storm troops.[5] After the passage of the Public Order Act it was announced that members would be required to wear the official badge – the flash and circle – on all B.U.F. occasions. Despite these formal distinctions, it is apparent that the real division was, as in most organizations, between active and inactive members.

It is difficult to determine the size of the membership, for Mosley never revealed the lists even to his closest associates.

* Only two members of the B.U.F.'s 'inner circle' were prospective Parliamentary candidates, Major-General J. F. C. Fuller and Alexander Raven Thomson.

The membership figures released by the B.U.F. were inflated and the contemporary accounts may not be accurate for the movement's political style was calculated to give an impression of exaggerated strength. Press estimates in 1934 and 1935 placed the membership between 17,000 and 35,000 and Dr Robert Forgan, the former deputy leader of the movement, claims a maximum membership of about 40,000.[6] Membership declined after 1934 and John Beckett, shortly after he left the movement in 1937, set it at 11,000.[7] Another former official, A. K. Chesterton, estimated 15,000 paying members in 1938, 3,000 of whom were activists.[8] Colin Cross quotes Chesterton as stating that 100,000 had passed through the movement by 1938.[9] The Home Secretary announced in 1940 that the number of persons who paid their last annual subscription to the B.U.F. was 9,000 of which about 1,000 were active. In contrast, the Communist Party nearly doubled its membership between 1935 and 1937 and reached a peak of 15,517 in 1936.[10]

It is equally difficult to locate their strength, and even if there were accurate figures as to the number of branches, they would tell little about the size of the membership for no conditions or terms for recognition were prescribed. In other words, a branch could consist of two members or one hundred members. The editor of *Blackshirt* claimed that in the spring of 1933 the B.U.F. had 370 branches and the usual figure quoted by the Fascists during the first two years was 400.[11] *The Daily Mail* in May 1934 reported forty-two branches and seven unattached centres in London and thirty-two main branches, seventy-four branches, and seventy-two sub-branches in the provinces.[12] This is probably nearer to the truth. *Blackshirt* listed thirty-four London branches with defence forces in June. A count of branch reports published in *Blackshirt*, through the summer of 1934, lists thirty-four branches in the London area, excluding National Headquarters, and 112 throughout the country for a total of 146.

It is possible to make some general statements about the centres of Blackshirt membership. Although they attempted to establish a movement on a national basis, they were successful

in only a few specific areas. Sir John Simon in winding up the
debate on the Public Order Bill stated that the whole House
would be interested in the legislation, 'yet the immediate crying
need for some of this legislation is really only felt in a very
limited number of constituencies'.[13] This was in 1936 and the
Home Secretary was referring to the centres of Jewish population where the Blackshirts had introduced political anti-
Semitism and political violence.

A month earlier the B.U.F. published a list of 100 constituencies which it planned to contest at the next General Election. The criteria for selection were the strength of the B.U.F.
organization in a constituency and/or the availability of a candidate.[14] Certainly from an analysis of election data, the choice of
constituencies was not governed by their marginality. The only
pattern that does emerge is a preponderance of Tory-held seats.
It is likely that the availability of a candidate took precedent
over the existence of a strong branch in a number of cases. Yet
candidates were announced for only eighty-one constituencies.
A rough measure of the location of B.U.F. activity, however,
can be suggested. Nineteen of the 100 designated constituencies
were in London while twenty were in close proximity. The
Fascists proposed to contest sixteen constituencies in Lancashire, twelve in Yorkshire, six in the Midlands and three in
Wales. The remaining constituencies were mainly located in
coastal and farming areas.

Another rough indicator of the degree of activity in the
eighty-one constituencies where candidates were announced
was devised by recording the number of meetings and incidents
reported in the Fascist and local Press. The B.U.F. had been
active in thirty-nine of the constituencies and some activity was
reported in eighteen others. But in twenty-four of these divisions, activity was seldom reported if at all.* Despite the shortcomings of this approach, the location of the active constituencies does correspond to the claims of the Blackshirts that
their largest and most active branches were in the industrial

* The categories are, of course, arbitrary and no claims are made in
terms of validity other than the lack of more substantial data.

centres of London, Manchester, Lancashire and Yorkshire.[15] During the formative stage of the B.U.F. there was also evidence of numerous branches in the seaside resorts, particularly on the South Coast.

It is significant that the B.U.F. made progress where there was some unemployment but had little success in the most distressed areas such as Scotland, South Wales, or the North-East.[16] This could possibly be explained in terms of the class structure. The B.U.F. attempted to project an image that was not based on class, yet it was popularly identified as a middle-class movement. The distressed areas were solidly working-class and Labour strongholds. The Communist Party also had its greatest successes in South Wales and West Scotland.[17] The B.U.F.'s appeal was thereby limited on all counts. Where the B.U.F. did recruit from among the unemployed – in London there was the attraction of jobs in the Defence Force – it was not along class lines. When the B.U.F. turned to anti-Semitism, its scope was narrowed to centres of Jewish population.

Mosley's closest associates arrived at British Fascism by several routes. Some had previous political experience or were already involved with Mosley. A few had been members of earlier Fascist organizations while for others the B.U.F. was their first political venture. The inner circle that formed around Mosley was given some formal status as the Policy Directorate, although there were a few influential Blackshirts who never served on it. The main function of the Policy Directorate seems to have been negative in that Mosley would not do anything that was strongly objected to by that body.[18] It was far more important, however, as an official line of communication to the Leader and its dominance became a prize in the battle between two factions – political and military – that grew up within the movement. The composition of this body also reflected the rapid turn-over of the whole movement, so that its exact membership at any one time cannot be ascertained.

Certainly one prominent member was Mosley's I.L.P. and New Party colleague, Dr Robert Forgan. Born in 1891, Forgan was educated at Aberdeen and Cambridge. After serving in the

First World War, he entered local politics. At the time of his election to Parliament in 1929, he was a Public Health Officer in Glasgow. His Parliamentary career, after an auspicious debut when he called for a ventilating system in the House of Commons to purify the stale air, was undistinguished.[19] The *Fascist Week* described Forgan, the Director of Organization, as Mosley's right-hand man.[20] Administration, however, was not his forte, and he was eventually put in charge of enlisting influential and financial support. He was promoted to Deputy Leader where he remained until the autumn of 1934 when he left the movement because of its turn to anti-Semitism.[21]

Another former M.P. who became an important figure in the B.U.F. was John Beckett, who joined in 1934 after an erratic political history. He was born the same year as Mosley, served and was wounded in the First World War, and then entered politics. He founded, with the blessings of the I.L.P., the short-lived National Union of Ex-Servicemen and became its chairman. It was refused recognition by the Labour Party and was dissolved after the formation of the British Legion in 1921. Meanwhile, Beckett had qualified as a Labour Party agent. He worked with Clement Attlee, then M.P. for Limehouse, and was a member of the Hackney Borough Council when Herbert Morrison was its leader. He unsuccessfully contested North Newcastle for the Labour Party in 1923, but won a seat at Gateshead the following year. He was re-elected in 1929, this time for Peckham, and served as an I.L.P. whip. He then made his mark in the House of Commons by seizing the Mace as a protest against the pending suspension of Fenner Brockway, during a debate on political prisoners in India. He was defeated as an Independent Labour candidate in the 1931 election and retired from active politics. During the next two years he visited Italy and was impressed by the corporate state.[22]

Beckett was appointed Director of Publicity and for a short period edited both *Action* and *Blackshirt*. Although he never achieved the eminence within the movement of Mosley or William Joyce, he still addressed what were considered to be key meetings throughout the country as well as smaller open-air meetings. His propaganda activities continually led to encounters with the police. During the abdication crisis he was arrested outside Buckingham Palace, and the following year he was fined for attacking a heckler who had interrupted one of his open-air meetings.[23]

W. E. D. Allen was one of Mosley's confidantes. He has been identified by former Blackshirts as a member of the Policy Directorate but his true position is less certain. Allen was two years younger than Mosley and was educated at Eton. He was the heir to a prosperous family business, but his interests were elsewhere. In 1922, he contested Tyrone-Fermanagh as an Ulster Unionist, and was returned for West Belfast in 1929. In the interim, he had travelled widely and served as a special correspondent for *The Daily Telegraph* in the Middle East. By the time the B.U.F. was founded, he had published four books. He crossed the floor to join Mosley in the New Party and stayed with him. On the formation of the B.U.F., Allen was occupied with the family business in Belfast, but found time to devote his literary skills to the movement. Under the pseudonym 'James Drennan' he wrote *Oswald Mosley, BUF and British Fascism*, and contributed occasional articles to the B.U.F. weeklies and the *Fascist Quarterly*. He seems to have drifted away from the B.U.F. after 1936.

A number of political activists who had previously worked with Mosley also joined the inner circle. Wilfred Risdon, a Somerset man in his middle thirties, had contested South Dorset for the Labour Party in 1924. He was appointed divisional organizer for the I.L.P. in the Midlands, where he came into contact with the future Fascist leader. He later joined Mosley in the New Party and was the electoral agent for the Ashton-under-Lyne by-election as well as for Gateshead in the 1931 General Election.[24] Risdon held a succession of posts within the B.U.F. including those of the first Director of Propaganda, Deputy Director of Political Organization, Deputy Director-General and chief political agent. F. M. Box had also been prominent in the New Party where, along with Leslie Cumings, he had taken charge of organization following the resignation of Allen Young. He had previously been a Conservative Party agent. Box succeeded Forgan as Director of Organization and, along with Beckett, attempted to reconstruct the B.U.F. on the lines of a conventional political party. As a result of organizational strains and clashes of personality and interest, Box was replaced early in 1935.

The National Defence Force was organized under the supervision of Eric Hamilton Piercy, who had the imposing title of Officer Commanding National Defence Force Control. A full-time Blackshirt in his early thirties, he had formerly been a salesman. He had also been an inspector in the special constabulary, but was forced to resign as a result of his Fascist activities.[25] In the New Party, he had been in charge of stewarding meetings, and was thus a logical choice to train and command the National Defence Force. During the early years of the B.U.F., Piercy was very much in the limelight and newspaper pictures often showed him at Mosley's side. By 1935, however, no more was heard of him, which was surprising considering the supremacy gradually gained within the organization by the more militaristic elements. The Blackshirt with the longest association with Mosley was, perhaps, George Sutton who had acted as his private secretary since 1920. A First World War veteran, he had also been a member of the North St Pancras Labour Party and I.L.P., serving as the chairman of the local branch of the former and on the General Council of the local branch of the latter.[26] He acted as a research assistant to Mosley, Strachey and Young in their collaborations and was eventually appointed the B.U.F.'s Director of Research.[27] He did not leave his employer until the early 1950s.

Two former British Fascists played prominent roles in the development of the B.U.F. – one as a speaker and the other as an administrator. A great deal has been written elsewhere about William Joyce, who subsequently became the infamous Lord Haw-Haw.[28] His Fascist career began in December 1923, when he joined the British Fascisti. At that time he was a student at Birkbeck College and later took a first-class honours degree in English. The following autumn he was in charge of a British

Fascisti unit acting as stewards at a meeting in support of the Unionist Parliamentary candidate for Lambeth North when his face was slashed by a razor. Joyce described his assailant as a 'Jewish Communist'.[29] He was praised in the *British Fascist Bulletin* as 'a loyal and steadfast member whose services at G.H.Q. have always been appreciated'.[30] He joined the B.U.F. in 1933 and, motivated by an intense patriotism and fanatical anti-Semitism, he established a reputation within the movement as a platform orator, second only to Mosley. He resigned from a post at the Victoria Tutorial College to accept a full-time position with the movement, first as Area Administrative Officer for West London and then as a Director of Research.[31] He was promoted to Director of Propaganda and became a not very powerful Deputy Leader.

Although Joyce's popularity and prestige were widespread within the B.U.F., his influence was limited. A second former British Fascist who did not present a potential challenge to Mosley's authority was more successful in the movement's hierarchy. Neil Francis-Hawkins had been a salesman of surgical instruments. As a member of the Council of the British Fascists, he had conducted negotiations with the B.U.F. in an attempt to reach an agreement on a merger. On joining the new movement, in his early thirties, he was appointed National Defence Force Adjutant and he immediately built up a following amongst its personnel. Francis-Hawkins proved to be a first-class administrator. He was quickly promoted to Officer in Charge of the London Area, Chief Administrative Officer and finally to the number two position in the movement as Director-General of Organization. As he climbed the ladder, he brought his Defence Force followers with him. These included B. D. E. Donovan, Captain U. A. Hick, Lieutenant-Colonel C. S. Sharpe, J. H. Hone and John Sant. Donovan, an ex-Indian Army officer and former school-master, succeeded Francis-Hawkins as Officer in Charge of the London area. He was subsequently promoted Assistant Director-General of Organization for the South and was assisted by Sharpe. In the North, J. H. Hone, another ex-officer who had also been a civil servant in South Africa, was placed in charge of Scotland at the beginning of 1936 and was appointed Assistant Director-General of Organization for the North at the end of the year. Hick eventually succeeded to Donovan's former position in London which was, of course, the centre of B.U.F. activity. After a purge in 1937, *Action* described Donovan and W. W. Wilson, the movement's accountant, as Francis-Hawkins's right-hand men.[32]

Alexander Raven Thomson was the Alfred Rosenberg of British Fascism. Thomson, who had a modest independent income, had attended universities abroad and had had a brief spell in the Communist Party before joining the B.U.F. at the age of thirty-four.[33] He had also written a pretentious book, *Civilization as Divine Superman*, in which he set out to refute Spengler and point the way for the survival of Western civilization. He was appointed Deputy Director of Publicity and after a reorganization he was promoted to director of a new research department. He then became the Director of Policy and as the movement's philosopher contributed lengthy and pompous articles to its publications and published theoretical pamphlets. As a member of the Policy Directorate, he became an intimate of Mosley and a close associate of Francis-Hawkins.

Representative of the movement's accent on youth was the Chief of Staff, Ian Hope Dundas. An early recruit to the B.U.F. at the age of twenty-four, he assisted Mosley in the publication of *The Greater Britain*.[34] He was the second son of Admiral Sir Charles Dundas, the twenty-eighth chief of Dundas. Educated at the Royal Naval College, he resigned his commission in 1929 and became private secretary to Brenden Bracken, the Conservative M.P. for North Paddington.[35] As Chief of Staff, Dundas was at first responsible for discipline within the movement and for organizing and stewarding meetings. He later performed special missions for the Leader and provided him with a secretariat. It was rumoured, for example, that Dundas spent long periods in Italy.

The men who assisted the Chief of Staff were also notable for their youth. A. G. Findlay was a former bank clerk in his early twenties.[36] By 1935, Findlay had become responsible for the supervision of the financial affairs of the movement, as a result of difficulties that had arisen over the control of funds both at Headquarters and at the branch level. He was made Deputy Chief of Staff the following year. John Sant had been a civil servant in the Near and Far East. He joined the B.U.F. in 1933 at the age of twenty-seven and was appointed a National Headquarters' Staff officer.[37] In 1935, Sant was appointed National Inspecting Officer for Yorkshire and the North-East. Shortly thereafter, he was promoted to Assistant Director-General for the North of England.

As well as political and organizational skills, there was a need for journalistic talent. The relatively rapid succession of editors of the B.U.F. papers suggests the difficulties in fulfilling these needs satisfactorily as well as the movement's instability. The original editor of *Blackshirt* was Captain Cecil Courtney Lewis. In addition to being a solicitor and the author of two books, Lewis had held a regular commission in the Indian Army and a Foreign Office post in the Middle East. Before returning to England, he spent some time in Italy where he acquired his Fascist convictions.[38] Lewis bears a partial responsibility for enlarging the labels 'old gang' and 'Communist' to conspiracy proportions. After he relinquished the editorship to Rex Tremlett, he remained in the B.U.F. until 1937 acting as Mosley's legal adviser.

Tremlett was a South African in his early thirties and, although a journalist by profession, he had little idea of how to run a paper. Before joining the B.U.F. he had been a prospector for gold and had held twenty-six different jobs, mostly on trade papers in Johannesburg.[39] Soon after his promotion, he had several clashes with Mosley and was replaced by W. J. Leaper. He left the movement at the end of 1934, and eventually became the manager of the Dolman Printing Company, which printed both *Action* and the *Blackshirt* until the end of 1939. Leaper, the third editor, entered politics as a member of the I.L.P. and the Labour Party. He joined the New Party immediately on its formation, and contested the Shipley Division of Yorkshire in the 1931 General Election. He subsequently joined the B.U.F.

and helped to found the Newcastle upon Tyne branch. When the *Fascist Week* commenced publication, Leaper resigned his post on the *Newcastle Evening News* and joined the staff.[40] Leaper considered Mosley a genuine radical and was impressed by the possibilities of the corporate state. He remained convinced until 1936 when he left the B.U.F. after a dispute over the rabid anti-Semitic tone of the new weekly, *Action*.[41]

Beckett, as Director of Publicity, took over the responsibility for editing both *Blackshirt* and *Action* on Leaper's resignation. But Beckett left the B.U.F., along with Joyce, six months after Leaper in the spring of 1937. Both publications were then edited by Geoffrey Dorman, but A. K. Chesterton soon took over the editorship of *Blackshirt* and in 1938 the editorship of *Action* for a short period. Dorman had been educated at Tonbridge and Cambridge and had been a fellow-officer with Mosley at the Royal Flying Corps School at Shoreham. After the First World War he joined the staff of *Aeroplane* where he worked until 1930.[42] He then became a free-lance and began a career as a writer of adventure stories. Dorman joined the movement in 1933 and did organization work in South London until he joined the National Headquarters staff as an editor. He contributed weekly columns on aviation and motoring to *Blackshirt* under the pseudonyms 'Blackbird' and 'Bluebird'. On the publication of *Action*, Dorman was appointed assistant editor. Following Chesterton's resignation in April 1938, Dorman resumed the editorship of *Action*, a post he held for a little over a year until he was replaced by Raven Thomson. Dorman was described in 1937 as one of the key figures of the B.U.F. However, he does not seem to have been permitted to assume any responsibility, for even when he served as an editor Raven Thomson was deputed to assist him.

A. K. Chesterton, a cousin of G. K., was born in South Africa in 1899. He was educated there and in England and served in the First World War. After the war, he worked in the gold mines for a short time prior to taking up journalism. He worked on the *Johannesburg Star* before returning to England, where he held jobs on provincial and national newspapers.

From 1929 to 1933, he was editor of a group of newspapers in Torquay. When he joined the B.U.F. late in 1933, he had been employed as a publicity agent for the Shakespeare Memorial Theatre in Stratford-on-Avon.[43] He was appointed Area Administrative Officer for the Midlands, but after six months Mosley brought him to National Headquarters.

Not all the members of the inner circle of the B.U.F. held titled positions. This was true of two ex-officers, Captain Robert Gordon-Canning and Major-General J. F. C. Fuller, who served on the Policy Directorate. Gordon-Canning, a distant descendant of George Canning, the Prime Minister, was educated at Eton and served in the army from 1906 to 1919, mainly in the Middle East. He was a romantic in inclination, modelling himself on Lawrence of Arabia and publishing several volumes of poetry. A self-proclaimed expert on Middle East affairs, with a pronounced bias for the Arab case, he found in the B.U.F. an outlet for his anti-Semitism. It was rumoured that he gave generously to the movement, and even that he served as Mosley's contact man with Hitler. Shortly after leaving the B.U.F., he became the treasurer for the British Council for Christian Settlement in Europe, and achieved notoriety after the Second World War by his purchase of a bust of Hitler at an auction at the German Embassy in London.

The most prominent ex-officer recruited to the B.U.F. was Major-General J. F. C. Fuller, who joined the B.U.F. shortly after his retirement in 1933. Fuller was an expert on tank warfare and a military historian of rank, who had published a dozen books. He then crusaded for Fascism and, until the end of 1938, took an active part as a member of the Policy Directorate, Headquarters worker, prospective Parliamentary candidate and occasional speaker. As a contributor to Fascist publications he wrote a series of pro-Franco articles from Spain.

These then were the men who formed the inner circle of the B.U.F. and, in as far as they were given collective recognition, Mosley formed the Policy Directorate from their ranks. The exact composition of this body at any one time is unknown for its membership was fluid, depending on internal power

struggles and upon who was in Mosley's favour. At first, it
seemed to have included Mosley, Forgan, Joyce, Beckett,
Fuller, Gordon-Canning and Leaper. The Directorate probably
did not exist when Risdon was Director of Propaganda and
when Lewis was editor of *Blackshirt*. Raven Thomson, Francis-
Hawkins and Chesterton were added later. Dundas, Tremlett
and Piercy, as far as is known, were never included in this
select group; nor was Forgan's immediate successor, Box.
After Beckett and Joyce resigned, Francis-Hawkins replaced
them with two of his followers, Donovan and Hick. The political faction countered, insisting that Risdon and Findlay be included.

In addition to the Leader and his lieutenants there was a sub-
stratum of paid and voluntary workers, many of whom also
possessed pretentious titles, prospective Parliamentary candidates and members of some reputation, both active and inactive
who were willing to let their names be associated with the
B.U.F. Together they formed something of a Fascist *élite*. Data
is insufficient to formulate more than crude generalizations
about the social composition of this *élite*, but if accepted with
caution they are instructive.

The movement's accent on youth was reflected in its leadership. Mosley was thirty-six when he founded the B.U.F.; Allen,
Beckett, Chesterton, Francis-Hawkins, Risdon, Raven Thomson and Tremlett were in their thirties when they joined; while
Dundas, Findlay, Joyce and Sant were in their twenties. W. F.
Mandle's sample of 103 members of the B.U.F. *élite* reveals that
fifty-seven of the eighty-four whose ages could be ascertained
were under forty in 1935. This is verified by a sample of prospective Parliamentary candidates (hereafter, p.p.c.s) as given in
1936 and 1937. If a General Election had been called for 1937,
the B.U.F. would certainly have given an impression of youth.
Thirty-seven out of fifty-five of the candidates were under
forty, and fourteen were in their twenties.

The B.U.F. leadership taken as a whole was relatively well-
educated. Twenty-eight in Mandle's sample had received some
form of advanced education; fourteen had been at Oxford or

Cambridge while another ten were educated at universities in Great Britain or abroad. Fifty-one had had a secondary education, of whom thirty-four had attended public schools. The proportions were equally impressive in the more restricted P.P.C. sample. Twenty-three had some advanced education including nine who had been at Oxbridge. The number who had attended public school was twenty-two. This suggests that the best-educated were not necessarily the most active and this seems to be substantiated, at least in the case of the top leadership where only Joyce, Forgan, Raven Thomson and Dorman had received university educations.

Despite the educational level of its *élite*, the B.U.F. failed to draw support from intellectuals. This group is singled out not because intellectuals are particularly disposed to support extreme movements, but because their skills tend to be necessary for the success of such movements.[44] Certainly this is demonstrated by the difficulties incurred in editing the B.U.F.'s publications. British intellectuals, for the most part, had nothing to do with Mosley's brand of Fascism. Some intellectuals may have admired Continental Fascism, while others were truly alarmed. Those who admired, ignored Mosley, and those who were alarmed, opposed him. Although a substantial number of intellectuals flocked to the Communist Party or its associated organizations, the Blackshirts could claim few.[45]

The extent of military service is striking in that it includes sixty per cent of the Fascist *élite*. More precisely, sixty-two in Mandle's sample had been in the armed services and thirty-seven (fifty-six per cent) in the sample of P.P.C.s. In terms of ex-officers the proportions are fifty-eight per cent (thirty-six) and fifty-nine per cent (twenty-two) respectively. Mandle also points out that when age is taken into account the findings are even more impressive. It was unlikely that those under thirty-five in 1935 would have seen service in the First World War. Of the forty-seven known to be over thirty-five in his sample, forty-one had served.[46]

Certainly all the available evidence points to the prominent role that ex-servicemen, particularly ex-officers, played in the

B.U.F. Major-General Fuller and Captain Gordon-Canning were among Mosley's closest advisers. Captain Cecil Courtney Lewis, Lieutenant Ian Hope Dundas, Lieutenant-Colonel C. S. Sharpe, Captain U. A. Hick served in important capacities. Major George Tabor, one of Mosley's secretaries, and a director of several of the B.U.F. companies, was typical of a number of retired military officers who became Headquarters workers. These also included Major Leigh Vaughan-Henry and Captain T. D. Butler. For the most part, these retired officers remained in the background. Branch leaders included Vice-Admiral G. B. Powell in Portsmouth and Commander C. E. Hudson at Bognor and Chichester. They were also prospective Parliamentary candidates, as were Vice-Admiral R. St P. Parry, Sir Lionel Haworth, an ex-Indian Army officer, and Colonel James Walsh. Among the active organizers were Captain C. Bentinck-Budd, Captain Vincent Collier and Lieutenant-Colonel H. E. Crocker. Major E. Mathews, Major R. H. Brodie, Lieutenant-Colonel F. W. P. Macdonald and the former British Fascist leader, Brigadier-General R. B. Blakeney, contributed to the B.U.F. periodicals.

Unfortunately even less is known about previous political affiliations, and party identification as such reveals little about the extent of participation. With the exception of the inner circle the general impression is one of political amateurism. Even in the inner circle, however, those with political experience were usually recruited on the basis of a previous association with Mosley. This was true of Allen, Forgan, Risdon, Box, Leaper, Piercy and Sutton. The exceptions were Beckett, Raven Thomson, who had a brief stint in the Communist Party, and the two former British Fascists, Joyce and Francis-Hawkins. Joyce had also been president of the Conservative Society at Birkbeck College.

The previous political affiliations of twenty-four are identified by Mandle. These include eight former Socialists, eight Conservatives and three Communists. The remaining five had been in more than one party: two had been in the Labour and Communist parties, one had been a Liberal and a Conservative M.P., another had been in the Liberal Party and the Labour Party and one had been both a Conservative and a Socialist. The political affiliations of twenty-one P.P.C.S were ascertained and are of interest despite the obvious overlap between the two samples. There were nine Conservatives, five Labourites, five Communists, one independent and one former British Fascist, E. G. Mandeville Roe, the author of *The Corporate State*.

On the available evidence there does not seem to have been a mass exodus of activists or loyalists from the traditional parties. For example, the fears of some Conservatives that the B.U.F. was attracting large numbers of recruits from the Tory Right was at best only partly justified. Some Conservative voters, mainly readers of *The Daily Mail*, joined the B.U.F. or at least attended Mosley's meetings during the first seven months of 1934 in response to Lord Rothermere's brief flirtation with Fascism.[47] It was doubtful whether they ever left the Conservative Party as such. Within the movement they were known disparagingly as the 'Albert Hall' Fascists – those who viewed the B.U.F. as a ginger group of the Conservative Party.[48] That there were few Conservatives who broke officially with their party was suggested in the publicity given by the Blackshirts to those who did. The most prominent of the announced converts were Commander Carlyon Bellairs, a former Liberal and Conservative M.P. for Maidstone and author of *The Ghost of Parliament*, and the Hon. H. M. Upton, the only surviving son of Viscount Templeton. Others included the chairman of the Halberton Conservative Association, the Deputy Chairman of the Brightside Divisional Conservative Association, the Chairman of the Govan Conservative Association, a member of the Liverpool City Council, Vice-Chairman of the Swansea Conservative Association, the Chairman of the Hamworth Branch of the East Dorset Conservative Association, and the Chairman of the Women's Branch of the Whitechapel Conservative Party, who had been in charge of the Women's Convoy which had driven mail vans during the General Strike.[49] With one or two additions, this exhausted the list of Conservative small-fry willing to have their names linked to the B.U.F.

The Fascist *élite*, in terms of occupational breakdown, was distinctly middle class in character. This is discernible despite the difficulties in interpreting the available data. The three samples differ not only in size but in categorization. This seems to have been a result of a marked propensity towards instability in occupation on the part of the Fascists. Rex Tremlett, as already stated, was an extreme example in that he had held twenty-six jobs before joining the Blackshirts as a journalist. Hence Mandle found that twenty-three out of eighty-eight for whom he was able to ascertain occupations were engaged in business in some capacity, while Cross found only twelve of fifty-two in business. The sample of P.P.C.s classifies twenty-two out of seventy-eight, including eleven women, in business or managerial capacities. According to Mandle's sample, forty-one had some professional experience, eleven were farmers and eight were retired or had independent means. In the P.P.C. sample, only fifteen are classified as professional, five as farmers and ten with independent means.

There are two additional categories in the latter sample. Five and possibly nine (Cross cites ten) were full-time paid B.U.F. officials and four gave their occupation as housewife. What emerges from all three samples is the small number whose stated occupation was working class. Mandle cites sixteen, the P.P.C. sample fourteen, while Cross lists four.

Two other aspects of the Fascist *élite* bear consideration. The movement was successful in converting only a small number of publicly and socially prominent people even to the extent of letting their names be associated with the movement. This was evident in the pathetic publicity that they received in B.U.F. publications. Dundas, Fuller, Sir Lionel Haworth, Vice-Admiral R. St P. Parry and the Hon. H. M. Upton have already been mentioned. *Blackshirt* announced that the Earl of Errol, hereditary Lord High Constable of Scotland, had been appointed B.U.F. delegate to Kenya, where he spent most of his time.[50] It was reported that Lord Tollemache, a Cheshire landowner, had 'approved' the Blackshirt policy with the reservation that the House of Lords remained an exclusively hereditary body.[51] Lord Strathspey wrote a letter to *The Morning Post*, in which he stated that he favoured the B.U.F. and called for strong leadership.[52] Sir Alliot Verdon-Roe, the aviation pioneer, actually joined the movement in the summer of 1934.[53] Major Jocelyn Lucas, who was to become a Conservative M.P. in 1939, had a brief flirtation with Mosley's brand of Fascism.[54] As the Second World War approached, the novelist, Henry Williamson, joined the movement and wrote for *Action*.[55]

The Mitford-Freeman family was seen by the Press as closely linked to the B.U.F. Mosley was in a difficult position here as his personal life was involved. In October 1936, Mosley was secretly married to Diana Mitford in Germany. Hitler was a guest at the luncheon given by Frau Goebbels for the couple after the ceremony.[56] Diana's sister, Unity, had been cavorting with the Nazis for some time and the antics of the girl, whom Hitler described as the perfect Aryan type, were well reported in the British Press.[54] She was a member of the B.U.F., but it never publicized her membership or activities, although she was stoned at a Hyde Park meeting.[58] Partly as a result of his daughter's political identifications and activities, and partly because he was an eccentric reactionary, Lord Redesdale was charged by the anti-Fascists as being a B.U.F. supporter and a possible source of funds. But there was no proof to support these charges, with the exception of Lord Redesdale's admitted predilection towards Germany and Franco's Spain.[59] Shortly after Unity's return to England in 1940 following an unsuccessful suicide attempt, Lord Redesdale made a public confession. He stated that his 'crime', which he questioned, was that he had thought that the interests of England could best be served by friendly relations with Germany. He admitted that he had been wrong, and declared that he was not and never had been a Fascist, offering as questionable proof his motion for the rejection of Lord Salisbury's bill to reform the House of Lords.[60]

A small number of women also played leading roles in the B.U.F. and eleven were chosen as prospective Parliamentary candidates. These ranged from the rich Lady Pearson in the Canterbury area and Dorothy Viscountess Downe, a prominent

Norfolk Conservative, to Olive Hawks and Anne Brock Griggs
of the paid staff of the B.U.F. Among the candidates were four
who gave their occupation as housewife and two former suffra-
gettes, Norah Elam at Northampton and Mercèdes Barrington
at West Fulham. Lady Pearson and Olive Hawks provide good
contrasts. The former, a sister of Sir Henry Page-Croft, M.P.,
was the mainstay of Fascism in Sandwich, Canterbury, Deal and
Wolmer. Her car and chauffeur were at the disposal of the
B.U.F. Speakers were driven to meetings, leaflets were distributed and the car was used as both a loud-speaker van and a
platform for outdoor meetings. In Sandwich she owned a great
deal of property including a block of shops where the British
Union bookshop was located.[61] Olive Hawks, unlike Lady
Pearson, was an early recruit to the movement and worked her
way up through the ranks. After secondary school, she
worked for Press firms before joining the B.U.F. in 1933. As a
member she was at first employed as a secretary and later promoted to the Research Department where she was made responsible for replying to attacks against the B.U.F. in the Press.
She was eventually given occasional speaking engagements and
as a final reward was chosen as prospective Fascist candidate for
Peckham.[62]

The available data on the social backgrounds of the B.U.F.
leadership suggests a number of general characteristics. The
B.U.F.'s claim to be a movement of youth seems to have been
justified. There was also some justification for a popular anti-
Fascist stereotype since the leaders were for the most part
solidly middle class in terms of occupation and a high proportion had not only done military service but had been officers.
Although B.U.F. officials were relatively well-educated, there
was a noticeable lack of political experience. It might be instructive to employ again the method of personal histories to
illustrate these qualities in two members of the sub-*élite*, bearing
in mind that the above data characterized a composite type:
Captain Charles Bentinck-Budd, an early recruit who became a
paid, full-time Fascist official, and James Sheperd who did not

join the movement until March 1936 and remained an active volunteer.

Bentinck-Budd had been educated at St Edwards. In the First World War he was badly wounded and had to have an artificial leg. Following the war he took up farming although he also possessed a modest independent income. He then entered politics and, standing as an Independent, was elected to the Worthing Borough Council in 1930 and the West Sussex County Council the following year. In 1933, at the age of thirty-five, he joined the B.U.F. and was appointed West Sussex Area Organizer. He did not abandon local politics and was re-elected as an Independent although he publicized his Fascist affiliations. Thereafter he attended Council meetings in a black shirt until his resignation in 1935, when he took up a new assignment as Midlands Inspector for the B.U.F. In 1937, Bentinck-Budd became a full-time worker at the National Headquarters and was selected prospective Parliamentary candidate for Ladywood, Birmingham, a constituency that was not noted as a centre of Fascist support.[63]

James Sheperd was thirty-one years old when he joined the B.U.F. and managed a small family business. Unlike Bentinck-Budd, he had not seen military service and it is assumed that his education was limited since the B.U.F. was fairly diligent in reporting the educational backgrounds of its leaders who had been to university or to public or grammar schools. He had considerable political experience before joining the Fascists, however. He had been a member of the Communist Party, a Labour Party election agent and a trade-union organizer for two years in Sheffield. His motive for joining the B.U.F. was largely anti-Semitic and he put his organizing talents to work in West Islington where there had been little Fascist activity. Sheperd launched an ambitious anti-Semitic campaign with numerous street-corner meetings and house-to-house canvasses. A concerted effort was made to enlist the support of local shopkeepers by invoking the image of Mosley as their champion in the face of a Jewish conspiracy. After building up the constituency for three years and standing in a borough council by-election in

1938, Sheperd was rewarded – or he rewarded himself – by Parliamentary candidature in February 1939.

How far the social composition of the leadership reflected that of the membership is unknown. The B.U.F. records were seized in 1940 and along with other Home Office material are closed by order of the Lord Chancellor under Section 5 (b) of the Public Records Act, 1958, for 100 years. Contemporary accounts were not only unsystematic but highly impressionistic. Perhaps the most reliable report was that of the Advisory Committee on persons detained under Defence Regulation 18B to the Home Secretary in 1940. This suggested that the stable membership of the B.U.F. was composed of marginal members of all social and economic classes, occupational groupings and status and age groups. Their examination of individual cases of minor officers of the B.U.F. who were detained showed that many had little understanding of the aims and policy of the B.U.F. and that their understanding of any subject was often limited. Some appeared to be dupes who had been attracted to the B.U.F. for a variety of reasons, but who had no sympathy with what were described as subversive aims or with the movement's anti-war policy.[64] This statement must, of course, be treated with great care. Those interviewed were a hard core and were minor officers as distinct from members at large. Their lack of knowledge suggests that they were not members of the *élite* although some of them may have been. But given the small numbers recruited and the rapid turnover, it seems in order to assume (short of more substantial data) a high degree of social and economic marginality distinct from the middle-class bias of the leadership.

## NOTES

1. Colin Cross, *The Fascists in Britain* (1961), pp. 179–80.
2. W. F. Mandle, 'The Leadership of the British Union of Fascists', *The Australian Journal of Politics and History* (December 1966), pp. 360–83.
3. B.U.F., *Application Form*, 7 November 1932.
4. *The Manchester Guardian*, 19 May 1934.
5. *ibid.*, 23 November 1936.

6. Dr Robert Forgan, *Interview*, 13 December 1960. Cross quotes Forgan as placing the active membership 'nearer 5,000 than 10,000'. There is no conflict here for this was for October 1934 when the B.U.F. had lost a great deal of support. It is also an estimate of 'active' membership; *op. cit.*, p. 131.

7. *Salisbury Times*, 26 November 1937.

8. *Interview*, 4 January 1961.

9. Cross, *loc. cit.*

10. Henry Pelling, *The British Communist Party* (1958), pp. 104, 192; James Jupp, *The Left in Britain 1931 to 1941* (unpublished M.Sc. (Econ.) thesis), (University of London, 1956). The analysis of the C.P.G.B. also was dependent on economic disaster. Its increase in membership, however, can be credited to events abroad.

11. *The Daily Express*, 26 April 1933; *Blackshirt*, 5 July 1935; Cross refers to a statement by Mosley that there were 180 branches in the autumn of 1934 but gives no citation, *op. cit.*, p. 131.

12. *The Daily Mail*, 18 May 1934.

13. 318 *H. C. Deb. 5s.* (7 December 1936), col. 1779.

14. John Beckett, *Interview*, 14 December 1960; A. K. Chesterton, *Interview*, 22 December 1960.

15. Sir Oswald Mosley, *Interview*, 11 September 1959; Geoffrey Hamm, *Interview*, 14 December 1959.

16. Mosley claimed to be concentrating on quality in Scotland. *Glasgow Weekly Herald*, 25 September 1937.

17. James K. Pollock, *et al.*, *British Election Studies 1950* (1951), p. 111.

18. A. K. Chesterton, *Interview*, 22 December 1960.

19. 237 *H. C. Deb. 5s.* (26 March 1930), cols. 418–19.

20. *Fascist Week*, 15–21 December 1933.

21. Dr Robert Forgan, *Interview*, 13 December 1960.

22. John Beckett, *Interview*, 14 December 1960.

23. *News Review*, 21 October 1937.

24. Wilfred Risdon, *Interview*, 7 November 1960 (courtesy of Colin Cross by permission of Wilfred Risdon); *Action*, 23 January 1937.

25. *Fascist Week*, 12–18 January 1934.

26. *Fascist Week*, 16–24 March 1934.

27. Cross, *op. cit.*, p. 23.

28. For example see J. A. Cole, *Lord Haw-Haw* (1964); C. E. Bechhofer-Roberts (ed.), *The Trial of William Joyce* (1946); Rebecca West, *The New Meaning of Treason*, revised edn (1965), pp. 13–145.

29. Cole, *op. cit.*, p. 30.

30. *British Fascist Bulletin*, October 1924.

31. *Fascist Week*, 26 January–1 February 1934.

32. *Action*, 24 April 1937.

33. *Fascist Week*, 8–14 December 1933.

34. *The Sunday Dispatch*, 11 February 1934.

35. *The Evening News*, 23 January 1934.

36. *Fascist Week*, 2–8 February 1934.

LEADERS AND FOLLOWERS

37. *Action*, 30 January 1934.
38. *Fascist Week*, 29 December 1933; 4 January 1934.
39. *ibid.*, 9–15 February 1934.
40. W. J. Leaper, *Interview*, 9 November 1934.
41. *Action*, 20 March 1937.
42. *ibid.*
43. A. K. Chesterton, *Interview*, 4 January 1961.
44. William Kornhauser, *Politics of Mass Society* (1959), pp. 184–5.
45. See Neil Wood, *Communism and the British Intellectual* (1959).
46. Mandle, *op. cit.*, p. 362.
47. John Beckett, *Interview*, 14 December 1960; Geoffrey Hamm, *Interview*, 14 December 1959.
48. Hamm, *ibid.*
49. *Blackshirt*, 1 June 1934; 15 June 1934; *Fascist Week*, 2–8 February 1934; 4–10 May 1934; *The Daily Mail*, 15 May 1934; *The Sunday Dispatch*, 17 June 1934.
50. *Blackshirt*, 15 June 1934.
51. *The Daily Mail*, 12 May 1934.
52. *The Morning Post*, 2 July 1934.
53. *Blackshirt*, 13 July 1934.
54. *ibid.*, 29 March 1935.
55. *Action*, 12 November 1938; 7 May 1938.
56. Sir Oswald Mosley, *My Life* (1968), p. 363.
57. For example, see *The News Chronicle*, 27 July 1937; see also Mosley, *op. cit.*, pp. 367–8.
58. Jessica Mitford, *Hons. and Rebels* (1960), p. 60; Louis W. Bondy, *Racketeers of Hatred* (1946), pp. 158–9.
59. See *The Times*, 26 March 1935; *West London Press*, 29 November 1939.
60. Lord Redesdale, 'Letter', *The Times*, 9 March 1940; see Chapter 5.
61. *Board of Deputies of British Jews, Report of Investigations into BUF Activities in Sandwich and Surrounding Districts*, spring 1939.
62. *Action*, 12 June 1937. See also Cole, *op. cit.*, pp. 49–66, *passim*, for a description of what it was like to be a woman in the B.U.F. ranks in the provinces. Cole describes how Joyce met his second wife who was active in the Manchester branch.
63. *Blackshirt*, 23 August 1935; *Action*, 16 January 1937; Cross, *op. cit.*, p. 142.
64. 367 *H. C. Deb. 5s.* (28 November 1940), col. 310.

# 7. British Fascist Ideology

The publication of *The Greater Britain* marked the founding of the B.U.F. In order to understand how and on what terms the Fascists expected to gain power a number of considerations must be taken into account. First, the B.U.F. was founded to propagate a programme for economic and political reform. This was a departure from Fascist practice in that Continental movements came to power with only a series of projected goals. It was, however, in keeping with the British practice of requiring parties to state what they intended to do with political power, when and if achieved. A fundamental problem for the B.U.F. was how to make its programme palatable to a public which seemed to possess a high regard for the established institutions and traditions, or for the myths that sustained them, and yet whose commitment was not so fanatic as to foster a willingness to come out in the streets to defend them against real or supposed threats. Although the B.U.F. was articulating some genuine grievances, it was also handicapped by the stigma of Mosley's previous failure and by the exotic nature of the movement. B.U.F. policy was characterized by its duality. Mussolini had already capitalized on an ideological duality, engaging in myth-making to capture the loyalties of a mob and later relying on a more definite programme to secure the allegiance of sophisticated interests.[1] *The Greater Britain* was written for a politically educated minority, while particular themes in the movement's propaganda were emphasized in order to attract

support from possible sources of discontent. The most important were its appeals to youth, nationalism, anti-Communism,
anti-Semitism and its attacks on the political *élites*.

Policy was often manipulated with a callous disregard for
principles so that at least one of the themes, anti-Semitism,
gained ascendancy over the B.U.F.'s proposals for reform.
Policy was hinged to the likelihood of an impending economic
crisis and attempts were made to locate the causes and to pre-
scribe its resolution. As the probability of an economic crisis –
and hence political power – grew remote, the possibility of an
international crisis was stressed. At the same time, the reliance
on explanations that allocated responsibility to individuals and
groups increased in order to sustain the movement and rationalize its existence. Where the attacks on the 'old gang', the
Communists and the Jews had once been seen as means to an
end, they became ends in themselves.

Despite the ascendancy of Mosley's Fascist appeals, there
were definable policy positions which were dominant at different
stages in the development of the B.U.F. This was in response
to the changes in the movement's political fortunes and to the
dictates of a changing economic and political climate. If a particular scheme found little public support, which was true for all
B.U.F. schemes, it was de-emphasized and another scheme was
given prominence. This was justified on the grounds that
Fascism was a dynamic movement adaptable to rapidly changing circumstances. B.U.F. policy can thus be divided into three
loosely defined phases which overlapped in time. During the
first phase, from the formation of the movement until the
autumn of 1934, Mosley's policy was constructive in nature.
The substance of the programme was at least as important as its
propaganda. Despite the duality in B.U.F. policy, Mosley's
analysis of Britain's economic difficulties was serious in its
intentions. His solution was derived from his earlier Labour
Party and New Party pronouncements and from Italian Fascism.
The improvement in the economic situation and the loss of
respectability caused by the B.U.F.'s own tactics were
responsible for a change in direction.

During the second phase, political anti-Semitism with its theories of persecution and conspiracy characterized B.U.F. policy. Proposals for the corporate state and parliamentary reform were pushed into the background. Political anti-Semitism was more a weapon than a belief, although Mosley had become more a demagogue than a reformer. The Blackshirts maintained that the Jews were racially inferior, but they did not attempt to demonstrate it on biological grounds. Mosley often stated that he was against the Jews not for what they were, but for what they did.

From 1937 until June 1940, foreign policy was the most important consideration for the B.U.F. The idea of the corporate state was not discarded, however, and the Jews remained the chief Fascist enemy. The problem for the Blackshirts was to reconcile their support for Fascism abroad, while continuing to propagate an extreme form of nationalism. This led to a policy of selective pacifism which had three components: nationalism; opposition to war against a Fascist power, but not against Russia; rearmament and a willingness to fight if British interests were attacked, from whatever quarter. By this time, however, the Mosley movement was spent as a political force.

In tracing the changes in B.U.F. policy and the development of these themes, primary consideration must be given to Mosley's *The Greater Britain*, *Fascism*, and *Tomorrow We Live*, as he considered them his most important writings.[2] *The Greater Britain* was written in 1932 and revised two years later. *Fascism* was written during the second period and *Tomorrow We Live* at the end of it. Mosley's *The World Alternative* and *The British Peace* stated his position prior to the Second World War. The works of other Fascist writers and pamphleteers are referred to when appropriate.

## DOCTRINE

The *raison d'être* of the British Fascist movement was the crisis. According to the Blackshirts, the Government and the 'old gang' were bound to collapse. In the competition for power, the

Fascists and the Communists would clash. The Fascists would come to power and resolve the crisis. The only alternative was to give the Fascists power so that they could avert the crisis.

The duality in B.U.F. policy was reflected at the outset in its attempt to explain the causes of the crisis. Although Mosley tried initially to present a case, it was too involved for the unemployed, while those who feared Communism were not necessarily concerned with alternatives. Hence the Blackshirts interpreted their crisis at two levels.

First, Mosley attempted a serious economic analysis in *The Greater Britain* which, in fact, was marked by generalities and differed little from his earlier Labour Party and New Party pronouncements, despite the Fascist vocabulary. Mosley maintained that the faulty distribution of goods was at the root of Britain's economic troubles and that an excessive percentage of its energies and resources was expended on the production of goods for shrinking foreign markets to the detriment of the home market, which was still in need of development. This development would contribute to a more realistic solution to the unemployment problem. Parliamentary democracy was criticized for being outdated and inadequate. The structure of Parliament diverted attention from important issues to minor points which were endlessly debated. The M.P. was held to be too incompetent and ignorant to meet his responsibilities as a legislator. Finally, in addition to economic and political modernization, the moral social fibre of the nation was seen to be in need of regeneration.

The Fascists' second approach to Britain's economic difficulties and political shortcomings made no pretence to serious analysis. Instead blame was assigned to individuals and groups rather than to the policies, institutions and processes. The politics of conspiracy and persecution appealed for support not only to extremists but to those whose discontent was aggravated at a time of crisis. And, by placing the ultimate source of conspiracy outside Britain, prospective adherents were relieved of responsibility and the Blackshirts could hope to establish their 'British' credentials.

According to the Fascists, a certain group or groups, 'the old gangs', were undermining the interests of Great Britain for their own benefit or for the benefit of others. If the old gangs were today's enemy, they were preparing the way for to-morrow's Communism. Britain was not only being betrayed, but the Blackshirts, as the defenders of the national interest, were being persecuted. At its roots was a conspiracy which was at first described as International Finance, and later, as International Finance controlled by the Jews. The Jews also ruled Bolshevik Russia in the interests of a 'world conspiracy'. At times, the enemies of Fascism made strange bedfellows. *Blackshirt* quite early gave expression to this mentality, which should have served as a warning to many. It blamed pacifists, liberals, Jews, Communists, internationalists, capitalists, financiers, the British Press, unscrupulous propagandists, nasty hypocritical swine with axes to grind, for having supposedly conspired to conduct a war against Germany.[3]

The old gang was the political *élite* which, regardless of pronouncements and various party labels, carried out the same policies when elected.[4] This was essentially a 'policy of sub-servience to sectional interests and of national lethargy'.[5] The muddle-headedness of the old gangs had paved the way for Communist chaos. In order to resist change, the Tory old gang appealed to loyalty and patriotism, but Mosley charged that this was the reverse of true patriotism at such a time of crisis.[6] Where initially this may have been a genuine appeal to youth, it developed into a charge of conspiracy. One writer maintained that the Conservative Party was more dangerous than the Communist Party, because it was more insidiously international. It was described as the 'British Branch of the Financial International', which was controlled from Wall Street.[7] Later, it was claimed that International Finance was controlled by or was working in combination with the Jews and operating inside the Conservative Party.[8]

The Labour Party old gang did not profit from the past, according to Mosley. Moreover, it was aggravating its previous mistakes by stressing more committees, delegations, and talk.

Its leaders were mediocre middle-class intellectuals who bowed to the trade-union bosses.[9] In 1936 the Labour Party was fully identified with International Socialism, and International Socialism served only the interests of International Finance.[10] Needless to say, if the Finance working with and within the Conservative Party was Jewish, so was the Finance behind the Labour Party and International Socialism.[11]

The B.U.F.'s attacks on Communism also developed into diatribes against an alleged Jewish conspiracy. In *The Greater Britain*, Mosley declared Fascism to be the opponent of Communism which pursued 'class warfare to the destruction of all science, skill, and managerial ability'.[12] Then, as a part of the B.U.F.'s anti-Semitic attacks, Russia was described as a state controlled by the Jews. In one policy statement, it was asserted that the Jews knew that capitalism was breaking down, and that they were anxious to be prominent in whatever system took its place.[13] One of Mosley's most prominent supporters, Major-General J. F. C. Fuller, wrote of this supposed vast conspiracy:

Because he [Mosley] struck at the Empire of Money, its satraps, conservative, liberal, labour and communist shoulder to shoulder formed rank against him; which goes far to show their common origin and their common spirit. As was only natural, behind this united front there stood the Jew, the originator of the usury system, which has as its object, the economic enslavement not only of individuals but of nations.[14]

The Fascist instrument for obtaining power was the 'movement' and it would resolve the crisis by 'action' through which the corporate state would be instituted.\* The concept of a

---

\* 'Action' was one of the most frequently-used B.U.F. slogans. Mosley, in retrospect, admitted that one of his great mistakes was that he had sacrificed too much to the desire for action. He maintained that it was justifiable in certain instances – such as the need for housing and the resolution of the unemployment problem. However, he thought that action could become a vice, especially if pursued at all costs, for it might treat a minority unfairly: 'You can't have action by violating human decencies.' Mosley concluded that he had been young and in too much of a hurry. *Interview*, 11 September 1959; see also *My Life* (1968), p. 293.

movement was to distinguish the B.U.F. from the old gang and the political parties since it implied an organization above parties and politics but pragmatic enough to use constitutional means, when and if necessary. At first, when Mosley was looking to Italy for inspiration, Fascism, according to Blackshirt propagandists, was the name by which the Modern Movement became known to the world. Hence, Mosley named his movement the British Union of Fascists. Mosley then looked to Germany, as well as to Italy, and the name was changed to the British Union of Fascists and National Socialists. He considered Fascism and National Socialism to be the same movement, explaining that they found different expression in different countries in accordance with national and racial characteristics.[15] Finally, Mosley reversed the emphasis at the stage when his followers had been deprived of their uniform and when his movement was little more than an anti-Semitic band. The Modern Movement now manifested itself in terms of National Socialism and Mosley expressed its creed: 'If you love our country you are National; if you love our people you are Socialist.'[16] He pressed the abbreviation, British Union, not only because of this change in emphasis, but also in the hope of making his doctrine more palatable to the British public.

Mosley's movement, his 'instrument of steel', was based on authoritarianism. In the first edition of *The Greater Britain*, he wrote:

Its leadership may be individual or preferably in the case of the British character, a team with clearly allocated functions and responsibility. In either case the only effective instrument of revolutionary change is absolute authority.[17]

In the 1934 edition the passage on leadership was significantly altered:

Leadership in Fascism may be an individual or a team, but undoubtedly single leadership in practice proves the more effective instrument. The leader must be prepared to shoulder absolute responsibility for the functions clearly allocated to him.[18]

Perhaps no other passages revealed so clearly the development of Mosley's character. Once the Fascists achieved power, the movement would be absorbed by the state. Mosley wrote:

... you will need no more the strange and disturbing men who, in days of struggle and of danger, and in nights of darkness and of labour have forged the instrument of steel by which the world shall pass to higher things.[19]

The symbols of the Fascist movement were the emblem, the salute, and the uniform. The original emblem of the B.U.F. was the fascis. Its use was justified on the grounds that the tradition of civilization and progress was derived from Rome and that the British Empire had become the chief custodian of that tradition.[20] Later it was maintained that the fascis had been used in Great Britain for two thousand years, and that it was a fitting symbol for the Empire that had succeeded and surpassed the Roman Empire.[21]

Although the use of the fascis was never entirely discarded, its importance was gradually superseded by the flash and circle, which was irreverently referred to by the anti-Fascists as the 'flash in the pan'. Its use coincided with the Abyssinian crisis and with the B.U.F.'s peace campaign. The emblem represented the flash of action in the circle of unity. Although the B.U.F. maintained that the symbol belonged exclusively to British Fascism, it was similar to the Nazi emblem with the white flash substituted for the black swastika.

Two official salutes were sanctioned by the B.U.F. The first was a half-arm salute to be used by Blackshirts in uniform, while the full-arm salute was to be used in greeting royalty, the Leader, and the National Regimental and Fascist colours and during the performance of the last line of the National Anthem.[22] According to Mosley, the salute was neither Italian nor German, although the Germans had used it. He claimed that it was the oldest salute of 'European civilization and that it has been used in Britain many centuries before the founding of a Fascist party in Italy'.[23]

The black shirt was the symbol of Fascism. It was worn as an expression of faith and its colour was supposed to represent the iron determination of Fascism in the fight against 'red anarchy'.[24] It was also asserted that the uniform broke down class barriers within the movement and enabled it to act as a disciplined body especially in times of stress.[25]

In the pictorial records of B.U.F. demonstrations the uniforms appear unimpressive. The Fascists on parade were not fully outfitted. The first divisions wore black shirts, belt and matching trousers. They were followed by Fascists in black shirts and trousers that did not match. The women wore black shirts and matching or unmatching skirts. In 1936, the distinction became more obvious. The B.U.F. adopted a full military uniform with coat, peaked cap, belt and buckle and jack-boots. But the number who actually wore this outfit was small. This uniform was virtually restricted to the National Head-quarters officers and stewards.

The B.U.F. also developed its own *'kitsch kultur'*. Buckles, tie-pins, brooches, plaques, cuff-links, rings and arm-bands were marketed. Photographs, post-cards, song sheets, car stickers and slogans were printed. 'Greater Britain' cigarettes, 'a perfect blend of American and home-grown tobacco', were on sale. On Decca Records, one could listen to the Leader's speeches, 'Comrades in Struggle' and 'British Union'. One could sing 'British Awake' and 'The Marching Song' with the British Union Male Voice Choir and Orchestra. Finally, the uniforms, the flags, and the salutes were all part of the histrionics employed at the B.U.F. meetings, and especially at Mosley's demonstrations. Songs and chants were added. Mosley would appear, always a little late, and often announced by a fanfare of trumpets. He would march to the platform preceded by flags and flanked by stewards. Alone on the platform in his uniform, Mosley, the Leader, was British Fascism's most significant symbol.

The priority given to a paramilitary movement which forecast crisis, the provocative nature of its symbols and posturings and the tone of its propaganda suggested that the B.U.F. was prepared to take over the state by means of force. At no time, however, did the Blackshirts specifically state that they were organized to do this, short of a crisis. In deference to British traditions, the political habits of the electorate and the actual social and economic conditions in Britain in the 1930s, this would have been an extraordinary admission.

Mosley sought to make the position clear at the outset. In the conclusions to *The Greater Britain* he argued that in the final economic crisis organized force alone prevailed, and that the struggle *for* the modern state in such circumstances was between Fascism and Communism. The normal instruments of state were deemed inadequate and those governments and parties that relied on them would fall to the forces of anarchy. If such a situation arose in Great Britain, the B.U.F. was prepared to meet the 'anarchy of Communism with the organized force of Fascism'.[26] Mosley went on to state that immediate action would avert the catastrophe, but that under the present set-up such action was unlikely. Only by the acceptance of Fascism would Great Britain avoid disaster.[27]

Moreover, the willingness to use violence to curb the disturbances that began to take place at B.U.F. meetings added weight to the accusations of the anti-Fascists. And in 1933 Mosley wrote:

We hope to secure our Fascist Revolution by peaceful and constitutional means. By one road or another we are determined that Fascism will come to Britain. . . .[28]

The opportunity to challenge the B.U.F. on this issue publicly was provided by Mosley when he brought a libel action against the Daily News Ltd, in which he was awarded £5,000 in damages. The case arose over a leading article in *The Star* about a public debate between Mosley and James Maxton in which it was alleged that Mosley had said 'that he and his Fascists would be ready to take over the government with the aid of machine-guns when the moment arrived'.[29] According to the short-hand notes of his secretary, which were produced in evidence, Mosley had stated that at a time of crisis, 'if and when he [the organized Communist] ever comes out, we will be there in the streets, with Fascist machine-guns to meet them'.

Mosley was subjected to a gruelling three-hour cross-examination in which he stressed that the Fascists would not use force to capture political office and that this was different from obtaining power after force had been used. The B.U.F. was ready to meet force against the state by the use of force. When asked what the B.U.F. would do in the event of a Communist Government which had the assent of the King, he reiterated that in no case would he use machine-guns against a constitutionally elected government in power on the invitation of the King.[30]

Despite the denials that the Blackshirts saw force as basic to their struggle and not as a last resort, offending pages were deleted from the revised editions of *The Greater Britain* and the following explanation substituted:

The British Union seeks power by the vote of the people alone as declared always in our Regulations. The pages cut out of this book have been omitted because they have been misrepresented by opponents who allege that we seek power by unconstitutional means. Such action is rendered necessary by the clear intention of the Government who passed the Public Order Act to 'frame-up' the British Union with any evidence they can distort for this purpose.[31]

The circumstances in which the controversy could be conclusively settled never arose, but the fact remained that the B.U.F. was organized on a paramilitary basis. It was therefore reasonable to infer that the Blackshirts were willing to resort to violence, if necessary, to gain power, even by constitutional means.

## THE CORPORATE STATE

The Blackshirt revolution was to be both radical and conservative. It was to be radical in that the Fascists advocated the corporate state, parliamentary reform and a 'new morality'. On the other hand, Mosley wrote that the Fascist revolution differed from 'Communist anarchy' in that Blackshirts aimed to accept and utilize the useful elements within the state and weave them into the corporate state.[32] Hence, the B.U.F. slogan, 'We bring a saving revolution'.

The central feature of Mosley's constructive proposals was the corporate state. As used by the B.U.F., this was a broad concept which included not only the establishment of corporations but also many of the reforms suggested by Mosley in the Labour Party and the New Party. The corporate state was to be the machinery of central direction. It would set the limits within which individuals and interests would function. Within these limits all activities would be permitted and private enterprise and profit-making encouraged.

For the plans of the actual machinery of the proposed corporate state it is necessary to rely mainly on Alexander Raven Thomson's booklet, *The Coming Corporate State*. The booklet was an unofficial statement of policy, but it was the most ambitious attempt to work out the details of the corporate state. Moreover, Thomson, who was then Director of Policy, tried to work out these details in line with declared policy.* The economic system was to be divided into twenty corporations, ranging from agriculture, iron and steel, textiles and public utilities to professional, domestic and pensioners' sectors. All twenty corporations would be represented in a National Corporation.[33] Each corporation would in turn be split into smaller groups to deal with particular industries. At the base, there would be district councils of employers and workers, local employers' federations and trade-union lodges.

The employers, workers, and consumers were to be equally represented in each corporation. No one group was to be outvoted by the other two. The employers in each industry would be obliged to become members of their particular employers' federation. Similarly, membership in the industry-wide trade unions was to be mandatory. Although both groups would elect their representatives to the corporation, political activities

* In outline, it agreed with Mosley's proposals set out in *Tomorrow We Live* and those proposals credited to Mosley by Chesterton in his biography. Mosley in a later edition of *The Greater Britain* refers the readers to Raven Thomson's plan. For his reservations, however, see *My Life* (1968), pp. 332-4.

as such would be outlawed. The government, as representative of the nation, would nominate the consumers' representatives. The corporations were to be entrusted with the functions of planning, control and social welfare. Strikes and lock-outs would be forbidden. Instead, each corporation would regulate wages, hours and conditions of work. The employers' and workers' representatives would settle the question of prices, output and competition. The representatives of the consumers would be able to prevent any possible collusion between the employers and the workers. The corporation would plan production and the expansion or contraction of the industry. With the aid and advice of a National Investment Board, it would regulate investments, profits, interest and dividends. It would also be held responsible for welfare schemes, industrial insurance and pensions. A recreation programme modelled on the Italian Dopolavoro was envisaged.

The decisions of the corporations were to be binding and were to have the force of law. In the event of a dispute in the preparation of codes, the National Corporation could make suggestions, and failing that the disputes would go before a Labour Court for compulsory arbitration. Controversies within a single corporation and between corporations would be settled by the National Corporation. An industrial court would be set up to check unfair competition, and Labour was promised access to the courts as a substitute for the strike. As another gesture towards the workers, Raven Thomson included a 'Charter of Labour', dealing with working conditions and employee benefits.[34]

Although the corporate system was generally described in vague terms, if at all, attempts were made to apply the structure to problems that were peculiar to a particular industry. The retail and wholesale trades were a good example, for they were deemed vulnerable by the Blackshirts to Jew-baiting. Price-cutting in the grocery trade had precipitated anti-Semitic reactions in some quarters and this was exploited by the B.U.F. causing the Board of Deputies of British Jews to make representations to at least one grocers' association.[35]

A distributive corporation would be formed, which would protect and divide the market between the small shop-keepers and the cooperatives. All shops would be licensed to prevent cut-throat competition and every shop, with the exception of a strictly limited number of department stores and village shops, would be compelled to restrict its business to a particular line. The number of competitors in any line would be strictly controlled, and the places of business would be geographically distributed. The so-called 'alien multiple combines' would be liquidated and split into separate shops.[36] This was qualified in the *Fascist Quarterly*. British investors would receive compensation subject to Fascist review of past dividends earned at the shop-keepers' expense. Combines that were 'British' and did not sell foreign goods to the 'detriment' of home interests were to be dealt with less severely. However, steps would still be taken to prevent their further growth and to bring about their 'gradual' elimination. 'British' multiple shops that sold 'British' goods were to be allowed to remain open, but not to expand.[37] Other Fascist writers maintained that, in addition to the above functions, the distributive corporation would separate the retail, wholesale and manufacturing phases of trading and prevent any firm or combine from entering more than one of these fields. The corporation would limit excessive price discounts by law and would prohibit cooperatives from engaging in political activities. The cooperatives would also be split into smaller units and would only be permitted to trade with their own members.[38] Perhaps the most significant clue to the role of the corporation was that stated by one Blackshirt propagandist who, after detailing most of the above functions, wrote that the corporation should be able only to modify the above rules, but that the Government should be able to transcend them.[39]

The foregoing doctrine provides some insight into how the Fascist thinkers reconciled Fascism and capitalism. Private property, enterprise and initiative would not be eliminated. Private property would be subjected to the widest 'possible' distribution.[40] The ownership of land would be a public trust with no reward without service. This principle also applied to the large land-owner, in contradiction to the principle of 'widest possible distribution'. His land would be expropriated only for abuse of the public trust.[41] 'Services' and 'abuses' would be decided by the state. 'Thus,' Mosley wrote, 'most ownership of urban land will pass to the State, as that category of landlord is a great deal less likely than the leader of the countryside to justify his hereditary wealth by public services.'[42] Private enterprise would be regulated and private initiative controlled. The economic structure would be radically altered, but the foundation and the system itself would be preserved. The corporate state would be superimposed upon capitalism, rather than substituted for it.[43]

According to Mosley, the function of the National Corporation was 'to plan, regulate and direct the whole national economy, under the guidance of the minister, who himself would be ultimately responsible to Parliament'.[44] According to Raven Thomson, the first task of the National Corporation was to solve the problem of over-production. Several powers were to be vested in this body. The first was judicial in that the National Corporation would settle disputes that arose within and between the corporations. The second was the power of 'industrial planning on a national scale' which seemed to be defined as the adjustment of 'consumption to production by its control over wage rates throughout the industrial field'. In addition, the National Corporation was to exercise control over the Investment Board, a Foreign Trade Board and other corporate institutions. Third, 'all broad economic issues' would come before this body, but it would only sit as an advisory council to the Minister of Corporations, who would act as Speaker and control the deliberations of the assembly.[45]

The delegates to the National Corporation were to be elected on the same principle as in the individual corporations. Each corporation was to nominate equal numbers of employers and workers, although the number of representatives would be weighted in accordance with 'the importance of the industry to the national welfare'. It was not clear how this was to be done or on what basis. Nor was the position of the consumer representatives made clear. Finally, the subsidiary role of the National

Corporation was apparent in the proposal that it would be represented with other bodies and groups in the upper chamber that would replace the House of Lords.

Under Raven Thomson's plan, the National Corporation was to have a number of administrative organs. The Foreign Trade Board would regulate foreign trade under a policy of economic nationalism. The long-term objective would be to raise the standard of living in Great Britain and the Empire and hence build up adequate markets without relying on foreign trade. Until self-sufficiency could be reached, however, it would be necessary to import some raw materials and foodstuffs. Britain would buy only from those who would buy from Britain which would provide a balance of trade based not upon maximal but on minimal imports. This was in keeping with the idea of 'insulation' set forth by Mosley before he became a Fascist.[46]

An Investment Board would be created to control and regulate capital. Foreign investments without special sanction would be prohibited. The Investment Board would further regulate and control the responsibility for the planned development of Empire resources. Government officials, representatives of banking, insurance, the Stock Exchange and the Patents Office would sit on the Board. The role of the Investment Board, as explained by Raven Thomson, was more limited than that proposed in either *A National Policy* or *The Greater Britain*.[47]

Closely related to the problem of investment was that of finance, about which Fascist writers went on at great length because of its relevance to their persecution-conspiracy theories and because of Mosley's personal interests in the problems. Mosley, in *The Greater Britain*, discussed the need for financial control, but refrained from committing the B.U.F. to a financial corporation until his later works. The Bank of England, the joint stock banks and finance houses would be subject to the corporation. The export of capital and credit would be forbidden in contrast to proposals by Raven Thomson for licensing. Needless to say, the alien financier Jew would be deported.[48]

In order to implement these proposals an authoritarian political structure was deemed essential. Like the corporate state it would be superimposed upon the existing system, not substituted for it. The Crown, Parliament and the Government would be retained as institutions, but their structure would be altered, and the functions of the latter two would be radically revised so that only a hollow shell of the Constitution would remain. This conception of the political system placed the B.U.F. on the defensive, for the intention of establishing a dictatorship had to be denied. In *The Greater Britain*, Mosley wrote that Fascism as understood by the B.U.F. was not a creed of personal dictatorship as on the Continent, nor was it a creed of government tyranny.[49] The people, through Parliament, would retain the right to dismiss and change the government of the day. Mosley argued that since this power was retained, dictatorship was absurd.[50]

Yet with that remarkable duality that characterized Blackshirt policy, the B.U.F. shortly thereafter published a pamphlet by William Joyce, who asserted the need for a Fascist dictatorship in the Continental manner. In answer to the question of who shall rule, Joyce employed the circular justification of Italian Fascism:

The men who make Britain Fascist are the men whom all Britain cannot rule; and hence they must rule all Britain. Strength is the test of effective dictatorship and victory is the test of strength.[51]

Neither Joyce's statement, Mussolini's tactics in Italy nor the rise of Hitler convinced the anti-Fascists of the possible benevolence of a Blackshirt dictatorship, despite Mosley's reassurances. Denials were obviously insufficient, and Mosley attempted to set out a formula for a Fascist dictatorship based on the principles of 'modern dictatorship' and 'leadership'. Mosley claimed that, under modern conditions, dictators were not dictators, but leaders. The difference was that leaders had popular support. Hitler was described as the 'leader of enthusiastic and determined masses of men and women bound together by a voluntary discipline to secure the regeneration of their country'.[52] Moreover, leadership was seen as the substitute of individual responsibility for the collective responsibility of a do-nothing committee system.[53]

Under the corporate state, as described by Mosley in *The Greater Britain*, the government must have power to legislate by Order, subject to the power of Parliament to dismiss it by a vote of censure.[54] In effect, this differed little from the declaration in *A National Policy*. Mosley, however, made no statement as to whether Parliament would have the right to debate the general principles or policies, or the right to interrogate ministers as had been previously suggested. The House of Lords would be superseded by the National Corporation as a Parliament of Industry. The majority of the members of this Parliament were to be elected on an occupational basis. The remainder would be elected by the electorate in general, and they would represent the national interest.[55]

The position of Parliament was altered more radically by Mosley in the second edition of the B.U.F. bible. Under Fascism, the first Parliament would be called together at regular intervals to review the work of the government. At the end of that Parliament, an election would be held on an occupational franchise. Thereafter, the life of the Parliament would be dependent on a direct vote of the people held at regular intervals, which would not exceed the lifetime of a 'present' Parliament. The elector would have two votes: a yes-or-no judgement on the government; and a separate occupational franchise. Parliament would lose its power to dismiss the government by a vote of censure, and would be limited to assisting the government with 'technical and constructive criticism'. In the event of a government defeat by a vote of the electorate, the Monarch would send for new ministers, in whom he believed the nation would show confidence in a second vote. However, these too would presumably be Fascists since opposition parties would not be tolerated after the second general election.[56] When questioned at the Oxford University Fascist Association, whether after ten years he would allow the nation to change its mind, Mosley replied that no Fascist nation ever changed its mind.[57]

The plan to elect members to represent the national interests was also dropped.[58] Members of Parliament would have a new role. In between sittings they would be employed as executive officers in their local constituencies. They would be assisted by locally elected councils from which officers would be selected to head the departments in local government. The department heads would be responsible to the local M.P. who, in turn, would be responsible to the National Government. In this way, the leadership principle would replace the committee system. The fact that M.P.s would be elected on an occupational basis, rather than for a geographically defined constituency, never bothered Mosley. Raven Thomson and Major-General Fuller sought to correct this oversight. They argued that the corporations would assume the functions of local government bodies, and that the M.P. could carry out the executive work of his corporation.[59]

The National Corporation was no longer considered a suitable replacement for the House of Lords. Under the B.U.F.'s new scheme, it would be replaced by a second chamber of specialists and men of general knowledge. These would include representatives of the Dominions and Colonies, religious, educational, and military leaders, civil servants, foreign affairs experts, men who had rendered 'conspicuous service' to the state and representatives of a National Council of Corporations.[60]

It is necessary to turn to *The Coming Corporate State* to discover the nature of the Executive. According to Raven Thomson, Government office would be divorced from parliamentary representation, although Government ministers would be *'ex officio'* members of both houses. Cabinet reform was based on Mosley's Labour Party and New Party proposals. An inner cabinet invested with supreme power would be formed with the responsibility of planning national policy. It would include the Prime Minister (Leader) and three or four Ministers without portfolio. In addition, the existing ministries would be consolidated into eight or so ministries. It was not clear whether they were to meet as a body or not, but the 'Administrative Ministers' would be called into the Executive Cabinet from time to time for consultation.[61]

## THE JEWISH CONSPIRACY*

Mosley denied that he was ever an anti-Semite by offering his own definition of anti-Semitism. According to Mosley, an anti-Semite was a man who was opposed to all Jews because they were Jews '. . . I have never been against any man simply because he is a Jew'.[62] He repeated that the B.U.F. did not attack Jews because of their race or religion, but because of what they did.[63] The interpretation of 'what they did' was, of course, Mosley's own. Moreover, the Jews were not criticized because of their alleged acts, but because these acts were supposedly committed by them because of their Jewishness. In other words, Jewish landlords were not denounced as landlords, or even as Jewish landlords, but for being Jewish. In an interview given to *The Catholic Herald*, Mosley was alleged to have stated that it was impossible to differentiate between kinds of Jews, even those who were converted to the Catholic Church.[64]

According to John Strachey, Mosley's 'anti-Semitism was 100 per cent insincere'. He reasoned that Mosley used it to hold the allegiance of his followers and as the result of the influence of National Socialism.[65] Lady Cynthia Mosley's sister, Baroness Ravensdale, maintained that Mosley argued that Fascism would not survive without a scapegoat such as Jewry.[66] Certainly, the B.U.F. never really formulated an elaborate racial theory, although political racialism as distinct from biological racialism was exploited. Mosley had to construct a rationale to account for the failure of his movement, and at the same time to justify its continued existence and hold the allegiance of his followers. The Jews were a tangible object for projection and an outlet for frustration. Unlike the 'old gang' and the 'Communists', they could be located geographically, for many had settled together in particular sectors of urban areas. As far as the prejudiced and

* This section appeared in a different form as an unsigned article by the author, 'Mosley's Anti-Semitism, 1933–1939', *The Wiener Library Bulletin*, Nos. 3–4 (1959), pp. 33, 41; for Mosley's recent statement of his position, see *My Life* (1968), pp. 336–43. The belief in a world conspiracy is seen as complete nonsense, p. 443.

the resentful were concerned, the Jews were also physically identifiable. And since they were conspicuous in some trades and professions, if only as a minority, malcontents whether working or middle class could focus their aggressions on them.

Whatever the motivation, the B.U.F. concentrated much abuse on the Jews, and political anti-Semitism dominated the activities, as well as the policy of the B.U.F., after 1934. For example, the Blackshirts fought the L.C.C. elections of 1937 largely on anti-Semitism, Mosley having declared, 'East London will have to choose between us and the parties of Jewry. . . .'[67] Although the Communists and the Blackshirts continued to clash in the streets, there was no identifiable stronghold of Communism into which the Blackshirts could march and shout provocative slogans, intimidate the population or even destroy property. This was what happened in some areas of East London where a large number of Jews lived.

Theories of conspiracy and persecution were central to the propagation of political anti-Semitism. The politics of persecution was based on the propositions that Jewry was organized in various ways and that it was not only unduly influencing Great Britain and the world, but persecuting the Fascists. The Fascists, as the persecuted and as the defenders of the traditions and character of the British, must protect themselves from organized Jewry, and hence must prosecute the Jews. Finally, this persecution identified the Fascists with their audiences and also projected an image of the movement as less exotic than its opponents. This is well illustrated by the following passage:

When we have unmasked the real power behind Conservatism and Socialism, and see the corrupt influences which really govern, we are not surprised that the press they control, the cinema industry which they own body and soul, and the whole force of their finance and power is loosed upon us, when for the first time in the history of the nation a patriotic movement challenges the great Jewish interest of International Finance.[68]

Mosley launched his anti-Jewish campaign at the Albert Hall on 28 October 1934. His anti-Semitic outbursts, however, pre-dated this meeting at a time when the B.U.F. considered it necessary to issue pronouncements that it was not anti-Semitic, and private orders that Jew-baiting would not be tolerated. In fact, anti-Semitism was tolerated as Mosley himself engaged in it, and since the B.U.F. was an authoritarian movement such utterances, regardless of their origin, were ultimately his responsibility.*

The official line during the first phase was to deny the existence of a Jewish problem. Yet on the occasion of the first indoor meeting and Fascist parade in London, Mosley was reported to have said with reference to his questioners that, 'They are all from Jerusalem; they don't know any better.'[69] Following the meeting the Blackshirts marched to the Cenotaph where the police ordered them to disband following a shout, 'Down with Gandhi and to hell with the Jews.'[70] Early in December 1932, barely two months after the founding of the B.U.F., Mosley issued an order barring anti-Semitic activities and asserting the existence of a British race.[71]

On 1 April 1933, the entire front page of the fourth issue of the *Blackshirt* was devoted to an unsigned article on 'Fascism and the Jew'. The 'Jewish Question' was labelled irrelevant and the writer regretted, although later justified, the early Nazi attacks on the Jews. Meanwhile, Mosley, visiting Mussolini in the same month, went so far as to declare that British Fascism was in no way anti-Jewish, adding 'that Hitler had made his greatest mistake in his attitude towards the Jews'.[72] On his return to England, he announced that, although he disapproved of Jew-baiting, he would reserve judgement on Hitler's policy.[73]

From April until the autumn of 1933, the *Blackshirt* repeatedly assured its readers that the B.U.F. was in no way anti-Jewish.[74] Dr Robert Forgan, then second-in-command, said that there was no ban on Jews joining the B.U.F., although he did not say whether any Jews were actually members.[75] In an elaborate declaration of religious and racial tolerance published in *The Jewish Economic Forum* and in a Press interview – both in July –

* Mosley records the difficulty in exercising effective control and argues that the persistent anti-Semites were dismissed. Yet Joyce and Beckett, to name only two, persisted until 1937. See *My Life* (1968), p. 342.

Mosley claimed that racial and religious persecution were alien to the British character, and hence alien to British Fascism.[76] Articles tinged with anti-Semitism, however, began to creep into the Fascist Press. In September 1933, William Joyce, writing as 'Lucifer', drew a distinction between good Jews and bad Jews, and good-money Jews and bad-money Jews. He went on to claim that the 'low type of foreign Jew together with other aliens who are debasing the life of the nation will be run out of the country in double-quick time under Fascism'. The better type of Jew, according to this writer, who had become 'thoroughly British in outlook' would be glad to see him go.[77] Mosley put forth the same argument in Manchester on 16 October, and went on to claim that the Jews and aliens were not only debasing British life, but were attempting to dominate it in the interests of other countries. They used the 'weapons of the ghetto', daggers and razors.[78] There were other warnings. Mosley wrote that Fascism alone could deal with the alien menace, for Fascism alone put 'Britain First'. Aliens competing for British jobs would be debarred from the country, and those who abused British hospitality would be deported. Finally, Fascism would deal with 'The Great Alien Financier of the City of London'.[79]

Meanwhile, *Blackshirt* had printed various articles showing Germany and Italy, Hitler and Mussolini, in a favourable light.[80] In November 1933, one year before Mosley's official 'declaration of war' against the Jews, the latter were blamed for the mounting criticism against Germany. The *Blackshirt* on 4 November headlined an unsigned front-page article, 'Shall Jews Drag Britain to War?'. The author declared: 'We state deliberately that Jews are striving to involve Britain in war.' He continued: 'We do not fight Jews on racial or religious grounds. We oppose them because they have become an organized interest within the state pursuing a policy which threatens British lives and homes.' Mosley repeated the argument at a meeting in Ealing Town Hall that same week.[81]

Shortly thereafter, in the first issue of the *Fascist Week*, the Jews were attacked for taking over university posts. The Blackshirts claimed that they did not object to them as Jews, but as unwanted aliens who had left Germany because they were extremists.[82] The criticism continued for another week and was then dropped as suddenly as it had been begun. Most likely, the attack was halted pending the negotiations which were under way with Lord Rothermere; and during the first four months of the Mosley–Rothermere alliance there was a moratorium on Blackshirt Jew-baiting.

In the spring of 1934 Mosley resumed his campaign. At a meeting in Liverpool, he admitted that the B.U.F. no longer, if ever, allowed Jews to join the movement, and claimed persecution at the hands of 'certain Jewish interests'.[83] He gained the approval of Julius Streicher, the Nazi Jew-baiter. After Streicher's paper, *Der Stürmer*, had accused the B.U.F. of being 'a Jewish catchup movement', the editor explicitly retracted.[84] Streicher later stated that he had obtained information about the B.U.F., 'from a person I sent to the spot', and went on to state: 'The fact that the Mosley movement has positively defined its attitude toward the Jewish problem suggests that Mosley has now realized that the tactical reserve hitherto observed by him in this question is no longer expedient.'[85] By the autumn of 1934 *Der Stürmer* was calling Mosley 'a great speaker, an intrepid fighter and especially a fine diplomat'.[86]

The notoriety gained as a result of the B.U.F. meeting at Olympia in June ushered in a new stage in B.U.F. policy. The sometimes brutal methods employed by the Blackshirt stewards in combating the organized interruptions had alienated many of Fascism's more responsible and influential adherents. The B.U.F. received a further set-back when, a month later, Lord Rothermere withdrew his support, allegedly over the issue of anti-Semitism. Mosley now attacked the Jews more vehemently.

In Sheffield, towards the end of June 1934, Mosley announced that it was not the Fascists who had started the row. A few weeks later, he declared that 'behind the Communist and Socialist mob is the alien Jewish financier supplying the palm-oil to make them yell'.[87] More anti-Jewish outbursts occurred at a Fascist meeting in Manchester. And then, Mosley, at the

Albert Hall, on 28 October, 'accepted the challenge of organized Jewry'. In his declaration, he utilized the conspiracy and persecution theories. He spoke about the power of organized Jewry in Great Britain, and how it was mobilized against Fascism. Mosley claimed that they were not attacking the Jews on racial or religious lines, but only because the Jews were fighting against them and Great Britain. The Jews had assailed Fascism in three ways: they had physically assaulted the Blackshirts; Fascists had been victimized by their employers; and the 'organized power of Jewry as a racial interest' was trying to drag Britain into war.[88] At Leicester, the following April, he announced a new crusade:

For the first time I openly and publicly challenge the Jewish interest in this country commanding commerce, commanding the press, commanding the cinema, dominating the City of London, killing industry with the sweatshops. These great interests are not intimidating, and will not intimidate the Fascist movement of the modern age.[89]

This speech considerably impressed Streicher, who congratulated Mosley in a telegram. The British Fascist Leader replied:

... I greatly esteem your message in the midst of our hard struggle. The forces of Jewish corruption must be overcome in all great countries before the future of Europe can be made secure in justice and peace. Our struggle is hard but our victory is certain.[90]

Three methods were vital to the politics of conspiracy and persecution. The first was political racialism – the Jews as a racial interest. In Mosley's policy statement, *Fascism*, the Jews were described as foreigners, and blamed for almost all Britain's economic troubles. Mosley also stated that it would be bad for the Empire to stigmatize by law the other races in it as inferior or outcast. But British Fascism stood for British racial purity, and Mosley claimed that certain racial mixtures were bad, although he did not explain which were bad or why. If legislation was necessary to preserve the race, Fascism would not hesitate to introduce it.[91] This was never developed into anything that could properly be termed a racial theory, but new grounds had been found on which to attack the Jews.[92]

A second Fascist method attempted to demonstrate Jewish control of a particular industry or sector of public life. The Press, for example, was frequently cited, and one result of this was an expensive libel suit.[93] The Press was a particularly sensitive issue as, for the most part, it either attacked or ignored the Blackshirts. It was, therefore, not surprising to find that the B.U.F. blamed the defection of Lord Rothermere, in the summer of 1934, on the pressure exerted by Jewish advertisers. The usual argument was that the national Press was Jewish-owned and largely staffed by Jews. Where the Press was not owned by Jews, it was supposedly controlled by Jewish revenue.[94] A third method was that of derogatory or provocative reference to the Jew often accompanied by physical intimidation and violence. Attacks on the 'strong', 'ruthless' Jew were combined with attacks on the 'weak' Jew in the streets. It was a common practice for the Fascists to march through East London chanting, 'The Yids, the Yids, we gotta get rid of the Yids'.

As the Second World War approached, B.U.F. policy drew nearer to Nazi policy and the anti-Semitic campaign was intensified. A. K. Chesterton quoted a speech of Mosley's which gave the impression that the primary and sole purpose of the B.U.F. was to 'break for ever in Britain the power of the Jew'.[95] One speaker was alleged to have said that 'I am a disciple of Julius Streicher'.[96] In July 1937, twenty Blackshirts visited Streicher. His welcoming speech was full of admiration and praise for Mosley and his movement. He told his guests that he considered them 'as brothers and comrades in the fight' against Jewry.[97] The spokesman for the Blackshirts was reported to have said: 'We rejoice that we have seen the world leader in the fight against Semitism. From his *Stürmer* we forge the best weapons for our fight in England.'[98] The visitors raised a threefold '*Sieg Heil*' for Hitler and Streicher and sang the '*Horst Wessel Lied*' in English.[99]

It was not enough to attack the Jews. The B.U.F. had to find a solution to their problem. Raven Thomson stated, 'Our problem must be to get the Jewish genii back into the bottle of the ghetto in which our forefathers in their wisdom kept him, before his money power strangled the world.'[100] Mosley's first plan was to stop immigration and deport those Jews guilty of 'anti-British' conduct. By this, he meant those Jews who had allegedly organized themselves as a nation within a nation, and set their interests before those of Great Britain. Jews who were considered innocent of those charges would be allowed to remain, but only as foreigners; they would not possess the full rights of British citizenship.[101]

The initial solution created a problem. If the Jews were really a sinister conspiracy, no other nation would accept those Jews whom Great Britain deported. Mosley eventually recognized this. In *Tomorrow We Live*, he suggested that a suitable territory would have to be found, where the Jews could escape the 'curse of no nationality', and have the opportunity of becoming a nation. Mosley maintained that, if the Jews had been sincere in their pronouncements, and did want to become something more than 'the parasite of humanity', they would accept the offer.[102] The new territory would evidently be found by a conference of European nations.

## NATIONALISM

Nationalism was also a major theme in B.U.F. policy. In *The Greater Britain*, Mosley wrote that the B.U.F. was 'essentially a national movement' and, if policy could be summarized in two words, they would be 'Britain First'.[103] This, however, was not intended to mean 'Britain alone'. At first, Commonwealth development and Anglo-Saxon cooperation were advocated and later the creation of European unity based on a Fascist power *bloc*. A problem for the B.U.F. was how to reconcile the contradiction between its nationalist appeals and the defence of Fascism on the Continent. When foreign policy became an important consideration, the B.U.F. adopted a position of selective pacifism which set the tone for the third phase much in the same way that the corporate state and anti-Semitism had dominated the previous ones. The Blackshirts were not against war, but against war with the Fascist powers. Selective pacifism did not stand for disarmament for this surely would have conflicted with Britain First, which also stood for Britain First in defence. Mosley called for a vigorous defence policy when the B.U.F. was founded and later advocated an alliance of Fascist powers to include Britain.

Alfred Rosenberg, the philosopher of the Nazi movement, recognized the error of the duality of loyalties in B.U.F. policy. He considered it a psychological mistake for Mosley to have called his movement 'British Fascist'. He felt that the use of a label of foreign origin conflicted with the pride that England possessed for her own traditions. More important, he considered a Fascist party unsuitable for England. Rosenberg maintained that the B.U.F. had damaged its moral position during the Italian–Abyssinian war. The British Government, he argued, had taken a decidedly anti-Italian position and probably had the support of a majority of the British. Yet the Mosley movement, even though it stood for 'British interests exclusively', by supporting the Fascist cause could not help but be suspected of being in league with Mussolini. This discredited the B.U.F. from the very first.[104]

Blackshirt foreign policy developed along three lines during the first policy phase: a Fascist plan for peace; the promotion of Mussolini's and Hitler's regimes; and a 'British First – Empire First' campaign. Mosley devoted four pages to foreign policy in the first edition of *The Greater Britain* but he had a good deal more to say in the second. The preservation of European peace was given a high priority. He argued that the existence of Fascist governments in all great countries and the resulting cooperation between them would be the surest guarantee of peace.[105]

Mosley wanted a reconstructed League of Nations so that the 'effective leadership' of the great powers could be established and not obstructed by the small powers. In this way European reconstruction could be undertaken. A Fascist Europe would be responsible for removing the causes of war which were deemed largely economic. The desire for universal disarmament was expressed, but until that time a review of Britain's defence was urged, along with an immediate build-up of all the services. This, in fact, differed little from the policy set forth in *A National Policy*, minus the Fascist trappings and with the exception that here Mosley demanded special attention for the air force.[106] The emphasis on national security was directed towards the 'patriot' and the ex-serviceman to whom Fascist propaganda frequently made special appeals.[107] During the third policy phase, the B.U.F. attacked the Government for the ill-preparedness of the army and, at the same time, attacked Leslie Hore-Belisha, the Secretary of State for War, for trying to modernize it.

Meanwhile, B.U.F. publications continually paid homage to National Socialist Germany and Fascist Italy. Both Hitler and Mussolini were portrayed as the messengers of peace. The *Blackshirt* claimed that jingoism in Germany and Britain had been restrained by the 'moderate' and 'pacific' utterances of Hitler.[109] The same paper asserted that after Hitler had re-modelled Germany 'the so-called atrocities and harshness' would end. It insisted that three-quarters of the reports were not true and those that were true were the result of the uncontrolled exuberance of the revolution and could not be avoided, for the Reds had begun the violence.[108] Mussolini was described as 'the one skilled architect' of European peace for he had proved that Fascism stood for world peace, although it was not explained how.[110]

Emphasis was also placed on Empire development. Joyce defined Fascism as imperialism, while Mosley was anxious to reassure the public that the Fascists were interested in Empire development, not expansion.[111] According to the Blackshirts, the main Empire priority was economic unity which would be fostered by the corporate state.[112] A British Fascist government would be pledged to raise the standard of living for the native populations of the Colonies, but it would not permit self-government nor grant independence. The Blackshirts argued that, if independence was granted, the new nations would fall prey to foreign capitalist exploitation. Moreover, these newly independent races would be unwilling or unable to develop their economic resources. Mosley wrote:

The earth can and will be developed by the races fitted for that task and chief among such races we are not afraid to number our own.[113]

The B.U.F. peace campaign began during the second policy phase. It was motivated by the aggressive actions on the part of the Continental Fascist powers. Nationalistic appeals were utilized to advocate non-intervention against the Fascist powers and to advocate cooperation with them in order to preserve peace. Blackshirt propaganda, which had formerly served to promote admiration for Italy and Germany, was now used to defend them. A campaign which was summed-up in the slogan, 'Mind Britain's Business', was announced in August 1935 as a result of the Italian–Abyssinian war.[114]

Mosley altered his earlier plan for the maintenance of world peace. The Empire was seen as a key factor, a United Fascist Europe was to replace the League, and his analysis of the problem was in terms of his conspiracy and persecution theories. First, the B.U.F. would protect Great Britain by removing the causes of war, which were described as the struggle for markets. This would be done by the establishment of a self-contained Empire. Mosley concluded, 'When other nations follow our example, there will be nothing left to fight for.'[115] Second, the maintenance of world peace was to be secured by the material and spiritual union of Europe led by a *bloc* of four Fascist powers – Germany, Italy, France and Great Britain. If, despite this, war occurred, Great Britain would be saved, for a Fascist Government would 'Mind Britain's Business'.[116] Third, the threats to peace were described as International Finance and International Communism with the Jews lurking in the shadows behind both. The current manifestation of International Jewry was Russia, but with a united Europe on the West and an allied Japan on the East, it would be kept in place.[117]

After Hitler consolidated his power, Mosley switched his primary allegiance from Italy to Germany. At the time, the B.U.F. did not abandon the Italian Fascist cause, but instead there was a shift in emphasis most marked by political anti-Semitism.[118] The Blackshirts praised Hitler and championed Nazi Germany far more than they did Mussolini or Italy. The Blackshirts also emulated the Nazi uniforms, their songs and their salute. Mosley referred to the Germans as 'Our Blood Brothers',[119] and could 'say without any hesitation . . . from the bottom of my heart, "Heil Hitler" '.[120]

Much of the Blackshirt propaganda was devoted to condoning the aims of German foreign policy. B.U.F. speakers and pamphleteers argued that Germany should be allowed to expand in order to unite the German people. Their objective was motivated by a 'natural' and 'irresistible' force. It was not the Germans who were responsible for the state of Europe, but Financial Democracy and International Socialism. There was no conflict between Great Britain and Germany, for Britain's 'world mission' was Empire-centred, while Germany's was a European union of German people. The British Fascist movement tried to reassure the public that the Germans did not want a world-wide Empire, for that could lead to 'racial deterioration'.[121]

The Spanish Civil War, which overlapped the second and third B.U.F. policy phases, provided the movement with additional scope for propaganda. Mosley summarized the B.U.F. position in a speech in London, when he stated that, although his whole sympathy was with Franco, the whole of Spain was not worth one drop of English blood.[122] Franco was portrayed as the bulwark against the corrupt government of anti-religious forces of Soviet atheism. The governments of the West that wavered or even considered the possibility of intervention were labelled, along with the individual volunteer, tools of International Finance and Jewry.[123] Even after non-intervention was announced, the Blackshirts were dissatisfied. The *British Union Quarterly* declared the Government's policy a 'shoddy cloak' for intervention of a 'moral kind'. Non-intervention, according to the Blackshirts, was in order to allay the Socialists and to afford the opportunity for 'Mr Eden to strike once again at the enemies he has so gratuitously made for Britain on behalf of international finance'.[124]

Selective pacifism was the outstanding feature of the third B.U.F. policy phase. The principles had been formulated, and they were moulded to the particular circumstances and propagated with the limited resources that the movement could command. Hitler was defended, and at the same time Mosley acclaimed his movement's allegiance to the Crown. An enemy conspiracy had been found, but eventually the Hitler–Stalin pact confused the Mosleyites just as it did the Left.

German troops crossed the Austrian frontier on 10 March 1938. The following week *Action* described their march:

The advance of the Nazis was like a symphony; the Saar was the allegro, the Rhineland the andante, Austria the scherzo, there remained the finale to be played.[125]

Mosley launched a 'Stop-the-War' campaign. *Action* told its readers that the politicians backed by International Socialism were sending them to war. It concluded that no British interests were involved in Austria, and millions of Austrians were celebrating the 'new brotherhood of the German people'.[126]

Munich was next. On 29 September 1938, the Munich conference opened and on 1 October German troops moved into Czechoslovakian territory. On the same day, *Action* came out with a 'crisis special' in which Mosley proclaimed, 'This is no war for Britain. This is a war dictated by the enemies and oppressors of the British people.'[127] In Manchester two days later, Mosley described Chamberlain's journey as an act of courage and common sense.[128] Munich was seen as the possible prelude to a four-power peace pact leading to the union of Europe.[129] The subsequent failure of the Munich Agreement was not blamed on Hitler, but on the 'democrats' who destroyed 'the spirit'.[130]

The Hitler–Stalin pact caught the Blackshirts unprepared. Mosley ignored the fact that Hitler was also a party to the agreement and analysed Russia's motives. He set forth four possible explanations involving the conspiracy theory. First, Mosley argued that Russia may have 'rid herself of Jewish control', and under Russian leadership was primarily interested in a national revolution concerned with the Russian people. Mosley's second speculation was that the 'Jewish leaders of Russian Communism' were trying to promote a world war, between the axis powers and Financial Democracy, to bring about the destruction of the Western world. Third, Mosley thought that perhaps Russia was simply in no position to wage a war. He warned that if they did so, the system 'left by the Jewish commissars would collapse'. Finally, Mosley asserted that if the 'Jewish influences' were still in control in Russia, they must be seeking to destroy the British Empire in the Far East.[131]

On 1 September 1939, Mosley issued a message to all B.U.F. members and supporters requesting them to do nothing to impede the war effort or to help an enemy power. At the same time, he announced that the British Union continued to stand firmly for peace. Since neither Britain nor the Empire was threatened, the Government had intervened in an 'alien quarrel', a war of 'Jewish Finance'.[132] Mosley continued to campaign for a B.U.F. Government and for a social revolution on the grounds that British democracy would never dare to come to terms with Germany, which had outstripped her domestically.[133] Finally, on the eve of his internment under Defence Regulation 18B, he declared that he was campaigning in the hope of providing an alternative Government, if and when the present Government desired to make peace, 'with the British Empire intact and our people safe'.[134]

## NOTES

1. A. Rossi, *The Rise of Italian Fascism* (1938), p. 36.
2. Oswald Mosley, *Interview*, 11 September 1959.
3. *Blackshirt*, 10 November 1933.
4. They were indeed old. For a breakdown by age see Sigmund Neumann, *Permanent Revolution* (2nd edn, 1965), p. 252; W. L. Guttsman, *The British Political Élite* (1963), p. 202.
5. Oswald Mosley, *The Greater Britain* (1932 edn), p. 147.
6. Oswald Mosley, *Ten Points of Fascism* (1933), pp. 2–3.
7. 'Lucifer' (William Joyce), *The Letters of Lucifer* (1933), p. 8.
8. *Fascist Quarterly* (January 1936), p. 16.
9. Oswald Mosley, 'Fascism: It's Here to Stay', *The Sunday Chronicle*, 23 July 1933.

10. Oswald Mosley, *Fascism* (1936), Q. 4, 5, 7, 9.
11. C. F. Wegg-Prosser, 'The Worker and the State', *Fascist Quarterly* (April 1936), p. 259.
12. Mosley, *The Greater Britain*, p. 30.
13. British Union, *Britain and Jewry* (n.d.), p. 7.
14. J. F. C. Fuller, *What the British Union Has to Offer Britain* (n.d.), p. 6.
15. Mosley, *Fascism*, Q. 4.
16. Oswald Mosley, *Tomorrow We Live* (1936 edn), p. 62.
17. Mosley, *The Greater Britain*, p. 24.
18. *ibid.*, (1934 edn), p. 30.
19. Oswald Mosley, 'The Philosophy of Fascism', quoted in James Drennan, *BUF, Oswald Mosley and British Fascism* (1934), p. 287.
20. Mosley, *The Greater Britain*, p. v.
21. Mosley, *Fascism*, Q. 5.
22. B.U.F., *Constitution and Regulations* (1936), p. 24.
23. Mosley, *Fascism*, Q. 5.
24. *ibid.*; Oswald Mosley, 'Why We Wear the Blackshirt', *The Sunday Dispatch*, 12 January 1934.
25. A. K. Chesterton, *Oswald Mosley: Portrait of a Leader* (1937), pp. 119–20.
26. Mosley, *The Greater Britain*, pp. 150–51.
27. *ibid.*
28. Oswald Mosley, *Fascism in Britain* (1933), p. 8.
29. *The Star*, 25 February 1933.
30. *The Times* (*Law Reports*), 6 November 1934.
31. Mosley, *The Greater Britain* (1939 edn), p. 181.
32. Mosley, *The Greater Britain*, p. 30.
33. See below, pp. 146–7.
34. A. Raven Thomson, *The Coming Corporate State* (1937), pp. 25–7. This charter bore little resemblance to the Italian charter of Labour.
35. Maurice Freedman, 'Jews in the Society of Britain', in Maurice Freedman (ed.), *A Minority in Britain* (1955), pp. 213–17.
36. A. Raven Thomson, 'Finance, Democracy and the Shopkeeper', *Action*, 6 March 1936.
37. John Beckett and A. Raven Thomson, 'Problems of the Distributive Trade', *Fascist Quarterly* (January 1936), p. 36.
38. F. D. Hill, *'Gainst Trust and Monopoly* (n.d.), p. 6.
39. P. Heyward, *Menace of the Chain Stores* (n.d.), p. 6.
40. Mosley, *Fascism*, Q. 59.
41. Mosley, *Tomorrow We Live*, p. 58.
42. *ibid.*, p. 58.
43. Mosley, *The Greater Britain*, p. 27; *Fascism*, Q. 35; *Tomorrow We Live*, pp. 55–6.
44. Mosley, *The Greater Britain*, p. 98.
45. Raven Thomson, *The Coming Corporate State*, p. 11.
46. 239 *H. C. Deb. 5s.* (28 May 1930), cols. 1354–5; Allen Young, John

Strachey, W. J. Brown and Aneurin Bevan, *A National Policy* (1931), pp. 19, 29; see also Mosley, *The Greater Britain*, pp. 83–113.

47. Young, *et al.*, *op. cit.*, pp. 33–4; Mosley, *The Greater Britain*, pp. 121–2.
48. Mosley, *Fascism*, Q. 45, 47, 48; *Tomorrow We Live*, pp. 49–53.
49. Mosley, *The Greater Britain*, p. 20.
50. *ibid.*, p. 21.
51. Joyce, *Dictatorship* (1933), p. 11.
52. *Blackshirt*, 23 September 1934; Mosley, *The Greater Britain* (1934 edn), p. 26.
53. Mosley, *Tomorrow We Live*, p. 12.
54. Mosley, *The Greater Britain*, p. 21.
55. *ibid.*, p. 33.
56. *ibid.* (1934 edn), pp. 39–43.
57. *The Morning Post*, 2 May 1933.
58. *Blackshirt*, 14 October 1933.
59. Raven Thomson, *The Coming Corporate State*, p. 42; Fuller, *op. cit.*, p. 14.
60. Raven Thomson, *ibid.*, p. 43.
61. *ibid.*, p. 30.
62. *Zionist Record* (Johannesburg), 2 February 1959.
63. Mosley, *Fascism*, p. 95; *Tomorrow We Live* (1936 edn), p. 64; see also Joyce, *Fascism and Jewry*, p. 3; E. G. Clarke, *The British Union and Jews* (n.d.), p. 7.
64. *The Catholic Herald*, 21 July 1939.
65. John Strachey, *Interview*, 7 April 1960.
66. Baroness Ravensdale, *In Many Rhythms* (1953), p. 144.
67. Quoted by J. Ginswick in a review of Colin Cross, *The Fascists in Britain*, *East London Papers* (October 1962), p. 111; see also *The Western Mail*, 24 August 1937 where a B.U.F. prospective Parliamentary candidate stated that he had been instructed that all elections would be fought on the issue of anti-Semitism.
68. *Blackshirt*, 18 April 1935.
69. *The Daily Herald*, 25 October 1932; see also 'Critic', 'London Diary', *New Statesman and Nation*, 29 October 1932, p. 506.
70. *The Daily Herald* (Northern edn), 25 October 1932.
71. *ibid.*, 10 December 1932.
72. *The Manchester Guardian*, 21 April 1933.
73. *The Morning Post*, 2 May 1933.
74. *Blackshirt*, 16 May 1933; 22 July 1933.
75. *The Sunday Express*, 30 July 1933.
76. *The Jewish Economic Forum*, 28 July 1933 quoted in James Parkes, *An Enemy of the People: Anti-Semitism* (1945), pp. 57–8.
77. *Blackshirt*, 30 September 1933.
78. *The Manchester Guardian*, 16 October 1933.
79. Mosley, *Ten Points of Fascism*, p. 7.
80. *Blackshirt*, March 1933, 1–17 April 1933, 1–16 May 1933, 1–16 June 1933, 15 July 1933, 19 August 1933.

81. *Middlesex County Times*, 11 November 1933. The report seems to have been prepared by B.U.F. Headquarters. This was a frequent Blackshirt practice.
82. *Fascist Week*, 10 November 1933.
83. *The News Chronicle*, 7 May 1934.
84. *Der Stürmer*, March 1934.
85. *The Manchester Guardian*, 4 June 1934.
86. *Der Stürmer*, November 1934.
87. *The Manchester Guardian*, 15 September 1934.
88. *Blackshirt*, 2 November 1934.
89. *The Manchester Guardian*, 15 April 1935.
90. *Frankfurter Zeitung*, 11 May 1935; *Blackshirt*, 17 May 1935.
91. Mosley, *Fascism*, Q. 47, 48, 51, 69, 77, 93, 95, 97–9.
92. See A. K. Chesterton, *The Apotheosis of the Jew* (n.d.), p. 3.
93. See Chapter 12.
94. A. K. Chesterton, *Fascism and the Press* (n.d.); Clarke, *op. cit.*, p. 4; R. Gordon-Canning, *Arab or Jew?* (n.d.), p. 22; Joyce, *Fascism and Jewry*, p. 5; *Fascist Quarterly* (January 1936), p. 16; *Action*, 2 September 1939.
95. Chesterton, *Oswald Mosley: Portrait of a Leader*, p. 127.
96. 'Letter' from Ronald Kidd to the Rt Hon. Reverend, the Lord Bishop of London, 19 January 1936.
97. *The Times*, 29 July 1937.
98. *The News Chronicle*, 28 August 1937.
99. *ibid.*
100. A. Raven Thomson, *Our Financial Masters* (n.d.), p. 15.
101. Mosley, *Fascism*, Q. 95–9.
102. Mosley, *Tomorrow We Live*, pp. 65–6.
103. Mosley, *The Greater Britain*, p. 13.
104. S. Lang and E. von Schenck (eds.), *Memoirs of Alfred Rosenberg* (1949), pp. 130–31.
105. Mosley, *The Greater Britain* (1934 edn), p. 153.
106. *ibid.*, pp. 151–7; Young, *et al.*, *op. cit.*, p. 60.
107. W. Risdon, *A.R.P.* (1939(?)).
108. *Blackshirt*, 1 June 1933.
109. *ibid.*, 16–23 September 1933.
110. *ibid.*, 1 June 1933; 17 April 1933.
111. W. Joyce, *Fascism and India* (1933), p. 2; Mosley, *The Greater Britain*, p. 146.
112. Mosley, *The Greater Britain*, pp. 132–5, 138–42; (1934 edn), p. 147.
113. *ibid.*, p. 138.
114. See Oswald Mosley, 'The World Alternative', *Fascist Quarterly* (July 1936), pp. 308–91; J. MacNab, 'Letter', *Romford Recorder*, 22 January 1937; *Croydon Advertiser*, 22 March 1937.
115. Mosley, *Fascism*, Q. 87.
116. Mosley, *Tomorrow We Live*, p. 71; see also R. Gordon-Canning, *Mind Britain's Business* (1938), p. 8.

117. Mosley, *Tomorrow We Live*, p. 73; Mosley, *The World Alternative*, *op. cit.*, pp. 391–2, 395.
118. See *Action*, 24 October 1936.
119. *The Sentinel* (Wood Green), 28 January 1937.
120. *Blackshirt*, 27 September 1935.
121. Mosley, *Tomorrow We Live*, p. 72; Gordon-Canning, *op. cit.*, pp. 11–12.
122. *Islington Gazette*, 25 February 1938.
123. *British Union Quarterly*, 'Notes of the Quarter' (January 1937), pp. 15–17; J. F. C. Fuller, 'The War In Spain: Its Character and Form', *British Union Quarterly* (April 1937), pp. 38–40.
124. *ibid.* (July 1937), p. 10.
125. *Action*, 19 March 1938, p. 4.
126. *ibid.*, p. 1.
127. *ibid.*, 1 October 1938.
128. *The Daily Telegraph*, 30 October 1938.
129. *British Union Quarterly*, 'Notes of the Quarter' (January 1939), pp. 8, 12–13.
130. *ibid.* (April 1939), p. 3.
131. *ibid.*, 26 August 1939; see also 'Notes of the Quarter', *British Union Quarterly* (July 1939), p. 11; (spring 1940), p. 11.
132. Oswald Mosley, *Mosley's Message to B.U. Members and Supporters* (1 September 1939), leaflet; see also Oswald Mosley, *The British Peace, How to Get It* (n.d.); Mosley has frequently attempted to justify his position that Jewish interests were trying to involve Britain 'not in a British but in a Jewish quarrel'. See, for example, his letter in *The Observer*, 22 August 1965; *My Life* (1968), pp. 339–41.
133. 'Notes of the Quarter', *British Union Quarterly* (spring 1940), p. 17.
134. *Action*, 23 May 1940.

# 8. Olympia

The B.U.F. demonstration at Olympia on 7 June 1934 was the watershed for British Fascism. It was also important in terms of the controversy it aroused over political violence and public order. Olympia was not only Mosley's largest meeting to date, but it was also the Communist Party's first large anti-Fascist demonstration. Anti-Communism was an important theme in B.U.F. propaganda and the Communists had been actively denouncing the 'Blackshirt Menace'. B.U.F. pageantry had been tried and rehearsed. The pattern of violence had been established, although on a smaller scale. In a similar fashion, Communist plans and techniques had been tested.

The Commissioner of Police had received information that the Communist Party intended to demonstrate against Mosley by organized heckling inside the meeting and by a mass demonstration outside the hall. In fact, the Communist Party issued a Press statement to that effect.[1] They printed illegal tickets. Groups of hecklers were stationed at strategic points inside the meeting, and Press interviews with their members were organized outside. First-aid stations were set up in near-by houses, and there were the inevitable parades, banners, placards and slogans. It was unlikely that weapons were officially authorized, but this would not have prevented anyone from carrying them. Philip Toynbee has described how he and Esmond Romilly selected their knuckle-dusters.[2] Moreover, one anti-Fascist demonstrator was found by the police to be in possession of an iron bolt.[3] Finally, the anti-Fascist demonstrators were by no means restricted to members of the Communist Party.

Mosley, preceded and escorted by his legions, entered the flag-bedecked hall thirty-five minutes late and was greeted by the usual songs, cheers, shouts and salutes. However, the unmistakable sounds of booing were also present. The spotlights converged on him as he once again stood alone on the platform. As soon as he began to speak, the interruptions commenced. The anti-Fascists were greeted in turn by black-shirted stewards, and fighting broke out throughout the hall. For two hours, with a monotonous regularity, someone would interrupt, the spotlights would switch from the speaker to the interrupter, stewards would converge, and the heckler would be forcefully ejected.

It is impossible to ascertain either the degree of violence or the apportionment of blame. One of the memorable features of the meeting was the number of people prominent in public life in attendance. Politicians, authors and journalists were on the scene, either roused by curiosity, or because they were politically sympathetic to one side or the other. The Fascists and the anti-Fascists published testimonials supporting their positions.[4] Statements were made in Parliament and to the Press. The national dailies also printed numerous letters, and these were widely reprinted in other papers. Neither side was satisfactorily vindicated. The opinions expressed, however, favoured the anti-Fascists, for although they came determined to provoke disorder, the Blackshirts used unnecessary violence to maintain order.

The following is a brief selection of the public statements beginning with those in support of the anti-Fascists. According to Geoffrey Lloyd, Stanley Baldwin's Parliamentary Private Secretary, Olympia was not an isolated incident, but a culmination of a series of organized interruptions by the Communists and provocative and outrageous behaviour by the Fascists. Interrupters were attacked by ten to twenty stewards. Sir Oswald stopped speaking at once for the most trivial interruptions, although he had a battery of twenty-four loud-speakers. His talk of defending the right of freedom of speech was pure humbug, and his tactics were calculated to provide an 'apparent excuse' for violence.[5]

W. J. Anstruther-Gray, Unionist M.P. for North Lanark, also attacked the Blackshirts: 'Frankly if anybody had told me an hour before the meeting at Olympia that I should find myself on the side of the Communist interrupters, I would have called him a liar.'[6] He was not against interrupters, nor their being ejected from a meeting, but he was against seeing a man beaten and kicked by eight to ten others.[7] T. J. O'Connor, Unionist M.P. for Central Nottingham, described a number of occasions on which interrupters were ejected by the stewards, and claimed that, he had seen a Russian pogrom, which was the nearest analogy to the Olympia meeting that he could remember.[8] Earl Winterton took issue with O'Connor, but felt bound to admit that in some cases, unnecessary violence had been used. He did not think that the interrupters were handled by the use of weapons, but 'in the good old-fashioned way by the use of a fist'.[9]

The Blackshirts, however, were not without supporters. Michael Beaumont, the Conservative M.P. for Aylesbury, began his defence of Mosley in the House of Commons with the statement that, although he was not a Fascist, he was an anti-democrat and an avowed admirer of Fascism in other countries. He accepted Geoffrey Lloyd's statement, but maintained that his experience had been different. From what he observed inside the meeting, no one there 'got anything more than he deserved'.[10] T. F. Howard, Unionist M.P. for Islington South, also attended the meeting. He was not a Mosleyite, but admired Mosley for one thing – his determination to maintain the right of free speech. He admitted that force had been used, but denied, in so far as he could see, any brutality. He claimed that in his constituency, young men were going over to the Blackshirts because they resented the constant prevention of free speech. In conclusion, he declared that he had no sympathy with 'maniacs', whether Sir Oswald Mosley or Harry Pollitt, but that he did admire 'the tens of thousands' of young men who had joined the B.U.F.: 'They are the best element in this country.' He was sorry that they were following Mosley, who had won their support by appealing to their sense of fair play and the right of free speech.[11]

Patrick Donner, Conservative M.P. for West Islington, described the weapons used by the 'Communists' at the meeting. He claimed that some of them were wearing black shirts and that they resisted the stewards with the utmost violence. A friend of his had seen a Blackshirt with a razor cut across her face. He argued that people were complaining because for the first time there was a political party determined to maintain order and the right of free speech.[12] And Sir Thomas Moore, M.P., who admitted that the treatment of the interrupters was unnecessarily harsh at times, felt that the violence with which they were treated was in proportion to their resistance.[13]

Regardless of the validity of such statements delivered in the heat of partisan arguments, it seems clear that both sides had deliberately organized to provoke disorder. Mosley later, under oath, stated that a small number of Blackshirts were 'seriously' injured and that 100 were treated by doctors.[14] At the same time, one doctor testified that he had treated between sixty and seventy people at Olympia, none of whom were Fascists, while another claimed that he saw several injuries that could only have been inflicted by weapons.[15] Sir John Gilmour informed the House of Commons that fourteen people including a Blackshirt had been treated for injuries in hospitals. The hospital authorities reported that in no case was there any evidence of razor slashes or wounds inflicted by other instruments with the possible exception of knuckle-dusters in two cases.[16]

The Press and the political parties reacted with indignation against both sides. *The Daily Telegraph* spoke for many conservative papers when it denounced the idea of private armies and organized violence employed against equally despicable organized interruptions.[17] On the Labour side, *The Daily Herald* supported the Government proclamation that such disorder would no longer be tolerated, but argued that they were bound to occur, so long as political movements were organized on a military basis. Although *The Daily Herald* did not wish to deny the right of Mosley to say what he pleased, it called upon the Government to take action. Finally, the paper blamed the Communist Party for doing the anti-Fascist cause a disservice. If there had not been disturbances, the meeting would probably have passed unnoticed.[18] *The Times* leading article on the morning after Olympia deplored the brutal tactics used by the Blackshirts, but its tone treated British Fascism as something of a joke.[19] The following week, *The Times* was more expansive. Two lessons were to be learned from Olympia: first, the right of free speech must be preserved; and second, the partisans were not the proper people to look after its preservation. It welcomed a Government announcement that new steps may have to be taken to allow the police to fulfil their duty in keeping order, especially if it permitted them to enter a meeting where disorder was anticipated. In place of banning a Fascist organization, which might affect other organizations, *The Times* called for the enforcement of those statutes already on the books to insure the right of free speech.[20]

*The Manchester Guardian* maintained that Mosley's tactics were not provocative to the Communists alone. If he was really interested in the maintenance of free speech and not personal advertisement, he could have recourse to the Public Meeting Act of 1908.[21] The *Guardian* later considered the possibility of legislation. It was doubtful about its effects and about an increase in police powers, but at the same time mentioned that the law might have to be extended to allow the police to enter a meeting, if a breach of the peace was anticipated. In general, the paper felt that the Blackshirts were a new phenomenon in British history, and that the fundamental complaint against them was their attempt to parallel public powers. Ridicule was no longer sufficient to defeat them, for the ridicule was becoming mixed with resentment. It concluded with the suggestion that Parliament should consider the root of the trouble, which was the B.U.F.'s paramilitary organization.[22]

The general mood of the House of Commons was not to give Mosley free advertising by debating the issue out of proportion.

Violence on both sides was deplored, but a general concern for free speech was expressed, and nine Conservative M.P.s tabled a motion for discussion of the problem.[23] Clement Attlee, the Deputy Leader of the Labour Party, claimed to have evidence to demonstrate that the Blackshirts used 'plain-clothes inciters to disorder' at their meetings, and that the Blackshirts used deliberate incitement as an excuse for force.[24] As for Mosley, self-proclaimed defender of free speech, most of the Members probably agreed with Lieutenant-Colonel E. G. H. Powell, Unionist M.P. for South-East Southwark, who remarked that Mosley stood for free speech only as long as it was convenient for him.[25] The Home Secretary stated the Government's position that the recent scenes of disorder could no longer be tolerated and that, if they continued, it might be necessary to enact further legislation to insure the preservation of public order. The Government was not prepared to allow any private and irresponsible body to usurp its responsibility for the maintenance of order and the preservation of free institutions.[26]

Outside Parliament, the Conservatives, possibly feeling that the time was ripe to break any threat of the Fascists attracting their extreme right-wing supporters, lost no time in denouncing political violence. On the week-end following Olympia, Walter Elliot, W. Ormsby-Gore, Sir Philip Cunliffe-Lister, and Sir Kingsley Wood spoke out against it.[27] Baldwin made the party position clear. Fascism was described as 'ultra-montane Conservatism'. He concluded, 'it takes many of the tenets of our own party and pushes them to a conclusion which, if given effect to, would, I believe, be disastrous to our country'.[28]

The Labour Movement had considered the problem of Fascism and dictatorship prior to Olympia. Its main concern, however, was with Fascism abroad and the Left at home. It rejected approaches from the I.L.P. and the Communist Party for a united front in opposition to Fascism.[29] In 1933 the National Council of Labour (representing the Labour Party and the T.U.C.) published a manifesto, *Democracy versus Dictatorship*, which denounced Fascism and likened Communism to it.[30] The National Joint Council sponsored a demonstration at the Albert

Hall in April to protest against the Nazi regime and published a pamphlet, *Hitlerism*. The annual conferences of both the Labour Party and the T.U.C. passed resolutions noting alarm at the growth of Continental and domestic Fascism, and requested their executives to frame a policy expressing their opposition.[31] At the beginning of 1934, the National Executive of the Labour Party, prompted by the emergency proposals of Sir Stafford Cripps and the National Socialist League, issued a statement denouncing dictatorship of the Right and the Left.[32] On the eve of the meeting at Olympia, the Labour Party published a manifesto attacking Continental Fascism, and warned the public that it had its imitators in Great Britain.[33]

At the end of the summer the National Council of Labour published another statement directed primarily at the Continental situation. In treating British Fascism, the Labour Movement's apparent lethargy was explained on the grounds that it had intentionally avoided giving the problem undue publicity. Lord Rothermere's support of Mosley had altered the position. A national campaign to counter Fascism was proposed as well as an investigation of the law regarding subversive movements and the desirability of new legislation.[34] The statement was endorsed by the annual conferences of the Labour Party and the T.U.C. Walter Citrine, the General Secretary of the T.U.C., in moving its adoption, warned that the Fascist movement at home should be neither exaggerated nor ignored. He demanded an end to 'the drilling and arming of civilian sections of the community' and deplored the inactivity of the police and the partiality of the Bench.[35]

The Government rejected a proposal for a public inquiry into the political violence at the Olympia meeting, but in doing so the Home Secretary gave several hints on the possibility of future legislation and invited the party leaders to consult with him on the Government's draft proposals.[36] He met with leaders of the Opposition, and there was a report of suggested legislation, but the matter was allowed to drop.[37] According to James Maxton, the Government proposals included powers to prohibit organizations of a military character, and the wearing of a uniform and drilling; to ban meetings which interfered with the transaction of public business, or which threatened clashes between different sections of the population; to control the routes of processions, and prevent large bodies of people marching from outside into a town; and to extend police powers at public meetings.[38]

It is understandable that any British Government would try to avoid the thorny problem of further suppression of liberties.* Olympia was a particularly bad time to bring in new legislation in regard to civil liberties because the Government was already occupied in trying to guide the Incitement to Disaffection Bill, which was being subjected to severe criticism from the Opposition, through Parliament. Moreover, many elements in the Labour Movement were smarting under the so-called 'Trenchard Ban' – the order made by the Metropolitan Police Commissioner in 1931 which forbade meetings outside Labour Exchanges in the Metropolitan area. In any case the Government's prudence seems to have been temporarily justified in terms of the reaction of public opinion to British Fascism.

The behaviour of the police at Olympia was also of consequence. About 760 police were detailed to control the traffic and the crowd outside the hall which was estimated at 5,000.[39] Twenty-three people were arrested on charges of assault, obstructing the police, using insulting words and behaviour and three were carrying offensive weapons.[40] The majority of those arrested had been demonstrating against the Blackshirts and twenty were subsequently convicted.

The police had been instructed not to enter the meeting, unless they had reason to believe that something contrary to the law was taking place.[41] In fact, on one occasion a small party entered the premises – but not the meeting – as a result of a request that a man needed attention. They found one man who

* Lord Trenchard, Commissioner of Police for Metropolitan London, advised the Government on the need for legislation in the autumn of 1933. He recalled that they were very reluctant. After the Swedish Uniforms Act had been passed in 1934, he called it to their attention. Andrew Boyle, *Trenchard* (1962), p. 652.

had been 'fairly severely handled', and they observed Black-shirts 'struggling with and pounding and beating up others'. Groups of Blackshirts dispersed, but individuals were removed.

The policy governing the responsibility of the police for preserving order at a public meeting on private premises was set forth in the recommendations of a Departmental Committee at the Home Office in 1909. According to the report, a public meeting was considered to include a meeting called for any political or municipal purpose to which the public was admitted, whether by ticket or otherwise. A distinction was then drawn between a public meeting held in a public place and one held on private premises. In the latter case, persons in attendance were considered to be there at the invitation of the promoters of the meeting, and had no more rights than if they had been invited to enter a private house by the owner. If they refused to leave at the request of the chairman or representatives of the promoters, they were trespassers and could be removed. The stewards were not liable for damage, 'so long as no undue violence is proved'.[42]

The Report considered the duties of the police, which were not defined by public statute, but were generally speaking, 'to keep the King's peace'. In the case of meetings held on private premises, the police had no power to enter, unless requested by the occupier of the premises or the promoter of the meeting or when they had good reason to believe that a breach of the peace was being committed. It was not the duty of the police to steward or police meetings, unless invited to do so by the promoters or his representatives. They could arrest a person charged by another for a breach of the peace, if there were reasonable grounds for apprehending the continuance or im-mediate renewal of the breach.[43] The practice in the Metropoli-tan Police District was even further restricted. The police were not to enter a meeting, 'unless called upon to suppress an actual breach of the peace, or to take into custody any person charged by another with committing an offence of which the police can take legal cognizance'.[44]

There was also the Public Meeting Act of 1908 which made

it an offence for any person to act in a disorderly manner designed to prevent the transaction of the business for which a meeting was called, or for a person to incite others to commit an offence.[45] However, the Departmental Committee of 1909 reported that the Chief Constables who gave evidence generally took the view that they were not bound to take any initiative under the Act. It was asserted that the police should assist the promoters of a meeting in obtaining the names and addresses of deliberate interrupters and should give the promoters every opportunity of making charges under the Act. The Departmental Committee agreed with this interpretation.[46] In other words, there was nothing in the Act that enabled anyone to be arrested or have his name and address taken. This was rectified by Section 6 of the Public Order Act of 1936. According to the interpretation given to the Public Meeting Act by the Metropolitan Police in 1913, the police ought to interfere to prevent a breach of the peace. Nevertheless, it may not be in their power to arrest the guilty party.[47]

It should also be noted that the Metropolitan Police Act of 1839 made it an offence to use 'any threatening, abusive or insulting words or behaviour with intent to provoke a breach of the peace, or whereby a breach of the peace may be occasioned'.[48] However, this did not apply to public meetings held on private premises. Although the police could charge offenders outside Olympia, they were powerless inside the hall. Finally, the possession or use of an offensive weapon, or being armed with any instrument with intent to commit a felonious act was subject to a maximum of six months' hard labour under the Vagrancy Acts of 1824 and 1898.[49] This legislation, however, did not apply specifically to public meetings or processions, until the enactment of the Public Order Act.

The law as stated above made the duties of police at public meetings on private premises fairly clear, but did it justify their discretion in not entering the meeting? The Fascists had declined in the first instance to have any police 'assistance' or 'intervention' inside the hall and the Home Secretary maintained that the police received no requests to enter the meeting.[50] Yet the police did receive a request, or information making it advisable to enter the premises, as distinct from the meeting hall, either to treat an individual or to investigate or stop an offence. In any case, on entering Olympia they did witness offences contrary to the law and, in all probability, undue violence on the part of the stewards. But the police evidently did not feel that the offences justified their remaining on the premises or entering the meeting, even though they felt it necessary to remove individuals. Even if the number injured on both sides was exaggerated, fourteen people were treated in hospital and it was inconceivable that they were taken away without being noticed by the police. The police either treated or removed one injured person themselves.

The Home Secretary's defence was unsatisfactory. He argued that effective control and apprehension of offenders was impossible without the police being posted beforehand.[51] If this was the case, then there was no reason for the police ever entering a meeting, and it also negated the so-called deterrent value of their appearance on the scene. The problem of undue violence on the part of the stewards was partially evaded on the grounds that the question of unnecessary force might come before the courts.[52] In fact, it already had, and Sir Gervais Rentoul, the Magistrate at the West London Police Court, remarked that, 'It may be that altogether excessive and indefensible violence was used in Olympia.'[53] But this remark was more in passing for he was hearing charges on behaviour outside Olympia not inside. The Home Secretary declared that the police proceeded on the assumption that the stewards would act without undue violence and would avoid illegal acts. If this assumption proved unwarranted, the policy of the police would have to be reviewed.[54] Yet in the Metropolitan District alone, the police were aware of thirty-one people injured at Fascist meetings in the first five months of 1934.[55]

Moreover, if there was occasion to arrest twenty-three people out of 5,000 demonstrators outside Olympia, what did the police think was happening inside the hall? Fifteen thousand people had assembled, including an organized opposition determined to interrupt of which the police were aware, as well as uniformed and provocative stewards determined that Mosley would get a hearing. No doubt the police had a difficult job in maintaining order outside Olympia, but given their instructions the question remains to what extent was the public to expect that the police needed to be satisfied that an offence had been committed or was being committed before they would enter a meeting? Gilmour, however, in his statement to the House of Commons, pointed out an important truth. Referring to a letter appearing in *The Times* on 11 June in which a Blackshirt steward described how a member of the audience slashed a Blackshirt's face with a knife, the Home Secretary remarked that the letter-writer should have turned the man over to the police.[56] As a Blackshirt steward, he clearly could have done so with the help of his colleagues. This leads to the further question that, if Sir Oswald Mosley was really interested in the preservation of free speech, why did his stewards not turn over to the police those members of the audience who had resorted to violent methods or vile abuse instead of giving them a 'going over'?

In regard to the law, the position was clarified in 1935. While the Metropolitan police were restrained from entering the B.U.F. meeting at Olympia, the police in Glamorgan, two months later, entered a number of meetings without invitations or requests and where no offence had been committed or was being committed, and refused to leave when asked. This led to the case of Thomas *v.* Sawkins, where the High Court decided that the police could enter a meeting where they had reasonable grounds for believing that a breach of the peace would occur. The conveners of the meeting were protesting against the In-citement to Disaffection Bill, then before Parliament, and demanding the removal of the Chief Constable of Glamorgan. The police based their case on the anticipation 'that the meeting would become an unlawful assembly or a riot or that breaches of the peace would take place, and that seditious speeches were likely to be made'. The Lord Chief Justice and his colleagues based their decision primarily on the preventive duty of the police.[57]

Mosley did not offer excuses nor disclaim personal responsibility. He broadcast on the B.B.C. with Gerald Barry, editor of *The News Chronicle*, on the evening following Olympia. Barry argued that undue violence had been used and that in no case had it originated with members of the audience. Sir Oswald claimed that the disorder had been caused by organized 'Red violence'. His stewards had been brutally treated in many cases and they had captured weapons from the 'Communists'. He maintained that the Blackshirts never attacked their opponents' meetings, but when the Blackshirts were attacked, they hit back hard and 'so would any Briton worthy of the name'.[58] At Shrewsbury four days later, Mosley stated that 'the Blackshirts offer no apology'.[59] The Rothermere Press, still loyal, echoed Mosley. Ward Price declared that the Reds got only what they deserved and the statements of Geoffrey Lloyd, Lord Berners and Anstruther-Gray were 'hysterical' and 'unfounded'.[60]

It is reasonable to conclude that the B.U.F.'s demonstration of force was deliberate. *The Daily Worker*, for three weeks prior to the meeting, provided indications of what was likely to occur, and the Blackshirts prepared for it. At the same time, it is possible to discern a change in the movement's style of politics involving an escalation of violence. The B.U.F. had been organized on a paramilitary basis with a stress on discipline and physical fitness. The methods of German and Italian Fascism, which utilized the techniques of political violence, had been studied. Each meeting had been, in a sense, a rehearsal for the next one. Olympia was different in that the opposition was organized and sizeable.

What is suggested is that the serious aspects of B.U.F. policy had made little impact and that the arguments for the corporate state and the need for action had lost their urgency and, indeed, their relevance. In so far as violence had been calculated, it had been defensive in nature. It was deemed necessary in order to secure a hearing and had publicity value. But the Press, by and large, had ignored the Blackshirts. It is difficult to deny that Olympia focused national attention on the B.U.F., whereas the meeting at the Albert Hall in April had passed off peacefully and almost unnoticed. There is also evidence of pressure from within the movement for a militant use of violence. The organization was undergoing some strain as a result of a re-structuring which divided Mosley's lieutenants into political and military factions. The type of person recruited by the appeal for action or the desire to wear a uniform may also have forced Mosley's hand in order to command their allegiance and reinforce their faith in him and the Fascist creed.

Finally Olympia proved to be more than an incident for it signalled a change from defensive to offensive violence and soon thereafter the movement's constructive policy was replaced in prominence by anti-Semitism. Mosley did not seem to have much to lose. The number of public or influential people who supported British Fascism in June 1934, the high point of the movement, seems to have been negligible. If members of a British ruling class flirted with Fascism, it was probably with the Continental version rather than with Mosley's brand. Rothermere and the support that he could muster was not to be confused with the influential. The B.U.F.'s middle-class supporters would probably go some way in excusing his actions, for they could be rationalized in terms of anti-Communism and nationalism. Mosley had already proclaimed to middle-class audiences that he had made free speech possible in England. At Olympia he announced:

Before the organization of the Blackshirt movement free speech did not exist in the country. . . . To-day their [Reds] power over English audiences has come to an end. The interrupters go out as you have seen them go out to-night.[61]

Where he miscalculated was in the reaction of many Conservative M.P.s, and in the reaction of such papers as *The Daily Telegraph* and *The Morning Post*, which unequivocally denounced his tactics. The B.U.F., viewed by some supporters and sympathizers as a street army of the Conservative Party, had destroyed its own usefulness.

The Government's caution in committing itself to new legislation seemed at first to have been a wise policy. Mosley did his best to restrain his stewards, restricting their duties to handing over interrupters to the police under the Public Meeting Act. The police, where they could, entered meetings. The active anti-Fascist opposition altered tactics and concentrated on demonstrations outside the meeting hall and on B.U.F. open-air meetings. Although the B.U.F. indoor meetings staged in the months following Olympia took place without serious incident, the anti-Fascist demonstrations outside the halls often resulted in disorder. The first important meeting that the Blackshirts held after Olympia was in Leicester. The police handled the anti-Fascist demonstrations outside the hall, and the Blackshirt stewards handled those inside. There was no disorder.[62] The same was true in Swansea.[63] Mosley's meeting in the Sheffield City Hall was attended by some 2,500 people. Under the terms for letting the hall, the police were given free access, and about 100 were on duty for the purpose of preserving order; 300 Fascist stewards were also present in uniform. Outside, an estimated 10,000 participated in an anti-Fascist demonstration called by the Sheffield United Action Committee, which included representatives of the Communist Party and other left-wing organizations. There were arrests, although good order was maintained. Inside the meeting, Mosley referred an interrupter to the Public Meeting Act, and warned him that if he failed to conform he would be handed over to the police. The police immediately escorted the interrupter from the hall.[64] In Ipswich, Mosley was speaking to an audience of about 300 at a greyhound track, when approximately 100 police entered the grounds and stationed themselves throughout the crowd. Although the size of the audience eventually swelled, there was no disorder.[65]

The majority of B.U.F. meetings were held out of doors. They were local soap-box, street-corner gatherings and were subject to the rough and tumble of street-corner politics. At Woolwich, for example, the police testified that a B.U.F. meeting was peaceful, until the anti-Fascists rushed the platform. The police made three arrests, and the meeting was closed down. The anti-Fascists then marched on the police station where three more arrests were made. Eventually, four anti-Fascists were fined and two dismissed.[66] In general it was true that more anti-Fascists were arrested and charged. Out of sixty-nine people prosecuted on charges of creating disorder at public meetings in the Metropolitan Police District, between July 1933 and July 1934, only sixteen were known members of the B.U.F.[67]

Although there was occasional bias on the part of the police against the anti-Fascists, the Blackshirts also experienced their share of discrimination. Such an instance arose out of a meeting at Worthing on 9 October. The actual meeting took place without incident. Mosley was accompanied by sixteen members of the Defence Force and they brought ambulances with them. It was claimed that the ambulances were a common feature of the B.U.F. meetings sponsored by National Headquarters. Outside the meeting a large boisterous crowd had gathered. Captain Charles Bentinck-Budd, the Fascist organizer of the meeting, anticipated trouble, and had notified the police three times during the day and once after the crowd had gathered. Considerable tension arose when the Blackshirts left the meeting. The prosecution claimed that, instead of dispersing or quickly marching away, they paraded around a traffic circle in a defiant attitude with hands clenched. The crowd surged forward and someone was pushed into Mosley, who was later charged with assault. After the Fascists were clear of the immediate vicinity and were proceeding towards their headquarters, a number of incidents occurred.

The police subsequently charged Mosley, William Joyce, Captain Bentinck-Budd and Bernard Mullins, a Blackshirt steward, with riot under common law. It was a minor offence, relative to the Riot Act, and involved 'common purpose' to attack and provoke others, thereby causing a riot. Additional charges of assault were brought against Mosley and the steward. The latter charge against Mosley was dismissed in police court. He testified that he may have raised an arm in self-defence. The alleged victim maintained that he was pushed into Mosley, who struck out. He had not complained, but ten days after the meeting the police approached him.

The prosecution based its case for riot on what it described as 'overwhelming evidence of common purpose'. Great significance was placed on Mosley's alleged remark, 'They have not got the guts to stand up to us,' until it was demonstrated that the remark was overheard by an admitted anti-Fascist with the declared purpose of countering Mosley. The prosecution also tried to demonstrate its case on provocative behaviour and the alleged assaults. However, the defence showed that the anti-Fascists were not casual passers-by. In the case of an attack on a Fascist, the police did nothing and refused to make a charge. The police as much as admitted this, stating that the man was not taken into custody because the blow had not been seen. Previously, they had maintained that they had told him to move along. The defence, which was conducted mainly by Sir Patrick Hastings, tried to demonstrate that the police arrangements were inadequate, and that the crowd was out of control. Where the Blackshirts may have struck out, it was in self-defence.

Mosley showed his contempt for the police evidence when first cross-examined at the police court. He maintained that at no time during the evening did the police speak to him, and that this suggested that the prosecution was an afterthought on the part of the authorities behind the police. When asked who the authorities were, he replied that he understood it was the Government of the day. Counsel then pressed him on whether he seriously believed that the Government brought about the prosecution. Mosley replied that it had been brought about by political considerations, and he agreed to the suggestion that some political party had influenced the West Sussex police to institute the prosecution. He replied to the counsel's inquiry that it was his impression that individual members of the Worthing police force had given false and contradictory evidence against him. It was stated later in the proceedings that all that Sir Oswald meant was that he could not conceive how any instructed member of the police force, without some good reason, could have brought about such charges.

At the Sussex Assizes, Mr Justice Branson directed an acquittal before the defence even answered the charge. He maintained that there was no evidence of common purpose in which they agreed to use violence. He then commented that he did not think the police had always given evidence during the trial 'with the fairness' to which he was accustomed from them. The prosecution offered no evidence for the steward's alleged assault and he was subsequently dismissed.[68]

Where notoriety and violence doomed support and publicity for the B.U.F. from some quarters, it was bound to attract it from others. An all-out anti-Jewish campaign was an obvious solution. But in addition, a show of bravado was needed to hold supporters and to keep the image of the movement before the public. The B.U.F. announced plans for a mass rally to be held in Hyde Park on 9 September. The *Blackshirt* described it as 'the greatest and most loyal demonstration any political leader has ever been accorded in Britain'. In the middle of August, the newly formed Co-ordinating Committee for Anti-Fascist Activities issued a circular signed by John Strachey, D. N. Pritt, Ellen Wilkinson, James Maxton, Lord Marley, the Chief Opposition Whip in the House of Lords, among others, to all London 'working-class' organizations, calling for a counter-demonstration at Hyde Park.[69] In a letter to the Press, the Co-ordinating Committee warned that an unorganized rally of workers would run the risk of being attacked by the Fascists with 'calculated brutality', which experience had shown that the Blackshirts would 'always use', if they could get away with it. They proposed to drown the Fascist rally in 'a sea of organized working class activity'. It might even be necessary to call one-day strikes.[70] The next day *The Daily Worker* printed a manifesto under the heading 'Deliver the Death Blow to Fascism in England'. It stated, 'Now the mighty assembly of London's workers and of all opposed to Fascism in Hyde Park can deliver the death blow to British Fascism and set the country ablaze with the determination to prevent a repetition in this country of the happenings in Germany and Austria'.[71] On 21 August, *The Daily Worker*, giving publicity to the anti-Fascist demonstration, urged people to 'strike a hammer-blow against Mosley's gangsters' and to 'organize themselves as shock-brigades'.[72]

These statements were unsuccessfully challenged in court by
William Joyce on behalf of the B.U.F. He alleged that they were
an incitement to disorder and thereby constituted a breach of
the Public Meeting Act.[73]

The 'official' Labour Movement instructed its followers to
stay away. The National Council of Labour sent a letter to all
affiliated organizations in the Greater London area, asking them
not to have anything to do with the anti-Fascist demonstration,
and repudiated all forms of organized opposition.[74] The following week, a manifesto, 'The Labour Movement and Fascism',
by A. M. Wall, Secretary of the London Trades Council, and
Herbert Morrison, as Secretary of the London Labour Party,
advised its readers not to become 'hysterical or neurotic' and
thus advertise Fascism, even if it was not to be underestimated.
The authors were against a united front and noted the simi-
larities between Communism and Fascism. Walter Citrine at the
Trades Union Congress, spoke along similar lines. On the eve
of the demonstrations, *The Daily Herald* advised its readers to
follow the advice of the National Council of Labour. Organizers
of the counter-demonstrations, according to the paper, wanted
a row and that would advertise Fascism.[75]

The *New Statesman* felt that a Communist demonstration was
undesirable, and that a Labour counter-demonstration would
be more appropriate.[76] Strachey answered that the demonstration had the support of the National Executive of the Chemical
Workers, Furnishing Trades Association, the London District
Committee of the Amalgamated Society of Engineers, the Pas-
senger Section of the London Transport Workers and a large
number of London Trades Councils and local branches.[77] The
*New Statesman* remained firm in its conviction that the demonstration was overwhelmingly Communist, and agreed with a
T.U.C. motion for Government legislation over uniforms,
which *The Economist* also advocated.[78] Finally, *The Manchester
Guardian* drew comparisons between Mosley's proposed Hyde
Park demonstration and Hitler's Nuremberg rally, and the
Attorney General, Sir Thomas Inskip, was quoted as saying
that the Government had, 'no intention of allowing any class

of people to organize themselves under military discipline in order to supplant Parliamentary Government'.[79]

The police had made elaborate plans to safeguard the peace at the demonstrations. It was reported that some 6,000 foot and mounted police were on duty in the park or kept in reserve in the vicinity. Lord Trenchard had interrupted his holiday and returned to Scotland Yard for the occasion. A small advance guard of the Blackshirts was first on the scene. Next came the anti-Fascists in four processions, each with its banners and bands. They held four meetings simultaneously. Strachey, Pollitt, John McGovern, Fenner Brockway, Leah Manning and John Gollan of the Youth Anti-War Council were among the speakers. Appeals for strict observance of public order were reiterated from every platform.[80]

The Fascists, with Mosley in the lead, marched into the park to be greeted by the hoots and jeers of the opposition crowds who rushed to their meetings. An estimated 2,500 to 3,000 uniformed Blackshirts lined up with military precision in front of their seven platforms. The Blackshirts were surrounded, and the opposition shut out, by cordons of police. By this time the crowds had swelled. Estimates were given up to 100,000, while more sober observers restricted their comments to the largest crowds seen in Hyde Park in years. B.U.F. speakers mounted the platforms and, deprived of loud-speakers, did their best to enlighten the crowd on the principles of Fascism. Mosley brought out his front-line talent including Joyce, John Beckett, Raven Thomson, and A. K. Chesterton. But no one could hear them. The hoots and howls of the anti-Fascists, the general din of the crowd and a police autogyro, which two newspapers described as the most effective noisemaker, made their remarks inaudible. At last, the Leader rose, and with his mother at his side dressed in a Blackshirt and beret, he denounced the so-called Jewish opposition's presence, although it was the eve of the Jewish New Year. The total opposition was seen as the greatest tribute to Fascism. The Fascist and anti-Fascist demonstrations ended at the same time, and their respective forces began to march away. At this point, disorder occurred for the first time in the afternoon, and although eighteen people were arrested it was not serious. A few attempts were made to break the Fascist ranks, but the police were in complete control of the situation. Of the eighteen arrested, seventeen were anti-Fascists.*

Satisfaction with the demonstration was expressed in almost every quarter. The police were particularly commended.[81] Strachey issued a statement on behalf of those who had called the counter-demonstration. He proclaimed that all their objects had been achieved, and that the maximum mobilization of the working class had prevented a repetition of Fascist attacks on workers, such as had occurred at Olympia. Mosley stated that the organized opposition was weaker than expected and that it was definitely a Fascist crowd. He congratulated the police for their handling of the 'organized interruption'.[82] The *Blackshirt* was even more jubilant, and the demonstration was pronounced a Fascist triumph over the Communists.[83] *The Daily Herald* maintained its position of heaping discredit upon the organized anti-Fascists. It declared that, 'the Mosley fiasco was mainly owing to splendid police organization and the good sense of the London workers, who observed the direction of the T.U.C. and took no part in the counter-demonstration'.[84] The liberal *Manchester Guardian* lauded the police, but asked whether this sort of demonstration should be allowed to continue. It suggested the need for legislation to deal with 'private military formations' and the wearing of uniforms.[85]

## NOTES

1. 290 *H. C. Deb. 5s.* (11 June 1934), col. 1343; see *The Daily Worker*, 21 May–7 June 1934.
2. Philip Toynbee, *Friends Apart* (1954), p. 21.
3. *The Times*, 18 June 1934.
4. 'Vindicator', *Fascists at Olympia* (1934); B.U.F., *Red Violence and Blue Lies* (1934). The B.U.F. pamphlet included a letter from William Joyce and one from a Mrs Joyce.

* Aldous Huxley anticipated the Hyde Park demonstration in *Point Counter Point* (1928) six years earlier when Everard Webley marched his green-shirted British Freemen there for a rally, pp. 396–9.

5. 290 *H. C. Deb. ss.* (14 June 1934), cols. 1935–8.
6. *ibid.*, col. 2003.
7. *ibid.*, cols. 2003–6.
8. *ibid.*, cols. 1951–60.
9. *ibid.*, cols. 1982–5; see also *The Daily Telegraph*, 11, 13 June 1934; *The News Chronicle*, 13 June 1934; Gerald Barry, *BBC Broadcast*, 8 June 1934.
10. 290 *H. C. Deb. ss.* (14 June 1934), cols. 1938–45.
11. *ibid.*, cols. 2009–18.
12. *National Review*, July 1934, pp. 119–22.
13. *The Daily Telegraph*, 14 June 1934; see also *The Times*, 13 June 1934; *The Morning Post*, 13 June 1934.
14. 'Mosley *v.* Marchbanks', *The Times* (*Law Reports*), 7 February 1936.
15. *The Times*, 9 June 1934.
16. 290 *H. C. Deb. ss.* (14 June 1934), cols. 1970–71.
17. *The Daily Telegraph*, 11 June 1934.
18. *The Daily Herald*, 12 June 1934.
19. *The Times*, 8 June 1934.
20. *ibid.*, 12 June 1934.
21. *The Manchester Guardian*, 9 June 1934.
22. *ibid.*, 12 June 1934.
23. *The Times*, 13 June 1934.
24. 290 *H. C. Deb. ss.* (14 June 1934), col. 1930.
25. *ibid.*, col. 2026.
26. *ibid.* (11 June 1934), col. 1945.
27. *The Daily Herald*, 11 June 1934; *The Manchester Guardian*, 11 June 1934.
28. *The Sunday Times*, 17 June 1934.
29. The Labour Party, *Report of the Thirty-Third Annual Conference* (1933), pp. 15–17, 177–8.
30. *ibid.*, pp. 135–6; T.U.C., *Report of the Proceedings at the Sixty-Fifth Annual Trades Union Congress* (1933), pp. 348–51.
31. The Labour Party, *op. cit.*, pp. 224–5; T.U.C., *op. cit.*, pp. 340–45, 174.
32. The Labour Party, *Report of the Thirty-Fourth Annual Conference* (1934), p. 9.
33. *The Daily Telegraph*, 11 June 1934.
34. National Council of Labour, *Statement of Fascism at Home and Abroad* (1934).
35. T.U.C., *Report of the Proceedings at the Sixty-Sixth Annual Trade Union Congress* (1934), pp. 247–9.
36. 290 *H. C. Deb. ss.* (14 June 1934), cols. 1972–91; see also (11 June 1934), cols. 1344–5.
37. 297 *H. C. Deb. ss.* (13 February 1935), col. 1932; *The Daily Telegraph*, 24 July 1934.
38. *New Statesman and Nation*, 25 August 1934, p. 225.
39. 290 *H. C. Deb. ss.* (11 June 1934), col. 1344.
40. *ibid.* (13 June 1934), col. 1693.

41. *ibid.* (14 June 1934), col. 1967.
42. *Report of the Departmental Committee on the Duties of the Police with Respect to the Preservation of Order at Public Meetings* (Cmd 4673, 1909), Vol. I, pp. 5–6.
43. *ibid.*
44. *ibid.*, p. 7.
45. 1909, *8 Edw. 7. c. 66.*
46. *Report of the Departmental Committee on the Duties of the Police, op. cit.*, p. 15.
47. Albert Crew, *The Conduct of and Procedure at Public, Company and Local Government Meetings* (1950 edn), p. 12.
48. 1839, *2 & 3 Vict. C. 14*, Section 54, Paragraph 13.
49. 1824, *5 Geo. 4. c. 38*, Section 4, 1898, *61 and 62, Vict. c. 59.*
50. 290 *H. C. Deb. 5s.* (11 June 1934), col. 1344; (14 June 1934), col. 1967.
51. 290 *H. C. Deb. 5s.* (14 June 1934), col. 1968.
52. *ibid.* (11 June 1934), col. 1344.
53. *The Morning Post*, 9 June 1934.
54. 290 *H. C. Deb. 5s.* (11 June 1934), col. 1344.
55. *ibid.* (13 June 1934), cols. 1692–3.
56. *ibid.*
57. *Thomas v. Sawkins* (1935), *2 K.B. 249*; see also A. L. Goodhart, 'Thomas *v*. Sawkins: A Constitutional Innovation', *Cambridge Law Journal* (1936), pp. 22–30; David Williams, *Keeping the Peace* (1967), pp. 144–9.
58. *The Times*, 9 June 1934.
59. *The News Chronicle*, 13 June 1934.
60. *The Daily Mail*, 8 June 1934.
61. *The Times*, 1 June 1934.
62. 291 *H. C. Deb. 5s.* (18 June 1934), col. 13.
63. *The Times*, 2 July 1934.
64. 291 *H. C. Deb. 5s.* (2 July 1934), col. 1564–5; *The Manchester Guardian*, 29 June 1934.
65. *The Manchester Guardian*, 6 July 1934.
66. *The Times*, 20, 27 November 1934.
67. 292 *H. C. Deb. 5s.* (24 July 1934), col. 1645.
68. *The Times*, 9, 13, 16 November 1934; 18, 19 December 1934; *The Manchester Guardian*, 5, 9, 13–16 November 1934; 14, 15 December 1934.
69. *The Manchester Guardian*, 25 August 1934; the Committee was Communist in sympathy but not in affiliation and attracted non-Communist, anti-Fascist support.
70. *The Daily Worker, The Manchester Guardian, The Morning Post*, 15 August 1934.
71. *The Daily Worker*, 16 August 1934.
72. *ibid.*, 21 August 1934.
73. *The Times*, 8 September 1934; *The Manchester Guardian*, 7, 8 September 1934.

74. See *The Times*, 23 August 1934; *The Manchester Guardian*, 23, 25 August 1934.
75. *The Daily Herald*, 8 September 1934.
76. *New Statesman and Nation*, 25 August 1934, p. 226.
77. *ibid.*, 8 September 1934.
78. Kingsley Martin (unsigned), 'Hyde Park', *ibid.*, 8 September 1934, pp. 283–5; T.U.C., *Report of the Proceedings Sixty-Sixth Annual Trades Union Congress* (1934), p. 257; *The Economist*, 8 September 1934, p. 436.
79. *The Manchester Guardian*, 8 September 1934.
80. *The Times*, 10 September 1934.
81. *New Statesman and Nation*, 15 September 1934, p. 318; *The Spectator*, 14 September 1934.
82. *The Manchester Guardian*, 18 September 1934.
83. *Blackshirt*, 14 September 1934.
84. *The Daily Herald*, 10 September 1934.
85. *The Manchester Guardian*, 10 September 1934.

1. Sir Oswald Mosley, founder and leader of the British Union of Fascists.

2. A contingent of
Blackshirts on parade in
Manchester, February 1934.

3. Sir Oswald Mosley inspects weapons that his Blackshirts claimed to have confiscated from anti-Fascists at the B.U.F. meeting, Olympia, June 1934.

4. Sir Oswald Mosley greets
a mass of saluting Blackshirts
in Hyde Park, September 1934.

5. Sir Oswald Mosley arrives at a
B.U.F. demonstration in the Albert Hall, April 1934.
6. Sir Oswald Mosley, in his new uniform, arrives to
lead the B.U.F. march into East London, 4 October 1936.
The march was subsequently banned.

7. Police disperse anti-Fascists near Aldgate, 4 October 1936.

8. 'The Battle of Cable Street.'
9. Police charge a crowd gathered in
Trafalgar Square, July 1937, to attend a rally
following a B.U.F. march from Kentish Town.

10. Police dismantle an
anti-Fascist barricade,
East London, 4 October 1936.

11. Deprived of their uniforms and banned from the East End, the British Fascists march into South London, 1 May 1938. Sir Oswald Mosley, in the centre of the photograph, is flanked by Neil Francis-Hawkins and Major-General J. F. C. Fuller.

# 9. Disenchantment and Disorder

Great Britain was on the road to economic recovery in 1935. The economic outlook was encouraging compared with that of other countries, including those that had undertaken reforms of the economic structure. Unemployment, however, remained a problem. But the B.U.F. did not possess the exclusive rights of criticism of Government action or inaction. On the contrary, criticism of Government policy was forthcoming from more influential, although hardly more effective, quarters. Back-bench M.P.s of all parties, as well as trade unions and town councils, filed protests. Yet despite the dissatisfaction with Government policy, and despite the Labour gains at by-elections, those who trembled in fear of a Socialist Government were reassured by the changes in the National Government following the Silver Jubilee. Stanley Baldwin became Prime Minister and, later in the autumn, led the National Government to victory at a General Election.

The foreign situation was confused. Although war was not an issue, Germany's and Italy's intentions were questionable. Hitler had announced conscription and revealed the existence of a German Air Force. At the same time, he was being con-ciliatory. Britain, in turn, expanded its military programme, especially the Air Force, and negotiated with Hitler for arms limitations. Trouble between Abyssinia and Italy had been brewing since December 1934, and reached a state of crisis the following autumn. The prestige, authority and effectiveness of the League of Nations was at stake. *The Times*, *The Spectator* and *New Statesman* urged the British Government to support the League. *The Observer*, the Rothermere Press and the Blackshirts stood opposed. Mussolini's forces attacked in October. Mosley, who had visited Italy in April, announced his 'Mind Britain's Business' campaign in August.

The B.U.F. was, by and large, a discredited movement. The economic crisis had not materialized. Political violence had not only created an opposition, but aroused widespread resentment. Moreover, the mass of the British public remained apathetic, and the B.U.F. had lost its novelty or curiosity value. Many were also confirmed in their suspicion that Mosley was little more than a political adventurer. Mosley's problem was to find a rationale for the B.U.F.'s failure and, at the same time, to justify its continued existence. Hitler and the Nazis provided a model and political anti-Semitism was given precedence. The persecution and conspiracy theories provided an explanation for failure, and created a new mission, if not the hope of a new crisis. The defence of Fascism in Europe was another reason for the continued existence of the B.U.F. Hence, the Blackshirts launched their peace campaign, which was a peculiar blend of pacifism and nationalism. At the same time, however, the growing power of Fascism on the Continent furthered the anti-Fascist cause in Britain.

Judged in terms of activity the B.U.F. lost momentum in 1935. This may have been a deliberate policy based on the assumption that a cooling-off period was needed after the unfavourable publicity of the second half of 1934. In so far as the Blackshirts were active, the national Press ignored them. It is difficult to ascertain whether this was a deliberate boycott or whether the B.U.F. ceased to be newsworthy. British Fascism had lost its relevance and the same speech propounded by the Leader and parroted by his colleagues could have been of interest only to their fanatical followers.

The movement was also experiencing financial difficulties.

Black House, for example, was closed down during the year. It is impossible to estimate the actual expenditure of the B.U.F. at any one time, although it is significant that as late as 1937 there was a salaried staff of 143. Provided that Mosley deployed his resources efficiently, it was possible to give an impression of greater resources than may have been the actual case. It is beyond doubt, however, that at the height of the movement in 1934, there was heavy expenditure. The following rough calculations are intended to give a general idea, rather than an accurate picture, and discount branch expenses. Dr Robert Forgan was paid £600 as Director of Organization and £750 as Deputy Leader.[1] John Beckett received £700 as editor of *Action* and probably £600 before then.[2] W. J. Leaper was paid approximately £400, and it is safe to assume that Rex Tremlett was paid the same.[3] William Joyce never earned more than £300.[4] A. K. Chesterton was paid £250 as an Area Administrative Officer and £300 as editor of *Action*.[5] There were approximately twenty officers of Chesterton's rank and their total salaries were in the neighbourhood of £5,000. In addition, there were at a conservative estimate fifty to 100 members of the National Defence Force, who received room, at least partial board and spending money, amounting to £10,000 a year. It is probably safe to assume that Mosley paid out £20,000 in salaries in 1934.

Beckett wrote in 1937 that Mosley had spent £3,000 a week for propaganda purposes.[6] Although the majority of meetings were open-air, there were meetings held at halls renting at £10 to £50 almost every night of the year, while Olympia rented at 250 guineas, and the Albert Hall at 150 guineas. It is probable, however, that many of the meetings were financed out of branch funds. But these meetings had also to be advertised and the National Defence Force, as well as local stewards, were transported long distances and received expenses. The returns on the meetings varied in that it was the practice to distribute free tickets.

Written propaganda, given the most generous estimate, barely paid its way. Up to June 1934, there were two weeklies selling at 2d. a copy with circulation orders of 25,000 to 30,000 claimed for each paper.[7] Setting aside papers given away and assuming 100 per cent sales for each paper, 60,000 papers at 2*d*. would gross £500. But total production costs would have been about £450 per issue, discounting distribution which at first included agents, as well as Blackshirts. Advertising was slight. There were usually 10,000 copies of each pamphlet printed, but the sale of these varied widely and probably off-set the marginal returns on the weeklies. Finally, there were the miscellaneous expenses such as court cases, the lease of National Head-quarters, which was rumoured to have been sold for a good profit, and the purchase of the four vans, though these may have been a gift to the B.U.F.[8]

The most sought-after information about the B.U.F. concerned finances, but this remains Mosley's most guarded secret. Formally, the finances of the movement were in the hands of a group of limited liability companies. In effect, these companies had little control over B.U.F. finance. Several of them were no more than convenient devices to protect the papers and publications from libel suits. They were formed with nominal capital of £100 or £1,000 in £1 shares. The majority of the allotted shares were in the hands of another private company, usually B.U.F. Trust Ltd.[9] The directors were officers of the B.U.F., but Mosley never delegated the effective financial responsibility to any of his lieutenants.[10]

The possible sources of funds were Mosley's personal investment, dues and subscriptions, contributions and money received from abroad. *The Daily Mail*, which was the closest public source to the B.U.F., claimed in January 1934 that the annual income was £70,000.[11] If this figure can be accepted, the income probably increased substantially by June 1934. The estimated maximum membership at that time was 40,000. If there were 35,000 employed members, their total annual dues would have amounted to £21,000, while the unemployed would have contributed an additional £1,000. Membership dropped after Olympia and never approached its former peak. In other words, dues provided a small proportion of the actual income of the B.U.F.

Mosley records his contribution to the B.U.F. as having been in the neighbourhood of £100,000.[12] It is doubtful whether there was any other single contributor who provided a large enough portion of the funds to have influenced the policy or the political style of the movement.* Mosley admits this, but in a grand manner. Thus he writes:

In the matter of funds it seems a sound and honourable rule only to mention those who so openly supported us that everyone would assume they assisted us in this way.[13]

Consequently, Mosley only mentions Sir William Morris (later Lord Nuffield), Wyndham Portal and Lord Rothermere. It seems that only Lord Rothermere donated a sum of money directly to the Fascists, and this in no way compared with Morris's contribution to the New Party.[14] According to Mosley, there was also support from industrialists and merchants – unnamed, of course – of more moderate means.[15] Moreover, the national movement could usually count on the branches for funds since a number of them were relatively rich.[16] Inevitably, the secrecy in regard to funds encouraged rather than curtailed rumours about industrial magnates who supported the B.U.F., and Mosley and Joyce boasted of the support of large industrialists. Among those rumoured to have contributed generously were Sir William Morris, Lord Inchcape, Sir Henry Deterding, Watney's Brewery and the Imperial Tobacco Company. These rumours were, for the most part, without foundation. Sir William Morris, as noted above, contributed generously to the New Party on the condition that the money be used for the establishment of youth clubs.[17] Several were founded, but it is doubtful whether they exhausted the funds that he contributed. Hence, there was the possibility that some of the money was used, without Morris's knowledge, for the Fascist movement. The rumours grew to such an extent that

* Joyce told the story how he rejected an offer from a Jewish businessman 'prominent in the tobacco trade' of £300,000 on the condition that the B.U.F. should not be anti-Semitic. He did not even bother to consult Mosley. J. A. Cole, *Lord Haw-Haw* (1964), p. 58.

Sir William Morris wrote a letter of denial to *The Jewish Chronicle* and contributed a sum to Jewish charity.[18] The rumour that Imperial Tobacco had contributed anywhere from £5,000 to £100,000 proved false.[19] Lord Inchcape, the shipping magnate, was the director of over twenty companies including five banking and insurance companies. *The Daily Herald*, in 1931, reported that, so far as could be ascertained, he was one of the backers of the Mosley movement.[20] This, of course, was the New Party and had nothing to do with the B.U.F. Nevertheless, unfounded rumour carried over to the Fascist era. Sir Henry Deterding was the Director-General of the Royal Dutch Petroleum Company. His name was linked with Mosley by both anti-Fascists and ex-Fascists, especially after the B.U.F. turned to anti-Semitism. This may have been no more than an extension of the reports of Deterding's relationship with Hitler. The accusations against Watney's were based on the weekly advertisements in the B.U.F. publications. Watney's also had the beer concession at the National Headquarters canteen and club.

There was also a rumour of support from a millionaire who later became a Conservative Minister. It is likely that the story referred to Wyndham Portal, who was associated with the New Party, and who, as Viscount Portal, was Minister of Works from 1942 to 1944.[21] As for Lady Houston, the eccentric nationalist and the publisher of *The Saturday Review*, the evidence indicates that she did not actually contribute money to the B.U.F. From 1933 onwards, there had been much speculation as to whether Lady Houston was financing the movement. Claud Cockburn published a story in *The Week* at the end of August 1933, that Mosley and Lady Houston had joined forces to publish a new periodical, *The Fascist Weekly*.[22] Two months later the *Fascist Week* appeared. But when the rumour became the subject of a Low cartoon in *The Evening Standard*, Lady Houston felt forced to publish a denial.[23] In any case, the *Fascist Week* was incorporated with *Blackshirt* in June 1934.

*The Saturday Review* was sympathetic to the B.U.F. Throughout 1934, it heaped praise on the movement, and thereafter refrained from attacking it.[24] In 1936 it defended Mosley's intrusions into East London.[25] But Lady Houston was careful to separate her admiration for Mussolini and Hitler from her support for Mosley. The attitude was that of an 'Albert Hall Fascist', and it was not surprising to find her defending both Mosley and Lord Rothermere at the time of their break.[26] Reports circulated after her death that she had planned to contribute large sums to a B.U.F. election fund. This was denied by the movement in a statement to the Press.[27] At one time, however, she had planned to give Mosley £200,000. But a Blackshirt writer had published a satire on her and *The Saturday Review*. When she demanded an apology from Mosley, she received a lecture on the give and take of political life.[28]

The very nature of the role of contributors makes it difficult to identify them. The financial backers – both large and small – similar to the bulk of the membership, were probably marginal members of a particular interest or status group who yielded little power in their profession or occupation. There was the manufacturer of sports cars who offered to give five per cent of the purchase price on all cars bought by Fascists to the election fund.[29] Joyce cultivated a department store proprietor in the North, an eccentric country squire and a stockbroker. The latter, Alex Scrimgeour, was deemed the most regular contributor among his personal converts.[30]

Members who were reported to have given generously included W. E. D. Allen, the chairman of David Allen and Sons Ltd, the poster painters, Captain Robert Gordon-Canning, James L. Battersby, and Sir Alliot Verdon-Roe. Allen and Gordon-Canning were counted among the inner circle so that there was probably some validity to the reports. Battersby was a member of a well-known family of Stockport hatters, but he was disowned and disinherited. Verdon-Roe was the famous aviation pioneer who with his brother founded A. V. Roe Ltd, and then sold it in 1928. He then bought an interest in W. E. Saunders Ltd, which was renamed Saunders–Roe Ltd, of which he became president. His main political concern was monetary reform. He quite openly lent his name to the B.U.F., and probably contributed to its treasury.

There is evidence to suggest that Mosley received funds from foreign sources. Stories were current among the inner circle of the B.U.F. about such funds. Italy was alleged to have been the main source, but there was disagreement over whether this money had been supplied during the formative period, or whether it had been restricted to the time of the Abyssinian crisis. It was alleged that a small amount of money came from Hitler and a rather larger sum from sources in Switzerland. Forgan relates how Mosley sent him to negotiate with Mussolini, who remained uncommitted. Shortly afterwards, however, large parcels of foreign notes arrived in suitcases, amounting in some instances to £10,000, which he believed to have been delivered through the Italian Embassy.

On a number of occasions in the House of Commons, the Government was pressed for information on the possibility that Mosley had received money from abroad. In 1936, Sir John Simon claimed to have evidence that both the Communists and the Fascists had received sums from foreign sources, but he did not elaborate.[31] Some evidence was produced after the Second World War by Chuter Ede, the Home Secretary in the Labour Government. He quoted from a letter from Count Grandi, the Italian Ambassador in London, to Mussolini dated 30 January 1934. Count Grandi relayed Mosley's gratitude for the considerable sum of money that the Italian Ambassador had turned over to him and for Mussolini's commitment for future material aid. The Home Secretary read a second letter dated 1 March 1935, in which Count Grandi had written that the £60,403 in a year which Mussolini had been giving Mosley was a waste of money.[32] Mosley immediately denied the contention and implied that the letters were forgeries. He maintained that the Government had had access during the war to the accounts of the B.U.F. and to those of everyone connected with the movement and yet been able to prove nothing.[33] In 1940, Richard Stokes, Labour M.P. for Ipswich, stated that the advisory committee on the detainees under the Defence Regulations, with the aid of Mosley's solicitors and all the banks, had inquired into whether the B.U.F. had received money from abroad. They found after a most 'exhaustive' search that no money had come from foreign sources.[34] With the exception of those letters quoted by the Home Secretary, the German and Italian documents relating to Fascist activities in Great Britain and captured by the Allies during the Second World War, reveal nothing about finances.[35]

The date of the second letter corresponded with the beginning of the economies undertaken by Mosley, commencing with the selling of the lease of National Headquarters and culminating in a purge of the headquarters staff in 1937. The actual cutting-back of funds may have been delayed, however, for the Abyssinian war began in May 1935, and lasted until October 1936. A cut-back of funds by Mussolini at that time could explain the financial crisis of 1937. In any event, the financial deterioration of the B.U.F. cannot be attributed to that one source, for with the amelioration of the economic crisis the B.U.F. may have lost some of its domestic financial support. The switch to anti-Semitism and Hitler's tactics, if public reaction can be taken as indicative, drove away others. This should not be over-emphasized, for Jew-baiting could have attracted a number of rich anti-Semites. Political violence probably disenchanted a larger number of financial contributors than anti-Semitism did since Olympia occurred prior to the movement's East London campaign. Finally Baroness Ravensdale has maintained that Mosley drove away many big industrialists by his high-handedness and tactlessness, a claim supported by a number of ex-B.U.F. officials.[36]

Neil Francis-Hawkins, the Director of Organization, in a review of the history of the B.U.F., noted only one important meeting in 1935 when Mosley launched his 'Mind Britain's Business' Campaign at the Free Trade Hall in Manchester in September.[37] The campaign was both pacifist and anti-Semitic. Mosley announced that the meeting was 'called in the support of peace'. He attacked the League of Nations, maintaining that a real league would only emerge from international Fascism. He declared that, 'over the whole of this Abyssinian dispute rise the stink of oil and stronger than even the stink of oil is the stink of Jews'.[38] The next night Mosley held a London rally at the Adelphi Theatre in the Strand. In the following weeks, Mosley made 'major' speeches at Southampton, Hanley and Basingstoke.

The General Election also created a dilemma for the Blackshirts. They had boasted of their organizational advances and increases in membership for three years and had claimed that they would seek power through the democratic process. So, by not contesting the election, the Blackshirts would further suspicions as to the goals of the movement and, by not contesting any constituencies, their intentions in East London would be open to question. The election also presented an opportunity for them to test their 'Mind Britain's Business' policy, their criticism of the Government's unemployment programme, as well as the progress of their anti-Semitic campaign in certain areas. It was significant that foreign policy and unemployment were the issues of a generally quiet election.

But it was also a strategically inopportune time for Mosley to have contested an election. The B.U.F. was held largely in disrepute and there was an apparent shortage of funds and personnel. Economic conditions and the political mood of the people were against a radical party while the unemployed already had a champion in the Labour Party, and in the distressed areas the Communist Party was better organized and had enlisted the support of many malcontents. Finally, Mosley could not afford an electoral disaster after the bitter experience of the New Party.

The B.U.F. decided on what amounted to an anti-General Election campaign: 'Blackshirts watch this futile farce and say "Fascism next Time".' Mosley wrote that three years had not been long enough to create an effective election machine as well as a nation-wide movement. For one thing, they did not have enough trained agents. The Conservatives, who were Fascism's chief challengers knew this and had called an early election to insure not only a victory, but a walk-over. In doing so, democracy was cutting its own throat, for it could not survive the present conditions. The B.U.F. must be ready and prepared for the crisis. He concluded that the B.U.F. would fight when the election machinery was ready and not before.[39]

Mosley returned to national prominence in 1936, not because of a revival in the fortunes of his movement but because of the renewed intensity of the anti-Fascist opposition, the problem of the control of public order by the police and the public's discovery of what was taking place in East London. Although economic recovery was on hand in 1936, it was a year of political storm and crisis. The death of King George V, at the beginning of the year, started a public outpouring of patriotism. The B.U.F. stood loyally by Edward VIII. In March, German troops moved into the Rhineland, and in May the hostilities 'officially' ended in Abyssinia. The Spanish Civil War began in June, and Zinoviev and Kamenev were executed in Russia. In Greece, a dictatorship was established. In Britain, there was a certain restlessness, and a revival in left-wing activity. The Spanish Civil War was the inspiration. Mosley was the domestic symbol for the advance of Fascism in Europe, and once again was vigorously opposed.

The B.U.F. announced it would hold a demonstration at the Albert Hall on 22 March. On 5 March, two days before Hitler's Rhineland *coup*, a circular was issued by John Strachey, presumably under the auspices of the Co-ordinating Committee for Anti-Fascist Activities, calling upon the opponents of Fascism to demonstrate outside the Hall.[40] *The Daily Worker* took up the cause and published articles and appeals.[41] But a full month before the meeting took place, the corporation of the Albert Hall had decided to submit the date and object of the meeting to the police.[42] It was left to the police to decide whether they should be present, an option permissible since the decision in Thomas *v.* Sawkins.

Prompted by the announcements of the proposed anti-Fascist demonstrations, the police not only prohibited demonstrations within half a mile's radius of the hall, but virtually excluded the public at large.* No traffic was allowed within that radius while the meeting was in progress, and pedestrians had

* Under powers derived from the Metropolitan Police Act of 1839.

to produce tickets or some other authorization before permission was received to enter the area. When anti-Fascists attempted to march into the area they were dispersed by the police. A number of demonstrators were directed to Hyde Park. Thirty police were stationed inside the hall, and another 100 were at the doors. A total of about 2,500 police and an additional 400 in reserve were involved in the Albert Hall and subsequent Thurloe Square demonstrations.[43]

Mosley spoke to a large audience and considerable disorder occurred during the meeting. There were a number of ejections, and about half a dozen were treated for minor injuries, although none was detained in hospital.[44]

The main anti-Fascist demonstration, outside the Albert Hall, was broken up by the police with considerable violence. The actual sequence of events and the allocation of the blame is open to interpretation, but the occasion raised the question of police behaviour. The anti-Fascist version of the incident was the most complete, for the National Council for Civil Liberties had forty observers inside and outside the meeting. Moreover, it instituted a public inquiry, although the evidence submitted was by no means impartial. The Home Secretary officially defended the police action. The Press, for the most part, overlooked the incident with the exception of the anti-Fascist *Daily Herald* and *News Chronicle*, which severely criticized the police.

According to Strachey, five days before the Albert Hall meeting, he and the London District of the Communist Party received letters from the Commissioner of Police informing them that no procession would be permitted to approach within half a mile of Albert Hall, and that no meeting would be allowed in the area. Hyde Park was suggested as an alternative.[45] Strachey maintained that, since the meeting place for the demonstrations had been publicly announced on numerous occasions, the announcement of a new place would only lead to confusion. Hence, the procession formed as scheduled and marched to within half a mile of the Albert Square, where they met the police cordons and were dispersed. Strachey proceeded to Exhibition Road, where he found a number of people already assembled for the meeting. Since Exhibition Road was also in the proscribed radius, and the police were already clearing the upper end of the street, Strachey approached the police officer who appeared to be in charge. He suggested that the meeting should be moved to the Thurloe Square area, which was considered to be just outside the radius. The police officer apparently did not reply. The decision was announced to the crowd, which moved along to the new meeting place.

Strachey chaired the meeting and was the first speaker. He was followed by R. McLennan of the National Unemployed Workers' Movement, Ted Willis of the Labour League of Youth, and the Reverend Leonard Schiff. Strachey maintained that no one said anything seditious or that could be construed as an incitement to violence, and that the crowd was orderly. During the Reverend Schiff's speech, the police assembled and, without warning, forced their way into the crowd. The chairman did not receive any requests or warnings from the police. Strachey wrote:

As soon as the mounted police were well inside the crowd, they drew their staves and began beating all those members of the public who were within their reach upon the head and shoulders. It was then observed that the foot police had also drawn their staves and were also using them on those members of the public whom they could reach. The crowd dispersed very rapidly making no resistance whatever to the police.[46]

*The Daily Herald* ran a story in sympathy with the anti-Fascists, and printed a picture showing mounted police in the crowd with staves raised.[47] *The News Chronicle* printed a number of eye-witness reports. An N.C.C.L. observer described how a youth was dragged away between two mounted policemen, who thought he had thrown a bottle. Although a bottle was thrown, the observer stated that it had not been thrown by this particular person. Another letter-writer described how Strachey had interrupted the speaker to advise the audience not to join a proposed demonstration outside the Albert Hall, when the 'mounted police charged down on us'.[48] Strachey's action was verified by the N.C.C.L.'s Commission of Inquiry.

Sir John Simon, the new Home Secretary, presented a different version in his defence of the police. According to the Home Secretary, the police had escorted several anti-Fascist processions into Hyde Park. Attempts were made to hold an anti-Fascist meeting in Exhibition Road and later a crowd collected in Thurloe Square. A body of twenty mounted and sixty foot police proceeded to the square. Before the police arrived there was disorder at the bottom of the road and members of the crowd were stopping cars. On one occasion, a bottle was hurled at a policeman, but it missed him and broke a shop window. Members of the crowd tried to stop the police as they approached the meeting. They informed the police that they had better not proceed any farther, or they would get 'more than they anticipated'. The Home Secretary stated that the officer in charge replied that they were in a prohibited area and causing serious obstruction. He appealed for the meeting to be closed and for the crowd to disperse. They refused and threw stones and earth. At this point, the officer in charge told the mounted police to disperse the crowd, and they advanced. In view of attempts made to unseat them, they drew their truncheons and in some cases used them. Of the twenty-four arrested, not one complained of injuries or requested to see a doctor while at least two police officers received severe kicks and one was still unable to resume duties.[49] This version was corroborated by Captain A. L. Hope, Unionist M.P. for Ashton, who was an eye-witness.[50]

The N.C.C.L. in its 'Report of a Commission of Inquiry' pointed out that the two incidents which the Home Secretary referred to evidently had no relation to the Thurloe Square meeting. Moreover, according to the report, he quibbled over the location of the Thurloe Square meeting and seemed to have made an issue over the distance. Chartered surveyors engaged by the N.C.C.L. reported that measured as the crow flies from the centre of Albert Hall, the meeting was held ten yards inside the radius, and if measured from the nearest point of the Albert Hall, was even farther inside. By the nearest route along a public thoroughfare, it was 'slightly' more than half a mile. It would seem that the police were technically right, and that in the absence of surveyors on the spot their desire to disperse the meeting was understandable. But it can be argued that Strachey as a private citizen should have had the benefit of the doubt. A meeting held so close to the radius could probably justly be deemed provocative. Yet it could be assumed that the natural wishes of the organizers would be to hold the new meeting in the vicinity of the original meeting so as to attract portions of the expected audience that might have remained unaware of the change.

The Home Secretary was on surer ground when he argued against the reports that described the meeting as quiet and peaceful: the formation of a cordon by members of the crowd denies these statements. Sir John Simon also contended that if the organizers thought that the instructions of the police were unlawful, they could have sought clarification. They failed to communicate with the police or with the Home Office. He went on to argue that if anti-Fascists assembled before and after a Fascist meeting disorder was likely to occur. He refused to hold an inquiry on the grounds that those who doubted the behaviour of the police, if they had sufficient evidence, could have gone to the courts or even to the Commissioner of Police for an inquiry.[51] This was unsatisfactory for the anti-Fascists, who argued that they wanted an impartial inquiry, not one by an interested party.

The N.C.C.L. was an active force behind the dissatisfaction with the behaviour of the police. On the day following the disorder at Thurloe Square, it arranged a meeting between a number of the observers and 'eye-witnesses', and Labour, Conservative and Liberal M.P.s at the House of Commons. When the Home Secretary refused to initiate an inquiry the N.C.C.L. announced that it would undertake its own. As a preliminary to the actual inquiry, the N.C.C.L. circulated a mimeographed document containing 113 statements by observers and eye-witnesses at the meeting, although some seem to have referred to incidents not directly related to Thurloe Square.

The members of the N.C.C.L. Commission of Inquiry were

Professor Norman Bentwich, the Chairman, Harrison Barrow, Professor F. M. Cornford, J. B. Priestley, and Miss Eleanor Rathbone, M.P. The inquiry was unsatisfactory in that it was conducted on the basis on which the anti-Fascists had criticized Sir John Simon's suggestion for an inquiry by the Commissioner of Police, that is, by an interested party. Moreover, they only heard evidence against the police. No representative of the police force testified, nor did any impartial eye-witness give evidence in support of the police, although special efforts were made to enlist such testimony.[52]

The Commission held two public sessions at which thirty-one witnesses testified. Of the thirty-one witnesses, nine were observers for the N.C.C.L., twenty were participants in the meeting, one was a by-stander and one witness left before the meeting began. The Commission claimed to have based its conclusions solely on the oral testimony, and to have confined the evidence to what would be admissible in a court of law. The conclusions supported the anti-Fascist case. First, it was admitted that cordons had been formed, but before the main contingent of police appeared, although a small number was present from the beginning of the meeting and made no attempt to interfere. Second, the Commission emphasized that the police did not attempt to convey a message to the chairman themselves, although they could have gone through or around the cordon or attempted to approach the platform from another direction. The Commission agreed that no instructions reached the platform, but argued that a man who attempted to convey a message was not allowed sufficient time to reach it. The Home Secretary stated that ten minutes had elapsed, but the Commission was 'convinced that the police did not wait for more than two minutes at the most'. Regardless of whether the Home Secretary or the Commission was right, Sir John's statement could be taken as an admission that no attempt was made on the part of the police to communicate directly with the chairman, as indeed it was taken by Harold Laski in his preface to the Commission's report.[53]

Perhaps the most significant admission by the Commission

was that incidents had occurred in the vicinity of Thurloe Square before, during, and after the meeting, although they had no direct connection with the meeting.[54] It could be interpreted that such incidents were likely to lead to further breaches of the peace, or that the speakers were inciting the crowd, although no prosecutions were brought against them. Moreover, there was a certain amount of obstruction. The police then had reason for dispersing the crowd, although the methods used were certainly open to question. The police may have been exasperated by the number of incidents, and may not have been able to judge how closely the disorder was related to the meeting, but again it should have been the duty of the police to exercise the greatest caution and discretion before acting in a manner likely to cause further disorder. What was important about Thurloe Square and what would have made an official inquiry desirable was that it was a culmination of numerous accusations against the police

Meetings at Oxford and Tonypandy in May and June resulted in some disorder. They demonstrated the nature of Blackshirt provocation, an increasing reliance on political violence and again raised the problem of police behaviour. At Oxford Mosley spoke to an over-flow meeting at the Carfax Assembly Rooms. The first hour of his speech was punctuated by good-humoured heckling but there were no incidents. Then a number of Blackshirts advanced as a unit down the centre gangway. A member of the audience rose to protest and persisted despite repeated warnings from the platform. Finally, the Blackshirts grabbed him in an effort to throw him out. This was the signal for a general uproar. Others came to his aid, and the centre of the meeting was described as a mass of struggling people. Members of the audience began throwing chairs. Order was eventually restored, and Mosley resumed his speech.

When he alleged that Labour Party members went into politics primarily to make money, Basil Murray, the son of Professor Gilbert Murray, stood up, asked a question in protest and immediately became involved in a struggle with the stewards. The acting Warden of New College, R. H. S. Crossman, jumped onto the platform and suggested that if Mosley would remove his Blackshirts he would get a fair hearing. Mosley in reply suggested that Crossman be removed. According to Crossman's account someone said, 'chuck him out', and the next moment he was on the floor.[55] Meanwhile Mosley demanded that Murray be removed. Mosley tried to maintain order, but it was several minutes before order could be restored by the police, who had been specially stationed at the rear of the hall, and by then several Fascists had been injured. The proctors were called in and several undergraduates had their names taken and were sent back to their colleges. A crowd collected outside and the 'International' was sung, both inside and outside the hall. Extra police were called, order was finally restored, and the meeting continued.

As for the injuries, the Hon. Frank Pakenham (Lord Longford), a Christ Church don, was roughly handled when he tried to 'rescue' an undergraduate. According to *The Oxford Mail*, the undergraduate was being horribly treated by the Blackshirts. Another undergraduate, Philip Toynbee, received a cut under the eye inflicted by a chair. Basil Murray and Bernard F. G. Floyd, the son of Sir Francis Floyd, the High Commissioner in Canada, were arrested and later fined.[56] In addition to several minor injuries, four Blackshirts were taken to hospital, and one was detained with multiple scalp wounds.[57]

Mosley described the fracas as the worst scene of hooliganism that he had experienced in hundreds of meetings and blamed members of the University.[58] Patrick Gordon-Walker, then a Christ Church don, in a letter to *The Oxford Mail*, stated that for all those present the mark of the meeting was the provocation of the audience beyond endurance. He described how the Blackshirts, whom he believed to be imported, lined the walls of the room and postured in an arrogant attitude. He felt that the audience was being deliberately intimidated and insultingly challenged. Mosley was accused of taunting and jeering at his audience. The first person ejected had been overwhelmed by the Blackshirts, and the effort to protect the interrupter led to the meeting being broken up.[59] As for the police, when a member of the audience attempted to enlist their aid, the Chief Constable told him to mind his own business and run along.[60] Pakenham's attempt to bring charges against his assailants was also dismissed in a cavalier fashion.[61]

One of the largest Fascist rallies to have been held in Wales took place when about 6,000 attended an open-air meeting at Tonypandy. The B.U.F. had never made any progress in Wales and usually encountered hostile opposition. For example, a B.U.F. meeting at Pontypridd had been broken up earlier that same month. At Tonypandy, the speakers, a local Fascist and Tommy Moran, a National Headquarters Propaganda Officer, were stoned and injured, and the meeting was closed after half an hour. The anti-Fascist leaders implored the crowd to desist but to no avail. Further trouble resulted from the distribution of a Blackshirt pamphlet, *The Miners' Only Hope*. The pamphlets were seized and torn to bits and, as a result, the Blackshirts began pushing them into people's faces. Thirty-six people were subsequently charged with riot, incitement to riot, unlawful assembly and breaches of the peace.

The accused, as a body, were brought before the Glamorgan Assizes at Swansea in December. It was alleged that hostile crowds had stoned the Fascist loud-speaker van, which was eventually driven away under police protection. The first of thirty police officers who gave evidence, when cross-examined by the defence, agreed that before the arrival of the Fascist van a number of people had been holding an orderly meeting. He further testified that after the departure of the van the anti-Fascists marched to Tonypandy in orderly procession. This was the main contention of the defence. Moran, under cross-examination, admitted that his head had been split open on eight occasions over the preceding months. The defence argued that wherever he and his Blackshirts went, disorder followed. Moran stated that the crowd was determined not to give him a hearing. The judge then asked him why he didn't go away. He replied that it was his job to promote Fascism. The defence finally submitted that out of a crowd of 5,000 to 6,000 people the police had not found a single independent witness to give evidence.

Three of the accused were discharged and seventeen were bound over. Seven were sent to prison for terms of two to twelve months. Five of these were unemployed and the sixth was the wife of one of the unemployed. Nine were sentenced to twenty days' hard labour, which being the period of the Assizes meant their immediate discharge. They were also bound over. Seven of them were unemployed. Of the seventeen others bound over, seven were unemployed, and four were women. Most of the others were colliers.

Many of the accused were stated by the police to hold extreme views against law and order and to have taken part in organized marches. One defendant, who was sentenced to twelve months' hard labour, had previously served fifteen months for endeavouring to seduce soldiers from their allegiance to the King. His wife, who was sentenced to three months' hard labour, had served two months for assaulting a police officer. Another of the accused, who was found guilty on four charges, was described by the police as a 'most violent and dangerous man, whose pet aversion seemed to be policemen'. It was further claimed that he was 'the most subversive agitator in the Rhondda, with a fanatical outlook on life'. At one point during the trial, he told the Judge that, 'The Fascists should be standing here on trial, not the workers'. When sentenced, he shouted 'Down with the Fascists'. A third anti-Fascist was described by the police as 'a most violent man and extremely lawless in outlook'. The police supplied this information after the defendants had been found guilty and before they were sentenced. Mr Justice Lewis, however, assured the defendants, 'I am not going to punish you for your extremist views but for breaking the law'.[62] The Executive Council of the South Wales Mineworkers' Federation sent a protest to the Home Secretary about this action on the part of the police and against the severity of the sentences.[63]

Harold Laski, in a letter to *The Manchester Guardian*, raised a number of questions about the problem of police neutrlaity and method of trial. He queried whether thirty people accused of different offences and tried simultaneously could lead to a 'sense of discrimination' by the jury, especially over six days of conflicting evidence. He also criticized the length of the judge's summing up. He expressed concern on these points for this had been the third 'mass' trial in Wales in recent years. Laski pointed out that the police denied that they could hear the provocative remarks attributed to Moran, although he had the use of loudspeakers. Yet, they were able to detail what the accused were doing and saying. Laski also criticized the police for drawing attention to the political views of the accused, which were not a crime, and suggested that the police differentiated between the 'extreme' views of the left and the views of the right. Professor Laski felt that it was dangerous to convict accused persons on the evidence of police, who assume that certain political beliefs make a man a bad citizen. He called for an inquiry into the habits of the police in these matters.[64]

Anti-Fascist opposition had increased in frequency and grown more violent. The week preceding the B.U.F.'s proposed East London march, which was to lead to the enactment of the Public Order Act, the Blackshirts planned a march through the predominantly Jewish sections of Leeds to Holbeck Moor, where Mosley was to speak to his followers. Petitions and letters of protest were sent to the Leeds Watch Committee, which was urged to forbid the march or place a ban on uniforms. The Watch Committee refused, but in deference to a request by the police the Fascists altered their route.[65] About 1,000 Blackshirts paraded, many of them in new uniforms styled after those of the Nazis. As at other meetings, the anti-Fascists waited until Mosley began his speech. They then pelted the platform with stones, and the Fascists were under attack all the way back to their headquarters. Scores of people, mainly Blackshirts, received minor injuries. The hospital treated fourteen people and one was detained with serious abdominal injuries. Mosley was struck on the body by stones several times and on the return march he was struck near the right temple by a stone. The police made only three arrests.[66]

Despite their political style and despite the resurgence of anti-Fascist resistance, Mosley had his followers well-disciplined in their relations with the police. This was indicated by the willingness with which the Fascists altered the routes of their processions at Leeds and, as was frequently the case, in East London. But this discipline held true in other circumstances. Earlier in the year, six Blackshirts were selling their newspaper outside a peace meeting at the Paddington Baths. Some of the people leaving the meeting obviously resented this action and it looked as if there might have been a disturbance. The police advised the Fascists to leave the vicinity and they immediately complied.[67]

Although no statistics are available, it was a rare occasion when the Blackshirts deliberately broke up an opponent's meeting. In answer to a question in June 1934, Sir John Gilmour, the Home Secretary, stated that there was no information available for the country as a whole and he could only cite the instances within the Metropolitan Police District. The first instance was in November 1933, when the B.U.F. broke up a meeting of the Imperial Fascist League. The following May, a party of Blackshirts attempted to break up a meeting held by the British Anti-War Movement.[68] Further instances were rare. In July 1936, a Fascist was fined and bound over for throwing soot and flour at an anti-Fascist procession.[69]

It was understandable that the B.U.F. would try and keep its members from opponents' meetings since a number of disturbances at anti-Fascist meetings, caused by Fascists, would deny Mosley's position as the self-appointed defender of freedom of speech. This policy also helped to draw the anti-Fascists to the B.U.F. meetings providing the Blackshirts with the excuse that their own brand of violence was purely defensive. Most important of all, B.U.F. meetings would no longer have been news if it were not for the violence attached to them.

NOTES

1. Dr Robert Forgan, *Interview*, 13 December 1960; Colin Cross's figures vary slightly, *The Fascists in Britain* (1961), p. 88.

2. John Beckett, *Interview*, 14 December 1960.
3. W. J. Leaper, *Interview*, 18 December 1960.
4. John Beckett, *Interview*, 14 December 1960; J. A. Cole, *Lord Haw-Haw* (1964), p. 44.
5. A. K. Chesterton, *Interview*, 4 January 1961.
6. John Beckett, 'Forward' to William Joyce, *National Socialism Now* (1937), p. 9.
7. W. J. Leaper, *Interview*, 9 November 1960; Beckett, *loc. cit.*
8. *Blackshirt*, 24 May 1935.
9. Inland Revenue (Company Searches Office), Records of B.U.F. Trust, Action Press, Abbey Supplies, B.U.F. Publications, Fascist Week Ltd, Sanctuary Press.
10. Mosley insists that he was constitutionally divorced from the financial side of the movement. *My Life* (1968), p. 344.
11. *The Daily Mail*, 18 January 1934.
12. Mosley, *op. cit.*, p. 348.
13. *ibid.*, p. 344.
14. *ibid.*, p. 346.
15. *ibid.*, p. 348.
16. *ibid.*
17. See Chapter 4.
18. *The Times*, 21 July 1934.
19. *Evening Chronicle* (Manchester), 10 September 1935.
20. *The Daily Herald*, 8 June 1931; even this remains unverified.
21. Mosley, *op. cit.*, pp. 344–5.
22. *The Week*, 30 August 1933.
23. *The Saturday Review*, 30 September 1933.
24. *ibid.*, 5 May 1934.
25. Warner Allen, *Lady Houston, One of the Few, a Memoir* (1947), p. 148; *The Saturday Review*, 14, 28 November 1936.
26. *The Saturday Review*, 22 December 1934; 11 August 1934.
27. *The Daily Telegraph*, 6 January 1937.
28. Warner Allen, *loc. cit.*; Mosley relates a somewhat different version of the same incident, *op. cit.*, p. 347.
29. *Action*, 17 September–1 October 1936.
30. Cole, *op. cit.*, pp. 46, 58–9.
31. 317 *H. C. Deb. 5s.* (12 November 1936), cols. 1029–30.
32. 423 *H. C. Deb. 5s.* (6 June 1946), col. 2140.
33. *The Daily Telegraph*, 7 June 1946.
34. 367 *H. C. Deb. 5s.* (10 December 1940), col. 839.
35. 'Fascism in England, 1934', Part of the *Confidential Report of the Ministry for Foreign Affairs on Fascist Movements Abroad*, 1934 (Job. 35–017749–59), Courtesy of the Warden, St Antony's College, Oxford. German Foreign Ministry: *Politik 29, England Band*, December 1925–February 1936. Serial 7602 H.
36. *In Many Rhythms* (1953), p. 141.
37. *Blackshirt*, 2 October 1937.

38. *The Manchester Guardian*, 2 September 1935.
39. *Blackshirt*, 25 October 1935.
40. *The Daily Telegraph, The Manchester Guardian, The Daily Worker*, 6 March 1936.
41. *The Daily Worker*, 11, 12, 17, 18 March 1936.
42. *The News Chronicle*, 20 February 1936.
43. 310 *H. C. Deb. 5s.* (25 March 1936), cols. 1229–30.
44. *Action*, 19, 26 March 1936.
45. N.C.C.L., *Report of a Commission of Inquiry into Certain Disturbances at Thurloe Square, South Kensington on March 22nd, 1936* (1936), p. 20.
46. N.C.C.L., *Sir Oswald Mosley's Albert Hall Meeting, March 22nd, 1936 – Extracts from statements of Eye-witnesses* (*mimeograph*), *1936 Statement 57*.
47. *The Daily Herald*, 23 March 1936.
48. *The News Chronicle*, 23 March 1936.
49. 310 *H. C. Deb. 5s.* (25 March 1936), cols. 1228–30.
50. *ibid.*, cols. 1365–8.
51. *ibid.*, cols. 1369–74.
52. N.C.C.L., *Report of a Commission of Inquiry into Certain Disturbances at Thurloe Square, South Kensington on March 22nd, 1936*, p. 18.
53. *ibid.*, p. 5.
54. *ibid.*, pp. 27, 29.
55. *The Manchester Guardian*, 26 May 1936.
56. *The News Chronicle*, 24 June 1936.
57. *The Oxford Mail*, 26 May 1936.
58. *ibid.*
59. *ibid.*, 27 May 1936; see also 28, 29 May 1936.
60. *ibid.*, 26 May 1936.
61. Letter to *The Times*, 11 July 1936; Lord Longford, *Born to Believe* (1953), p. 83; Geoffrey Marshall, *Police and Government* (1965), pp. 48–9.
62. Account based on *The Daily Herald*, 8–10, 14, 16 December 1936; *The Times, The Manchester Guardian*, 14, 16 December 1936; *Western Mail*, 12 June 1936; *Glamorgan County Times*, 20 June 1936; *South Wales Echo*, 9–14 December 1936.
63. *The Manchester Guardian*, 16 December 1936.
64. *ibid.*, 28 January 1937.
65. *The Times, The Manchester Guardian*, 26 September 1936.
66. *The Yorkshire Post*, 28, 30 September 1936; *Leeds Mercury*, 28 September 1936.
67. 310 *H. C. Deb. 5s.* (6 April 1934), cols. 2424–6.
68. 290 *H. C. Deb. 5s.* (13 June 1934), col. 1694.
69. *Blackshirt*, 18 July 1936.

# 10. The East London Campaign

As far as the Fascists were concerned, the Jews were different and readily identifiable. They could be attacked and intimidated physically as well as verbally. Like Communism, Jewry could be portrayed as possessing a mythical power, while Jews could be seen as too vulnerable and weak to counter paramilitary tactics. Where previously it might have been argued that the anti-Fascists made violence inevitable, political anti-Semitism deliberately invited its use. The Blackshirts concentrated their resources in East London, and their campaign, at its peak, approached a siege of terror. Moreover, they provided an excuse for the Communist Party, already active and well-organized, to intensify and focus its activities, so that East London was subjected to an outrageous political campaign accompanied by considerable disorder and violence. Stepney and Bethnal Green were the main centres for B.U.F. activity and to a lesser extent Shoreditch, presumably because of the lack of open space for outdoor meetings. None of the surrounding boroughs was in fact free from Blackshirt penetration. The important fact about these boroughs, for the purpose of this study, was that in the 1930s they still bore the scars of the rapid industrialization and over-population of the preceding century. The industrialization of East London and its subsequent stagnation left a legacy of derelict buildings lining narrow crowded streets filled with dirt and smoke. Over-population left behind unsanitary and often seemingly uninhabitable dwellings, and numbers of unassimilated immigrants. It should be noted that the arrival of foreigners in East London was not a phenomenon exclusive to the nineteenth century, for East London had always included among its population a large number of persons of foreign birth or descent.[1] But it was the economic decline and the increase in population of the nineteenth century that made these boroughs the worst slums in London.

More specifically, although the population of the three London boroughs declined significantly after the turn of the century and continued to do so during the 1930s, they remained densely over-populated. In terms of the number of people per acre Shoreditch, Bethnal Green and Stepney were ranked second, third and fourth among London boroughs. Measured by the conventional 'more than two persons per room standard' Shoreditch was again second with both the other boroughs ranked third in over-crowded housing.[2] As throughout East London, the population earned a livelihood from skilled and unskilled working-class occupations. Unemployment, although serious, was not a major problem for East London followed the pattern of London and the South-East in that unemployment never reached the proportions that it did in other regions and recovery was more rapid.[3] Yet the amount of poverty was distressing, despite amelioration during the three previous decades. The sample used in the *New Survey of London Life and Labour* revealed that eighteen per cent of the inhabitants of Shoreditch were in poverty, 17·8 per cent in Bethnal Green and 15·5 per cent in Stepney. They ranked second, third and fifth among East London boroughs.[4]

The population was heterogeneous but there was great variation among the boroughs. Stepney had the largest number of foreign-born residents of any borough in England with 30,032, most of whom were of Eastern European origin and 25,328 were aliens. On the other hand, the foreign-born population in Shoreditch was almost non-existent. Bethnal Green ranked seventh among the London boroughs. As for the Jews, they composed only 0·6 per cent of the total British population in 1931[5] and 0·7 per cent in 1936.[6] The number of Jews in Greater London was estimated at 234,000.[7] Whereas East London had accounted for ninety per cent of the metropolis's Jewish population in 1889, sixty per cent was concentrated there in 1929.[8] The *New Survey* house sample, located forty-three per cent of the Jewish families in Stepney, fifteen per cent in Bethnal Green and six per cent in Shoreditch.[9]

The political loyalties of the inhabitants of the three boroughs at the Parliamentary level was subject to some vacillation in the 1930s. At the General Election of 1935, Labour won Bethnal Green North-East with Dan Chater obtaining a majority of almost 5,000 votes over his Liberal opponent. In Bethnal Green South-West, the Liberal, Sir Percy Harris, barely defeated his Labour opponent, George Jager, a Jew, to hold the seat he had occupied since 1922. In Stepney, Clement Attlee retained his seat at Limehouse with a comfortable majority of 7,000. At Mile End, the Labour candidate, Dan Frankel, who was Jewish, regained the seat lost in 1931 to a Unionist. J. H. Hall regained Labour's seat at Whitechapel defeating Barnet Janner, a Liberal and a Jew. Ernest Thurtle had been the Labour M.P. for Shoreditch from 1923 to 1931 when he was defeated by a National Liberal. Thurtle regained the seat for Labour in 1935 with a majority of almost 7,000.

Turning to anti-Semitism in East London during the 1930s, it was evident that the antagonisms and resentments existed then in much the same way that they had existed before. The difference was that Hitler had made anti-Semitism a public issue, and that it was being exploited by an organized body of men headed by Mosley. Newspapers sent 'special investigators' into the East End after the public had been alerted to the situation as a result of a narrowly averted street war on 4 October 1936. The *Times* reporter was the most judicious. He warned his readers that they should remember that most observers saw and heard only what they wanted to see and hear. The danger in Fascism was seen as a mould for the East End working man's uncrystallized dislike for the Jew. They voiced

the traditional grumbles against Jewish price-cutting, clannish-
ness, supposed wealth and dirtiness, and the Jew as a stranger.[10]
Dudley Barker, for *The Evening Standard*, argued that anti-
Semitism had existed in the East End before the arrival of the
B.U.F. He felt it was attributable to the Jewish employer's
exploitation of his employees, the economic depression and the
different social habits of the Jew and the Gentile.[11] *The Morning
Post* correspondent came to a somewhat different conclusion.
He maintained that repeated and emphatic assertion, both in
private conversation and from the platform, had established in
the minds of some an 'identity between Jewry, sedition and
Socialist malpractice'.[12]

Assuming the presence of a latent anti-Semitism, the crucial
test is whether a political movement converted the sentiments
or antagonistic feelings into behaviour and, in particular, into
political action. Certainly the B.U.F. created an atmosphere of
tension and intimidation and the movement gained recruits.
There is little evidence, however, to substantiate a claim that the
B.U.F. mobilized local resentment against the Jews. This was
the case despite job and housing competition, despite the behaviour of the disreputable element in every community, and
in spite of antagonisms aroused by the resistance of some Jews
to assimilation. Again, in terms of recruitment figures, there is
no reliable data. There is clearly no foundation for the B.U.F.
claim of 4,000 members in Bethnal Green. At best it was
generally maintained that they made more headway there than
in other East London boroughs, yet it should be remembered
that the greatest concentration of Jews was in Stepney. Phil
Piratin, active as a Communist in East London, recorded how
the B.U.F. won recruits particularly from the younger people.
According to Piratin, they were attracted to Fascism not so
much by anti-Semitism as by the miserable conditions.[13] Mosley,
in attempting to explain away the B.U.F. defeats in the local
elections in 1937 and 1938, claimed that those who had been too
young to vote provided a main source of the movement's
strength.[14] It was reported, however, that canvasses of the
Conservative Party indicated that the number of electors willing

to reveal their allegiance to the B.U.F. was small even in the vicinity of local B.U.F. offices.[15] Labour Party leaders also disclaimed Fascist progress.[16] J. J. Mallon, the Warden of the Bernhard Baron St George's Jewish settlement, contended that the membership of both Fascist and anti-Fascist organizations in the East End was negligible.[17]

Despite this lack of conclusive evidence, it seems in order to argue that the B.U.F. failed in its mission. It has already been demonstrated that the movement's support at its peak was small and this peak was reached before Mosley's 'declaration of war' against the Jews. Indeed the East London campaign was associated with the decline of British Fascism. The B.U.F. was also slow in obtaining a foothold there in the course of its national campaign. In order to make an impact the movement had to concentrate its energies and resources and, given this concentration, the returns were minimal. The Blackshirts had continually to mobilize their members from outside the area to stage a demonstration within it. This is not to underestimate the serious disorder or discount the interaction between organized political violence and anti-Semitism. Although the majority of Fascist meetings and demonstrations were insignificant and the participants on both sides small in number, the provocation and violence were often of consequence.

The first large East End Fascist rally took place on Sunday, 7 June 1936. *Action* boasted that 100,000 people gathered in Victoria Park to hear the Leader.[18] The estimates of the East London newspapers ranged from 3,000 to over 50,000, while the police estimated 5,000. The Blackshirts, who came from all over London, were estimated at 500 strong. Some 500 foot police, sixty mounted police, and seven police vans were present. The crowd grew so hostile that they had to be dispersed by the police. This was followed by hand-to-hand fighting in which one Blackshirt was knocked unconscious. Most of the nine that were arrested were later discharged by the court.[19]

The constant political activity that took place night after night was more important than the periodically scheduled rallies. The Commissioner of Police, Sir Philip Game, reported that Fascist speakers in the East End had stimulated strong opposition, which came to a head in 1936, and that for several months organized heckling and disorderly conduct had been prevalent.[20] Geoffrey Lloyd, Under-Secretary of State for Home Affairs, announced that East London police had been present at no fewer than 536 meetings in August, 603 in September, and 647 in October. Nearly 300 police a day had been drafted into the East End between 5 October and 8 November.[21] In the House of Commons, Herbert Morrison described how Jews in Shoreditch had been threatened and abused.[22] In reply, the Home Secretary stated:

I say, and I am sure that the whole House will agree, that in this country we are not prepared to tolerate any form of Jew-baiting. We are not in the least disposed to look with an indulgent eye on any form of persecution. It is, therefore, necessary that public attention should be drawn to this danger.[23]

Sir John Simon went on to deny allegations that were being made against the police. He announced that police had already been drafted into the areas for meetings and parades and that additional police would be detailed.[24]

Mosley wrote to the Home Secretary requesting clarification. According to the Fascist Leader, Sir John Simon was suggesting that the Jews were the only people in Great Britain immune from attack, and that it was illegal to attack them. Sir Oswald argued that it was illegal to incite others to violence, but felt that he had as much right to attack Jews on their conduct in Great Britain as the Labour Party had the right to attack anyone possessing capital.[25]

The endless street-corner speeches and pamphleteering were bound to cause more resentment than large demonstrations where extra police could be detailed and the disorder minimized. Although demonstrations tended to get out of hand, they resulted in temporary disruptions and annoyance to the particular neighbourhood. Nightly activities were another matter. In the first place, they presented a dilemma for the Jews. If they stayed away, they would be the hapless victims of unfounded accusations. If they attended the meetings, they would often be provoked to disorder and thereby intensify an unsatisfactory situation. A *News Chronicle* correspondent described a situation of bolted doors, lighted fireworks being thrown into the windows of Jewish shops, threatening letters and people afraid to go out.[26] In the second place, the East End was an ideal place for street-corner politics. The prevailing conditions were suitable to a movement with limited finances and manpower. Substandard and over-crowded housing, poor working conditions, limited incomes, and inadequate recreational facilities drove people to the diversions provided by the street-corner politicians. In the third place, lack of activity on the part of the established political parties probably sent many to the meetings of the Blackshirts, who could not be ignored, and were a curiosity. *The Morning Post*, for example, criticized the Conservative Party on exactly these lines, and maintained that it was ineffective compared to the Labour Party.[27] Even so, the Labour Party tended to ignore the Fascists, advising its followers to stay away from Fascist meetings. There were the statements of Labour M.P.s in Parliament and of members of the local borough councils, but these statements were often made at a distance and removed from the actual scene, the street corner.

This left the Communist Party, and to a lesser extent, the I.L.P. to fill the vacuum. They became the champions of the Jews in the anti-Fascist cause. The extent to which they gained converts is not known. The Warden of Toynbee Hall, for example, wrote that there was a danger of younger Jews becoming militant Communists, while J. J. Mallon thought it was a reality.[28] The *Times* correspondent maintained that apolitical Jews were veering towards Communism, but that any estimate of their strength, 'must, if honest, be cautious to the point where it is no estimate at all'.[29] Membership figures of the Communist Party doubled between 1935 and 1937, but it was not solely due to Fascist intimidation of the Jews.[30] Just as many of the Fascists had come in from the outside, so did the Communists. However, anti-Fascist organizations did spring up in response to the Blackshirt 'invasion'. Some were, no doubt, Communist fronts, and hence a number of Jews may have joined unwittingly. This may have been the case of the Jewish People's Council Against Fascism and Anti-Semitism which was particularly active.[31] But the Jews had their own organizations. The Board of Deputies, somewhat late on the scene, also organized a campaign to counter anti-Semitic propaganda. Much of this activity was constructive and effective, while some was purely demonstrative.

For the most part, as stated above, the Blackshirts stayed away from anti-Fascist meetings. A significant measure of Fascist penetration in East London was the fact that anti-Fascist meetings and demonstrations were rarely attacked and were never mobbed by the residents of these districts. But counter-demonstrations aggravated an already explosive situation and gave rise to occasional incidents. In mid-July, the East London Trades Council organized a procession to Victoria Park where Herbert Morrison was to speak. Bags of flour and soot were thrown at the procession.[32] The Ex-Servicemen's Movement Against Fascism which had been formed in May 1936, scheduled a meeting for the end of August at Victoria Park. J. H. Hall and Sylvia Pankhurst, who were at the head of the procession which took place prior to the meeting, were struck by stones. Bags of flour were thrown at the marchers, and there were minor skirmishes. The police made nine arrests, seven of which resulted in fines. Only one was an anti-Fascist.[33]

Finally, an intensive political campaign was bound to try the patience of the police. The frequency of meetings and the tactics employed by both the Fascists and anti-Fascists did not create an ideal situation for the maintenance of law and order. Allegations were made against the Metropolitan Police, attempts were made to bring the situation to the attention of the public and questions were asked in the House of Commons.[34] In March, there was a full-scale debate on the problem of alleged attacks on East London Jews.[35] An incident at a Fascist meeting in Hampstead was publicized. The speaker referred to the Jews as, 'venereal-ridden vagrants who spread disease to every corner of the earth'. The crowd protested and a police inspector warned

them to be quiet under the threat of arrest for insulting behaviour.[36] The *New Statesman*, the following week, announced
that making such information public had had its effect, for at the
meeting on the following Sunday there were no attacks on the
Jews and the police had permitted heckling.[37] At a meeting of
the Stepney Borough Council in June, there were allegations of
police bias and of Jews being insulted in Stepney markets. The
Council sent a deputation to the Home Secretary.[38] Shortly
afterwards, D. N. Pritt, the new Labour M.P. for North Ham-
mersmith, raised the matter of police behaviour in the House
of Commons.[39] The Home Secretary denied that the police were
acting in a partisan manner, and claimed that the Fascists were
a terrible nuisance to the police.[40] Unfortunately, despite Sir
John's denial and assurances, the relationship between the
police and the Jews and the anti-Fascists deteriorated even
further in the following months.

This was the setting for a major B.U.F. march through East
London on Sunday, 4 October. The B.U.F. contingents were
to assemble in Royal Mint Street near Tower Bridge and then
march in four columns to meetings in Shoreditch, Limehouse,
Bow and Bethnal Green. Mosley was to address all four meetings. As soon as the anti-Fascists learned of Mosley's intentions,
they made their plans. The Communist Party and I.L.P. took
the lead, but there were also quieter forces at work. James Hall
led a deputation which included A. M. Wall, the secretary of the
London Trades Council, Father Grosser, J. W. Bentley and
J. Pearce, the chairman and secretary of the Jewish People's
Council, to the Home Office to request that the procession be
prohibited. The Jewish People's Council submitted a petition
of 100,000 signatures in protest against the march. Prominent
Jews called upon the mayors of East London boroughs to
receive deputations. Subsequently, a deputation of the mayors,
or their representatives, from Bethnal Green, Shoreditch, Stepney and Poplar met Sir Alexander Maxwell, the Deputy Under-
Secretary at the Home Office, in an effort to have the procession
prohibited or diverted. Meanwhile, George Lansbury wrote to
Sir John Simon asking that the march be diverted. He also

advised that all anti-Fascists should stay away.[41] This advice was supported by *The Daily Herald* and *The News Chronicle*.[42] Finally, on 3 October, the mayors of the East London boroughs and several rabbis made an appeal to keep away.

But their advice was not followed. The Communist Party and the Young Communist League originally planned a march from the Embankment to Trafalgar Square, where they were to hold a demonstration in support of Republican Spain. They then proposed marching to Shoreditch Town Hall for an evening meeting. On 2 October, they changed their minds, *The Daily Worker* announcing that they would congregate their forces in the East End. The attitude of *The Daily Worker* towards the anti-Fascist demonstration, however, was reserved compared with the space it had devoted to previous demonstrations. The I.L.P. was more active. Meetings were held, leaflets issued and slogans were chalked up. The I.L.P.'s pre-march campaign culminated in a meeting at Hackney Town Hall, where Fenner Brockway called for an overwhelming demonstration against the Blackshirts. A resolution was also sent to the Home Secretary in protest against the march.

On the morning of 4 October, the East End was transformed into an expectant Madrid. Red flags were draped from windows, and variations of the slogan 'They Shall Not Pass' adorned the walls throughout the district. Gangs of youths marched through the streets chanting 'Mosley Shall Not Pass' and 'Bar the Road to Fascism'. Members of the Jewish People's Council distributed a handbill which ended, 'This march must not take place'. Leaflets were distributed by the Communists calling for a demonstration at Aldgate. The Ex-Servicemen's Movement Against Fascism distributed handbills calling on its supporters to parade. The National Unemployed Workers' Movement boasted of a human barricade. The loud-speaker vans of the Communist Party and the Jewish Ex-Servicemen's Association echoed throughout the boroughs. Anti-Fascist rallies were announced for 2.00 P.M. at Cable Street and at 8.00 P.M. at Shoreditch Town Hall.

The propaganda had its effect, and by noon the streets of the

East End were filled with people. The crowds were swelled by outsiders from all over London, who answered the call of their leaders or came out of curiosity. One outsider, who had his nose broken by a bottle, claimed that the young politically committed went because it was considered 'good clean political fun'. By the middle of the afternoon, crowds had collected along the proposed Fascist route. Their numbers were estimated as high as 100,000.

The first contingent of Blackshirts began to arrive in Royal Mint Street about 2.00 P.M. where groups of anti-Fascists had already gathered. At first, there was good-natured jeering and singing, but before long the spectators grew unruly. The police drew their truncheons and the mounted police charged, driving the crowds into the side streets. By the time that Mosley arrived, an hour and a half later, several people had been injured, including some Blackshirts.

The police precautions paralleled the arrangements for the Hyde Park demonstration two years earlier. Some 6,000 to 7,000 police were recruited into the area including the entire mounted corps of the Metropolitan Police. Police wireless vans patrolled and an autogyro hovered overhead. Sir Philip Game set up his headquarters near-by. Nevertheless, the *East End News* was prompted to comment that the general impression was that if the Fascists had been allowed to march, 7,000 police would have been insufficient.[43] This may well have been the case. The demonstrators, who gathered at various points along the proposed route, for example at Gardiner's Corner, were in no mood to permit the Blackshirts to pass. People jammed the streets, blocked traffic and provoked the already harassed police into drawing their truncheons. This only excited the crowd further, and the police charged. Fighting broke out with subsequent injuries and arrests.

Perhaps the most dramatic sequence was at Cable Street, where London witnessed a close approximation to a political street war. The 'Battle of Cable Street' began when a number of people dragged a lorry from a near-by yard out into the middle of the road, and turned it over to form the base of a barricade. When the police charged, they were met with stones and bricks. Reinforcements had to be called before the barricade was captured. Attempts were made to erect other barricades, but these were quickly dismantled. A popular anti-Fascist legend was how an occasional policeman would surrender to the crowd, much to their embarrassment.

When Mosley arrived with a motor-cycle escort at Royal Mint Street, some 2,500 to 3,000 Blackshirts were assembled. Dressed in a black military-cut jacket, grey riding breeches, jack boots, a black peaked military cap and red arm band, he inspected his troops. After the inspection, Mosley consulted his lieutenants and then was met by Sir Philip Game. It was decided that the procession should be diverted. With drums and pipes playing, they set off in a westerly direction along the Embankment and shortly afterwards dispersed. According to *The Times*, the Commissioner of Police's decision had the full backing of the Home Office. After the deputation of the East London mayors, it had been decided that Sir Philip Game should be given the sole responsibility to make such a decision, if necessary.[44]

A serious riot was averted. It was some time, however, before the news drifted back to Aldgate and Cable Street, and it was still some hours later before the crowds were dispersed. The news was greeted as an anti-Fascist victory. Small processions began to return to the heart of Bethnal Green and Stepney with their arms raised in the clenched fist singing and chanting, 'They did not pass', and, 'We stopped them'. Wild tales and fantastic stories circulated throughout a jubilant crowd as they marched through the streets to Victoria Park for a victory rally.

The job of the police, however, was not over. The crowds had to be dispersed, the injured cared for and those who had been taken into custody charged. B.U.F. meetings had been going on at the appointed places throughout the afternoon, and near-by the anti-Fascists, particularly the Communists, were standing at their pitches. The crowds gravitated to these spots after the march had been prohibited, and in certain instances grew unruly. The mounted police were called to disperse them. Some eighty-six demonstrators, mostly anti-Fascists, were arrested.

Although a substantial proportion was discharged, many were fined and a number were imprisoned. Some 3,000 police remained on duty in the East End that night. Police behaviour seems to have been admirable, especially in terms of the provocative circumstances. It was a matter for speculation as to whether there would have been a riot if the Blackshirts had been permitted to proceed. In any case, the police had to handle a crowd that was aroused and expectant. Although repeated baton charges were necessary, and missiles of varying degrees of potency were thrown, the situation never developed into a mob scene or a riot. The Labour Mayor of Stepney, who had been outspoken against the police for allowing the demonstration in the first place, admitted in the instance of Limehouse, at any rate, that the behaviour of the police was extremely good.[45]

The B.U.F. attributed its failure to march through East London on 4 October to a Government surrender to Communism.[46] Scotland Yard issued a statement that due to fine weather a large crowd had been attracted to the demonstration and that, because of that crowd, the parade could not be permitted. Many breaches of the peace had occurred prior to Mosley's arrival, and there was a likelihood of more.[47] In the Commissioner's *Annual Report*, however, it was stated that the march had to be prevented, 'owing to strong local opposition', and that there was 'little doubt that serious rioting and bloodshed would have occurred had the march been allowed to take place'.[48]

What then did the newspapers say the following morning? *The Times* supported the police decision. The activities of both the Fascists and the anti-Fascists were described as a 'tedious and pitiable burlesque' making the lives of many of the residents of the East End 'unbearable'. *The Times* concluded, 'that this sort of hooliganism must clearly be ended, even if it involves a special and sustained effort from the police authorities'.[49] *The Manchester Guardian* also supported the decision and argued that the police had demonstrated that the Fascists had the right to hold a procession, but correctly banned it, when it showed signs of getting out of control.[50] *The Daily Telegraph* felt that the Commissioner's action had raised a serious question of what to do with those who wanted to preserve free speech, but threatened it by their own actions. The paper concluded that the Commissioner was on the side of free speech, and those who assembled to resist the march threatened it.[51] *The News Chronicle* and *The Daily Herald* supported Sir Philip Game's decision, but were critical in that he had had to make it in the first place. *The News Chronicle* argued that such scenes were intolerable, and blamed the Home Office for being 'perilously vacillating'. It was called upon to review the whole situation.[52] *The Daily Herald* maintained that the responsibility for the situation had rested entirely on Sir John Simon's shoulders. He had chosen to disregard the warnings and was left with a foolish policy. It was not a question of the right of free speech nor of the rights of peaceful citizens in a democratic country, but a deliberate attempt to import into Great Britain, not only the theories, but the practice of Fascism.[53] *The Daily Mail* did not comment editorially.

The B.U.F. received sympathetic treatment in those papers that saw Communism as the primary evil. 'Sentinel', in *The Morning Post*, began his column by stating that he was not in favour of the B.U.F. because of its importation of foreign symbols. But he went on to declare that he did not feel that Mosley's 'young men' were getting fair play. Developing this theme, he wrote, 'They are decent, clean-living young fellows – some of them Public School products, but most of them drawn from every rank and vocation, and they are loyal to King and Country'. He praised them for not assaulting the police, but felt that if their processions were likely to cause breaches of the peace, they should be banned. He was more emphatic, however, about taking action against the Communists who were described as the 'germ-carriers of the revolution'. He described the district east of Aldgate as where the names over shops and polyglot talk 'often' gave the illusion of a 'foreign town', and blamed the trouble on the 'East End mob'. The Socialists did not try to get rid of them, and this was proof of their 'un-English mentality'. Because they did not allow their opponents the right of free speech, they were seen as the 'real Fascists'.[54] *The Daily*

*Sketch* reported that according to secret and confidential reports made to 'the Yard', the responsibility for East End violence rested not with the political partisans, but with criminals of alien origin, who exploited both the Communist Party and the B.U.F. Both were viewed as rackets to cover up stealing, looting and pick-pockets. According to the article, the 'authorities' were also alarmed at the number of aliens in the country and about the influx of refugees. The article was broken by a box in which there was an announcement of two Mosley meetings.[55]

The anti-Fascists tried to make the most of what they considered a Fascist set-back while the latter by no means deserted East London. The following week the anti-Fascists staged a 'victory' march through the East End to a mass meeting in Victoria Park. The march was organized by the London District Committee of the Communist Party, but received the support of other groups including the I.L.P. Morgan Phillips, then the organizing secretary of the Whitechapel Labour Party, stated its position:

To-morrow's demonstration is awaited with some anxiety. Despite the claims of support which the Communists and the I.L.P. have made, this march too should be banned. We are the largest political organization in the district – our membership is more than 3,000 – and we will not join in the demonstration.[56]

The march proceeded as scheduled with the participants, variously estimated from 3,000 to 10,000, protected by some 2,000 to 3,000 police. There was much jeering, and apples and other missiles were thrown. The procession, however, was reasonably orderly until Victoria Park, where there were skirmishes and four were injured. Although nine were arrested, the police were able to announce that there had been no serious disorder.[57] However, the East End was not free from violence at other points that day.[58] After the meeting, crowds of thugs smashed and looted stores of Jewish shopkeepers in Mile End Road. One East London newspaper reported that 'Never before in the history of the East End has there been such frenzied victimization'.[59] On the following day, an attempt was made to burn the B.U.F. headquarters in Stepney.[60] Finally, during the middle of the week, the Blackshirts marched to Victoria Park and Limehouse where Mosley addressed the meetings. The audience was small at Victoria Park, but crowds collected to watch about 400 Blackshirts march to Limehouse where, according to estimates, between 4,000 and 15,000 people had gathered. Once again, some 3,000 police were on duty. Although there was a great deal of noise, excitement and traffic congestion, the meeting and march passed off almost without incident. It was obvious that the Fascists had no intention of leaving the area. On the contrary, the B.U.F. intensified its activities and, as noted above, 300 police had to be drafted into the East End every day, between 5 October and 8 November. The intense political atmosphere did not taper off until the winter and after the Public Order Act came into effect.

Relations between the police and the anti-Fascists, however, did not improve during this period. Ronald Kidd, the secretary of the N.C.C.L., described an incident at the Blackshirts' Victoria Park meeting on 14 October. An interrupter was forcibly ejected from the meeting by the police although his questions were legitimate and his manner unprovocative.[61] At the end of 1936 after Mosley addressed a meeting in the East End, his supporters, shouting 'Down with the Jews', marched to the offices of the Blue and White League, a Jewish anti-Fascist organization. They broke up the premises and assaulted members. This occurred, despite the fact that the secretary of the League had telephoned the police prior to the meeting to request protection.[62] On the other hand, anti-Fascists often attacked the police as well as the Blackshirts. Two days earlier two anti-Fascists had been charged with assaulting a police officer. They were given three and four months' hard labour respectively.[63] Later, still another anti-Fascist was given three months' hard labour for his part in the same affair. It was alleged that he had struck a police officer on the head with a piece of metal tubing.[64]

## NOTES

1. J. H. Robb, *Working Class Anti-Semite* (1954), p. 193.
2. *Census of England and Wales – County of London* (1932), tables 3, 11–13, XIX.
3. British Association for the Advancement of Science, *Britain in Recovery* (1938), p. 107; *Report of the Unemployment Assistance Board for the Period ended 31st December, 1935* (Cmd 5177), p. 84; 1936 (Cmd 5526), pp. 62–3; 1938 (Cmd 6021), p. 75, appendix 5.
4. *The New Survey of London Life and Labour*, Vol. III (1930–35), pp. 345–6, table III, p. 151. Poverty was set at an income of 40s. a week for a moderate family, p. 101.
5. *Census of England and Wales* (1931), *General Report* (1950), p. 178, table LXXVII; *County of London*, table 26, table 30.
6. *Jewish Year Book* cited by Hannah Neustatter, 'Demographic and Other Statistical Aspects of Anglo-Jewry', in Maurice Freedman (ed.), *A Minority in Britain* (1955), p. 58.
7. M. Kantorowitsch, 'Estimate of the Jewish Population of London, 1929–1933', *Journal of the Royal Statistical Society* (1936), p. 378.
8. Henrietta Adler, 'Jewish Life and Labour in East London', in Sir H. Llewelyn Smith (ed.), *The New Survey of London Life and Labour* (1934), Vol. VI, p. 271.
9. *ibid.*, p. 293.
10. *The Times*, 20 October 1936.
11. *The Evening Standard*, 5 November 1936.
12. *The Morning Post*, 21 October 1936.
13. Phil Piratin, *Our Flag Stays Red* (1948), pp. 16–18.
14. See Chapter 12. The East London boroughs did contain a higher percentage of residents between the ages of 5–19 than the rest of London. *Census of England and Wales – County of London* (1932), table 26.
15. *The Morning Post*, 21 October 1936.
16. 317 *H. C. Deb. 5s.* (16 November 1936), cols. 1375, 1384.
17. *The Daily Telegraph*, 28 October 1936.
18. *Action*, 11 June 1936.
19. *East London Advertiser, City and East London Observer, The Eastern Post and City Chronicle*, 13 June 1936.
20. *Report of the Commissioner of Police of the Metropolis for the Year, 1936* (Cmd 5457), pp. 25–6.
21. *The Times*, 19 November 1936.
22. 309 *H. C. Deb. 5s.* (5 March 1936), cols. 1595–603.
23. *ibid.*, col. 1605.
24. *ibid.*, cols. 1605–11.
25. *The Times*, 9 March 1936; *Action*, 12 March 1936.
26. *The News Chronicle*, 10 October 1936.
27. *The Morning Post*, 22 October 1936.
28. Basil Henriques, *The Indiscretions of a Warden* (1937), p. 96; J. J. Mallon,

'Fascist Provocation in East London', *The Daily Telegraph*, 28 October 1936.

29. *The Times*, 20 October 1936.
30. See Chapter 6.
31. Andrew Sharf, *The British Press and Jews Under Nazi Rule* (1964), p. 105, claims it was a front organization.
32. *The Manchester Guardian*, 13 July 1936.
33. *East London Advertiser*, 5 September 1936.
34. 308 *H. C. Deb. 5s.* (13 February 1936), cols. 1121–2.
35. 309 *H. C. Deb. 5s.* (5 March 1936), cols. 1595–634.
36. *New Statesman and Nation*, 23 May 1936, p. 797.
37. *ibid.*, 30 May 1936, p. 850; 312 *H. C. Deb. 5s.* (26 May 1936), cols. 1859–60.
38. *East London Advertiser*, 27 June 1936.
39. 314 *H. C. Deb. 5s.* (10 July 1936), cols. 1547–70.
40. *ibid.*, cols. 1616–29.
41. *The Morning Post*, 1 October 1936.
42. *The News Chronicle*, *The Daily Herald*, 3 October 1936.
43. *East End News*, 10 October 1936.
44. *The Times*, 5 October 1936.
45. *East End News*, 10 October 1936; for a comparative perspective consider the right-wing political activity in the streets of Paris on 6 February 1934 and 4 October 1936. See Edward R. Tannenbaum, *The Action Française* (1962); Herbert Tint, *The Decline of French Patriotism* (1964); Max Beloff, 'The Sixth of February' in James Joll (ed.), *The Decline of the Third Republic* (1959).
46. *The Manchester Guardian*, 5 October 1936.
47. *The Times*, 5 October 1936.
48. *Report of the Commissioner of Police of the Metropolis for the Year 1936*, p. 26.
49. *The Times*, 5 October 1936.
50. *The Manchester Guardian*, 5 October 1936.
51. *The Daily Telegraph*, 5 October 1936.
52. *The News Chronicle*, 5 October 1936.
53. *The Daily Herald*, 5 October 1936.
54. *The Morning Post*, 10 October 1936.
55. *The Daily Sketch*, 14 October 1936.
56. *The Sunday Chronicle*, 11 October 1936.
57. *The Times*, 12 October 1936.
58. *The Manchester Guardian*, 12 October 1936.
59. *The City and East London Observer*, 17 October 1936.
60. *ibid.*
61. Ronald Kidd, 'Anti-Semitism in East London', *Left Book Club News* (November 1936), p. 150.
62. Ronald Kidd, *Disturbances in East London* (1937), p. 2.
63. *The Manchester Guardian*, 13 October 1936.
64. *The Times*, 16 October 1936.

# 11. The Public Order Act

The lasting result of the 'Battle of Cable Street' was the Public Order Act. This does not necessarily mean that the events of 4 October alone were responsible for the Government's decision to bring in legislation. The rapidity with which the bill was introduced and the willingness of the Government to enact legislation suggested that the problem had already been studied and the broad outlines considered. It has been shown that legislation had been considered after the Olympia meeting and that party leaders had met to review the problem. After the debate in the House of Commons on 10 July 1936, in which the alleged attacks of Fascists on the East London Jews were discussed, it was reported that the Cabinet was considering the banning of all political uniforms.[1] The concern shown by the police, not only in the Metropolitan area, but throughout the country was also important. The Fascists and anti-Fascists were causing considerable disruption and were a drain on the resources of the police. At one point, during the debate on the Public Order Bill, Sir John Simon stated that it was, 'the unanimous view of the chief officers of police in the areas principally affected that the wearing of political uniforms is a source of special provocation'.[2]

The Labour Party had a splendid opportunity to give a lead to public opinion by calling for anti-Fascist legislation at their annual conference, which began in Edinburgh on 5 October. It took full advantage of the situation, and Herbert Morrison brought in an emergency resolution for the National Executive at the very beginning of the conference. The resolution expressed concern about the proceedings in East London the previous day, condemned the Government for its unwillingness to ban the procession in spite of the danger of a breach of the peace and condemned the Fascists for their tactics. The resolution expressed the view that, although freedom of speech must be preserved, deliberate provocation, racial strife and the militarization of politics should be prohibited. Finally, it called upon the Government to institute an inquiry into the disturbances and into the activities and finances of Fascist organizations.[3] Morrison, in retrospect, felt that this resolution was responsible for the introduction of the Public Order Bill, for the Home Secretary had resisted the idea of legislation 'all the way' and hence it was necessary to fight him.[4]

Sir John Simon's reply was immediate. He maintained that the police had no power to ban processions, and that if anyone wanted to invest the executive with such powers, the law would have to be changed, but in such a way that it would apply to the left as well as to the right.[5] The first announcement that the Government proposed to deal seriously with the situation was made less than a week after the march. Ramsay MacDonald, then Lord President of the Council, in an interview, defended the Home Secretary's action in regard to the Fascist march on 4 October but stated outright that steps would be taken to deal with the problems of political uniforms and the maintenance of liberty and public order.[6] Five days later, the Cabinet decided to set up a special Cabinet sub-committee on the question of legislation dealing with uniforms and processions.[7]

Meanwhile, pressure from the Labour Movement had not only mounted but had become more organized.[8] A conference was called and attended by members of the Executive Committee of the London Labour Party, Labour M.P.s, members of the L.C.C., mayors of the East London boroughs, leaders of the local borough councils and secretaries of local Labour parties of East and North East London. The Government was urged to take effective action and a decision was made to send a deputation. This was led by Herbert Morrison and met with the Home Secretary, the Under-Secretary, Geoffrey Lloyd, the Minister of Health, Sir Kingsley Wood, and Sir Philip Game.[9] Pressure was also forthcoming from other quarters. The National Executive of the Liberal Party sent a resolution to the Prime Minister and to the Home Secretary.[10] At another level, the Jewish People's Council continued its agitation in East London. It drafted bills, which were to be submitted to a conference which all Jewish organizations had been invited to attend in mid-November.[11] Not only was a political uniforms bill drafted, but a racial incitement bill as well, which would have made it an offence to arouse hatred against a racial community.*

The King's Speech, in early November, gave prominence to the introduction of a bill for strengthening the law on meetings and processions, 'without interfering with legitimate freedom of speech'.[12] The Prime Minister in the Debate on the Address declared that the Government regarded the Public Order Bill as a matter of great importance and urgency. He argued that the elements responsible were unimportant in themselves, but that they were provocative of great disorder. In the House of Lords, Viscount Halifax, the Lord Privy Seal, described the provocations as a nuisance and, in that sense, the Government would deal with them.[13] The Bill was introduced the following week. Despite Baldwin's emphasis on its importance, Simon made it clear that it was to be a minor, although necessary, task of the session.[15] By the time the Bill was presented for a third reading in December, it was not of first importance either politically or in news value. This was due primarily to the constitutional crisis of the King's abdication, which was first aired in the Press on 3 December.

The publication of the text of the Bill was greeted with general approval.[15] The consensus of opinion was that, however

---

* Campbell Stephen, I.L.P., M.P. for Camlachie, Glasgow, introduced an amendment to the Public Order Bill to make it an offence to use insulting words or behaviour to incite racial or religious prejudice. It was rejected by the House. 318 *H. C. Deb. 5s.* (26 November 1936), cols. 630–54.

much regretted, legislation was necessary. Both the Labour Party and the Liberal Party made it known that they would support the second reading of the measure, although they would seek some amendments. Some Conservatives and a few newspapers felt that legislation would only serve to flatter the Fascists or felt that the Fascist movement was not serious enough to justify the restrictions on liberty. In any event, *The Times* noted that there were 'few parallels in the archives of Parliament of so smooth a passage through the second reading of legislation of an essentially political complexion'.[16]

The most vocal opposition came from the political extremes. The Communists and the I.L.P. feared that the Act might eventually be used against them.[17] The moderate but actively anti-Fascist National Council for Civil Liberties was concerned that it would place too much power in the hands of the police and the Executive.[18] Mosley issued a statement to the Press. He began with his old argument that no member of his organization had been convicted of interfering with their opponents' meetings, while over 400 anti-Fascists had been convicted. Yet, the Bill discriminated in favour of his opponents. He admitted that prohibition of uniforms deprived the Blackshirts of a successful propaganda device but maintained that the prohibition of paramilitary organizations did not affect them. The B.U.F., according to its leader, was only organized to gain power through a majority at a General Election. Mosley also charged that the drafting of a bill suggested a deliberate attempt to 'frame-up' the Fascists by methods alien to British law and tradition. He was most worried about Clause 2, Section 4, of the Bill, claiming that it impaired the principle that the onus of proving guilt rested on the prosecution, and that the onus of proving innocence did not rest upon the accused. He asserted that the action enabled any opponent to put agents into an organization for the very purpose of contravening the law. Moreover, convictions could be obtained on evidence adduced by the prosecution from statements or activities by self-professed adherents, who were unknown to the accused.[19]

Mosley was referring to the section of the Bill which stated that in any criminal or civil proceedings concerned with the prohibition of quasi-military organizations, proof of things done or of words written, spoken or published by persons appearing to be members or adherents of an association, 'unless it is proved that those persons were not members or adherents thereof', shall be admissible as evidence.[20] Moreover, evidence was to be admissible if it came from pamphlets, speeches or actions of members or adherents of the organization. According to Mosley, the prosecution would be allowed to cite as evidence, for the purpose of demonstrating the object and manner in which the association was organized and operated, evidence that would otherwise be inadmissible at a criminal trial. For example, it would not be necessary to show that drilling was done in the presence of the accused.[21]

Mosley was by no means alone in his concern. Sir John Simon anticipated trouble, for he had remarked in his speech in the House of Commons that several people were uneasy about the language of this section. The Home Secretary argued, however, that the British law of evidence was so strict that it was necessary to some extent to depart from it in order to obtain fair results.[22] Indeed several Members did express concern during the debate that followed and most of their objections were met.[23] It was agreed that the accused had to be a person taking part in the management or control of the association not just a member or an adherent, which limited the possibility of planted agents or the 'agent provocateur'. Moreover, since it was necessary to demonstrate that the person had taken part in the direction of the organization, the onus of proof was not necessarily shifted.[24]

The Bill and subsequent Public Order Act created new offences under the law, besides amending and changing it. It was not aimed against particular political creeds or beliefs but was concerned solely with methods.[25] The primary object was to prohibit the wearing of uniforms for political purposes. No attempt was made to define 'uniforms', that being left to the courts. The Chief of Police, with the consent of the Home Secretary, could permit uniforms to be worn on ceremonial anniversaries and other special occasions, if it did not involve a risk to public order. Moreover, it was made clear that the uniforms of such organizations as the Salvation Army and Boy Scouts would not be affected.[26] The wearing of military uniforms by non-authorized personnel was already an offence under the Uniforms Act of 1894. The Public Order Act made it an offence to wear a uniform only in a public place or at a public meeting. Finally, no prosecution would take place without the permission of the Attorney General. This was a proviso obviously included to prevent the misuse of the new power.

The prohibition of uniforms was not unknown at this date. Denmark, Sweden, Norway, the Netherlands, Switzerland and Finland had already enacted legislation. Ireland had to stop the wearing of blue shirts when they took on a political significance. Pre-Nazi Germany and Austria had made attempts to forbid the wearing of symbolic shirts. In France, a few months earlier, it had been found necessary to institute prohibitions. *The Morning Post* reported that the British law would probably be based on the Swedish law passed in August 1933.[27] The Swedish law was so designed as to make it clear that it was legislating to preserve order, not to outlaw political creeds, and was cautious in the way it handled the definition of 'uniforms'. On the other hand, it went so far as to ban badges and armlets as well as uniforms.[28] It is necessary to consider one other point – the Blackshirts, although they were the most conspicuous, were not the only group that had adopted uniforms. The Social Credit Party had green shirts, a Jewish anti-Fascist organization, the Blue and White League, had white shirts, the I.L.P. wore red shirts, and the Young Communists tended to wear khaki shirts.

The second object of the Public Order Act was to prohibit paramilitary organizations. Two possibilities were cited: those who might organize to usurp the functions of the police or the armed forces; and second, those who organized and trained or organized and equipped to employ or display physical force in promoting a political object. The danger foreseen in the first case was a general and more vague possibility, and in the latter event the Government would be dealing with a certain class of case. The Home Secretary, in regard to the former, was willing to concede that the danger of usurpation at the time was not very great, but that it was necessary to set down the principles by which it might be judged.[29] As far as the latter case was concerned, proof of organization was insufficient in itself. Hence, there must be reasonable fear that a group was training or equipping for the use of force in promoting a political object.[30] The test of 'reasonable apprehension' was seen as the reaction produced on innocent members of the public.[31] The Act did not hold the members responsible. Instead, those who participated in the control or management of the organization were held liable for an offence under the law. The section was later amended to protect the right of organizations to use stewards. But the language of the same section prevented a corps of stewards from developing into a private army by limiting them to a 'reasonable' number and by restricting their activities to public meetings on private premises. In France, the situation was handled more drastically by the Popular Front Government disbanding the Fascist leagues. Sweden had passed a law in 1934 prohibiting private armies. The law was designed to check the activities of, and to deny arms to, any organization seeking to exercise the functions of the public authorities, or acting as a defence corps for any political party or group.

Third, the Public Order Act was intended to regulate and control public processions. The relevant provision stated that, if a chief of police had reasonable grounds for believing that a procession might occasion serious public disorder, he could impose necessary conditions on the organizers and participants in the march. The stated conditions included the power to alter the route of the procession, or to prohibit it from entering a public place, and the power to ban all public processions or any class of public procession for a period not exceeding three months. The latter ban could only be instituted on application to the borough or district council and had also to be approved by the Home Secretary. The requirement for 'reasonable' grounds and the limitation to three months were added by amendment to the original Bill. A further qualification was added to safeguard the right to display flags, banners or emblems provided they did not provoke a risk of a breach of the peace.

There were certain problems concerning these restrictions. Sir John Simon made it clear that the Government had no intention of prohibiting processions as such, on the grounds that they caused a great deal of inconvenience, especially in crowded places, and that there were many other ways by which the public could express their feelings.[32] Moreover, the police already possessed the power to alter or, if necessary, ban the route of a procession. The powers were available to the Metropolitan Police in the Metropolitan Police Act of 1839, and throughout the country in the Town Police Clauses Act of 1847.[33] Nor was there an unrestricted right under common law to hold street processions. Although street processions were commonplace, they could be viewed technically as an obstruction, or the police could have reasonable grounds for believing that a breach of the peace might be committed. And there were many local acts throughout the country giving the police power to control and regulate processions.[34] It has already been shown that the police used such powers, particularly in Manchester. Moreover, the police had banned the proposed Fascist East End march, and had also refused a left-wing demonstration in Oxford Street. The Home Secretary fully recognized this, but defended the clause on the grounds that the Acts of 1839 and 1847 were in archaic language and that they were passed before the establishment of a modern police force. Hence, there had been difficulty in their operation. Sir John argued for the need to insert a 'plain provision on the subject'.[35]

Another difficulty was the possibility of arbitrary application of the control and regulation of processions by the police. In part, this was negated by the insertion that the Chief of Police must have 'reasonable' grounds for believing in the likelihood of a breach of the peace, by Sir Philip Game in his reluctance to ban the Fascist East End march and the Home Secretary's defence based on the argument that a procession could not be banned by mere threat of opposition. Moreover, the Chief of Police was only to take necessary action in the event of the possibility of 'serious' public disorder. Finally, the Home Secretary defended the provision in favour of investing the authority in the Chief of Police rather than the local council, on the grounds that it was undesirable that the question of the regulation of processions, which might arouse political and religious hostility, should become a topic at local elections throughout the country.[36]

The investment of power in the authorities to forbid processions in a particular area for a limited period of time raised other problems. Hence, the Chief of Police was not given arbitrary power. It was specified that the relevant local authority would make the actual decision with the consent of the Home Secretary upon the application of the Chief of Police. London, however, was excepted. The Commissioner of Police required only the consent of the Home Secretary, not that of the borough councils. Moreover, it was not necessary to ban all processions though, in fact, all processions were banned. In other words, an attempt was made to apply the act to all organizations without discrimination. However, should all groups be penalized for the actions of one? Yet, the prohibition applied to processions only. It was permissible, and indeed it was to be the case that meetings and rallies continued to be held in a district where processions were banned. Furthermore, the Blackshirts continued to circulate leaflets, sell their pamphlets and papers and even put forth candidates in the L.C.C. elections the following spring. And they were permitted to hold processions elsewhere in London and throughout the country.

The Public Order Act went further. The possession of offensive weapons at public meetings and processions was prohibited. The Act left it to the courts to define 'offensive weapons', but made provisions for exemption of those who might carry weapons in the course of their official duty or as provided under the Firearms Act. The Act also made uniform throughout the country the laws making it an offence for a person in any public place or at any public meeting to use threatening, abusive, or insulting words or behaviour with an intent to provoke or threaten a breach of the peace. Sir John admitted that the

Government was not making a new law, but was setting down a rule that ought to apply generally.[37] The provision incorporated into the Public Order Act was almost identical to that in the Metropolitan Police Act of 1839, except that the latter had applied solely to London. The maximum penalty was raised from a 40s. fine to three months' imprisonment or a £50 fine. Moreover, the law was extended to cover any public meetings, including a public meeting on private premises.

Finally, the Public Meeting Act of 1908 was amended so that a person at a lawful public meeting who acted in a disorderly manner for the purpose of preventing the transaction of business for which the meeting had been called, would be liable to have his name and address taken and to arrest. The Home Secretary argued that the Public Meeting Act had been seriously restricted for want of machinery. If interrupters were from outside the area, it was difficult to identify them. It was also impossible to invest the chairman with the legal power to demand a person's name and address. The proper authority was the police. Thus, under the law as amended, if a police officer reasonably suspected a person of committing an offence, he could, if requested to do so by the chairman, demand the person's name and address. If this person refused or gave a false address, he would be guilty of an offence, and could be arrested if necessary. The Home Secretary, however, stated that it would be undesirable for the police throughout the country to have the responsibility of bringing charges under the Public Meeting Act. They would have the information, however, and if the injured party desired to press charges, he could.[38]

At the time of the passage of the Act, the Blackshirts were preoccupied with the abdication crisis. They expressed an unusual degree of sympathy for the abdicating King. In a sense, they were capitalizing on the issue to display their loyalty. Some ex-Blackshirt officers, however, maintained that Mosley suffered from a delusion that, in the event of a crisis, Edward VIII would have called him to the Palace. But the Fascists soon turned their attention to challenging the Public Order Act.

On 24 December 1936, the Commissioner of Police wrote to

all political organizations which had worn some type of distinguishing garment. He called attention to the new Act and to the fact that it went into effect on 1 January 1937. Fenner Brockway, the Secretary of the I.L.P., replied that the red shirts and red blouses of the Guild of Youth were in no sense uniforms. They were worn mostly on rambles, for sport purposes and for week-end outings.[39] Communist Party headquarters stated that its youth organization had abandoned khaki shirts a year before and that none of its members was now wearing a uniform.[40] Francis-Hawkins, the Director-General of Organization of the B.U.F., requested the police to provide a test case on the legality of wearing a black shirt under a plain jacket. At the same time, he issued a public statement that counsel's advice had been taken and that a black shirt with tie under an ordinary suit of clothes was legal and unaffected by the Public Order Act. The B.U.F. denied it was challenging the law, but stated the intention to wear the black shirt in the prescribed fashion, until it was proved illegal in the courts. The police replied that they did not feel that it was their duty to provide the opportunity for a test case. The letter went on to point out that it was up to the courts to decide what constituted a uniform, but warned that the wearing of a black shirt had signified association with a political organization and that the court might find it illegal. The B.U.F., determined to have the last word, stated that the refusal placed upon the Home Office the responsibility for a widespread infringement of the law should the courts decide that the undress black shirt was illegal.[41]

On 2 January, a police inspector took the names of two Fascists who were wearing the undress black shirt and one who was wearing a black polo sweater. No action was taken in this instance and the B.U.F. undoubtedly gained confidence from it. Three weeks later, Mosley addressed a meeting at Hornsey Town Hall wearing a black shirt and black tie under his suit.[42] This set the fashion for his speakers. But it was important to note that the Fascists refrained from appearing in public *en masse* in the undress uniforms. Photographs of Fascists at private gatherings, however, showed them dressed in their former attire.

The first uniforms case came before the court when a twenty-five-year-old Fascist was summonsed when selling *Action* in Leeds. He was wearing a black peaked cap bearing emblems, a black shirt and tie and a black motor-cycling overcoat. The case against the Fascist was that on first impression the police had thought that he was wearing a uniform. The defence argued that the accused was selling papers as an employee of Action Press Ltd, and that he was wearing the livery of a selling agent. The flash and circle badge was a trade mark of Action Press, and the livery also included riding breeches and high topped boots. The defence argued that by the terms of the contract the uniforms were received by vendors after a month's probation during which they were responsible for the disposal of 2*s.* 2*d.* worth of papers each week. The distribution for *Action* testified that the Leader disposed of his weekly quota. It was then stated, in contradiction to earlier testimony, that the B.U.F. badge was worn because Action Press received a lot of volunteer help from the British Union. If the stated quota was not sold, the uniform was withdrawn. The magistrate agreed that the man in the street would consider the livery to be a uniform. The defendant was found guilty, but fined only 40*s.* because it was a test case.[43]

The second case to come before the courts arose from an incident in which four Blackshirts had appeared at a public meeting in Hull during January. Two of the defendants, including the chairman, were dressed in navy-blue sweaters, black trousers, black belts with the movement's emblem on the buckles and red arm-bands. A third Fascist wore a black jacket and the red brassard. The defence maintained that the clothes had been purchased during the ordinary course of their lives. The armlets and the bands were the only apparel identifying them with a political organization. Council for the defence argued that the object of the Public Order Act was to prevent the wearing of a complete outfit. The magistrate pointed out that if Parliament meant by a uniform a complete outfit they would have defined it in those terms. Therefore, it must be something less, but he was not going to be trapped into defining the limits. He did not, however, feel that they were trying to break the law. Hence, they were bound over for six months and ordered to contribute towards the costs.[44]

Members of the Social Credit Party were also summonsed before the courts.* The first incident occurred in Luton, where the Green Shirts had staged a demonstration. According to police evidence, they apprehended a procession headed by five men beating green drums and five people carrying banners inscribed with the party emblem. They were dressed in green shirts, and green collars, ties and armlets. The majority were wearing coats. Three appeared in court, two of whom were the speakers. One admitted that they had been wearing the outfits in London and on occasion had had their names taken. The defence argued that they were wearing substantially the same clothes on the day of meeting, and that they were not wearing a 'distinctive dress of the same pattern, colour and appearance'. The case was dismissed.[45] The second summons was issued to a Green Shirt speaker in London. He had worn a light green shirt, green collar, a green tie bearing an inscription or initials, a black belt, grey flannel trousers and a green armlet. The defendant argued that the shirt was not that worn by members of the party and that he was not wearing the recognized green beret. Although the magistrate declared that this constituted a uniform the summons was dismissed under the Probation of Offenders Act on payment of costs.[46]

These cases were of more than usual interest. As far as the first case was concerned, the Blackshirts complained of discrimination. Two Mosleyites had also appeared before the courts the same month. At Birmingham, the defendant had worn a sports coat and grey flannel trousers with a black shirt. He had two B.U.F. badges on his lapel and an armlet. The Fascist was bound over and ordered to pay costs.[47] In a case at Coventry, the Fascist was fined 10*s*. He had been wearing a black shirt, collar, and tie, and breeches and riding boots. He had a Fascist

* The Green Shirt movement, later the Social Credit Party of Great Britain, was an off-shoot of Major C. H. Douglas's Social Credit Movement and had his approval for a short period.

badge as a tiepin. The Blackshirts argued that they were being found guilty, while Green Shirts were being let off free, and maintained that the Public Order Act had been aimed at them.[48] The second Green Shirt trial was interesting in that the magistrate attempted to define a uniform. In dismissing the summons, he held that the shirt, tie and armlet constituted a uniform, but that he did not take this particular case seriously.[49]

Another provision of the Public Order Act that hindered the cause of British Fascism was Section 3, which empowered the police to control and regulate processions. Blackshirt activity centred in, although it was not restricted to, East London. In March, the B.U.F. contested the L.C.C. elections in Bethnal Green, Limehouse and Shoreditch. On the first Sunday in May, which Mosley had adopted as National Socialist Day, the Blackshirts paraded from Limehouse to Bethnal Green. It passed off quietly, probably because there was a bus strike, which must have kept many Fascists and anti-Fascists away. The atmosphere in the East End, however, had again reached a peak of tension so that when the B.U.F. announced a proposed march from Limehouse through the East End to Trafalgar Square on 4 July, the Home Office invoked Clause Three of the Public Order Act forbidding marches of a political character through that area for a period of six weeks. Sir Samuel Hoare, who had succeeded Sir John Simon at the Home Office, announced the decision in the House. He stated that it was necessary in order to prevent a recurrence of what happened on 4 October 1936, and in view of the proposed anti-Fascist opposition.[50]

*The Manchester Guardian* remarked that the proposed march was not so much to provoke anti-Semitism as to test the Government.[51] The B.U.F. issued a statement in protest. They blamed the Home Office decision on an article in *The Daily Worker*, which was headed, 'Ban the Fascist March', and which ended 'Let the Home Office not wait this time until the people in London take the preservation of liberty and order into their own hands'.[52] According to *Action*, what the Home Secretary's decision amounted to was that whenever the anti-Fascists decided to organize violence to prevent their opponents' propaganda, they would be aided by the Government. The Government, instead of taking action against the organizers of riot, were taking action against the Blackshirts. The result was to give hooligans a free hand to prevent free speech. This, according to Mosley's weekly, was a complete 'abdication of Government'.[53] Nor was the Communist Party satisfied. It accused the Government of using the opportunity to ban all political marches.[54]

The B.U.F. decided to alter the route rather than postpone the march. A meeting would be held in Kentish Town, after which they would march to Trafalgar Square for a rally. Opposition formed against the newly-proposed demonstration. In St Pancras, the local Labour Party, Co-operative Society and trade unions organized a march of nearly 500 to the Town Hall to demand that the procession be banned. A deputation was received by the Borough Council, but a Labour resolution demanding that the march be banned was defeated. Instead, an amendment was passed demanding that the Home Secretary be informed and that a petition be organized.[55]

Sir Samuel Hoare issued a public statement. The 'particular circumstances' envisioned in Section 3, which made it desirable to ban processions, existed in East London as the result of Fascist and anti-Fascist activities and because of the nature of the area. The circumstances in St Pancras were quite different. A mere threat of hostile opposition was not a sufficient ground for banning a procession. To do otherwise would place a premium on disorder. As far as the police were concerned, their primary function was the maintenance of public order, 'and if opposition was organized to lawful processions or demonstrations, the police have no alternative but to take such steps as may be necessary to deal with disturbances of the public peace'.[56] Mosley interpreted this last statement as an admission that the Government had full power to prosecute those who 'organized opposition against a lawful procession'.[57] The actual march took place without serious disorder. The police had taken elaborate precautions, and some 2,400 officers were on duty. Numerous minor scuffles, however, did take place at both

Kentish Town and Trafalgar Square and some twenty people, mostly anti-Fascists, were arrested. Of these, eighteen were convicted of insulting words and behaviour, one was given a month's imprisonment and one discharged.[58]

The prohibition against political processions through the East End was extended for another six weeks in August. The anti-Fascist left began to grow more alarmed. Sir Walter Citrine, the General-Secretary of the T.U.C., in a statement to *The Daily Herald*, said that the Labour Movement feared that the authorities were trying to hamper political activity.[59] *The News Chronicle*, however, sent an investigator into the East End, and he concluded that if a plebiscite were taken in Stepney Green it would approve the ban.[60] The B.U.F. announced plans to march through East London on 3 October. The march was to celebrate the fifth anniversary of the founding of the B.U.F. and, of course, the first anniversary of the battle of Cable Street. The Jewish People's Council and the London Trades and Labour Council had already made representations to the Commissioner of Police in support of an extension of the ban.[61] The ban was subsequently extended for the maximum period of three months and was renewed every three months until the B.U.F. was disbanded in 1940.

The Mosleyites announced a new route through Bermondsey and South London. As in the case of the Kentish Town march, the result of the change in the route of the procession was a shift in the anti-Fascist struggle. The consequences, however, were somewhat more serious. The Communist Party demanded a protest meeting and march. The Executive of the London Labour Party refused to approach the Home Secretary with a view to banning the march. It urged supporters to boycott the demonstration on the grounds that it could not protest against the route, since the special circumstances of the East End were not in evidence in South London. Modifications in the route were favoured and these were accepted.[62] Nevertheless, trouble was forthcoming. The Communist protest was supported by the I.L.P., Bermondsey and Rotherhithe Trades Council.

South London had its own version of the battle of Cable

Street on 3 October. As in the previous year, the Fascists may have been the cause or the excuse, but the anti-Fascists and the police were the belligerents. An estimated 2,500 Blackshirts, some wearing false 'Jewish noses', assembled in Westminster. They were reported to have been unimpressive without their uniforms.[63] The anti-Fascists rallied their forces to Bermondsey and their objective was to prevent the Fascists from passing through a particular main thoroughfare. They achieved this for at the last minute the procession was diverted, but not before there had been 106 arrests and twenty-eight casualties including two policemen.

By comparison, the actual procession and meeting were less eventful. No disorder occurred until the Mosleyites reached the heart of Bermondsey. Then an empty taxi was pushed into the line of marchers and several people were knocked down. The police charged the crowd in order to restore order. At the new meeting place, more violence occurred when the anti-Fascists tried to prevent Mosley from getting a hearing, in addition to holding their own protest meetings. Some 2,500 police had been used to maintain order, and at the meeting place they were reported to have been striking out indiscriminately. Mosley stood on the platform with a police officer by his side watching the fray. He began his speech, 'Brother Fascists we have passed'.[64]

The Bermondsey march had its sequel in the courts. Charges including the possession of offensive weapons, throwing of missiles, insulting language and behaviour, setting light to fireworks, wilful damage and assault of police officers were brought against 106 anti-Fascists. Of the sixty-four cases reported in *South London Press*, half the defendants were fined, twenty-three imprisoned and nine discharged.[65] Most of those imprisoned were charged with assaulting police officers. One of the magistrates voiced his approval of the Public Order Act. In sentencing an anti-Fascist to six weeks' imprisonment for leading an attack on the police, he declared, 'I am thankful that the newer provisions of the Public Order Act enable me to inflict greater punishment when language is used by the leader of a mob which puts the police in such an ugly situation as they were in this case'.[66] The Fascists were jubilant. In addition to claiming that they did 'pass', they jumped on the side of the authorities and attacked the anti-Fascists for assaulting the police, demanding that the inciters be brought to trial.[67] The Bermondsey and Rotherhithe Trades Council, armed with the evidence of N.C.C.L. observers as well as their own and with a report from *The Manchester Guardian*, launched an inquiry into police behaviour.

The report of the Commissioner of Police for 1937 made it quite clear that Sir Philip Game wanted a ban on all political processions in the Metropolitan area.[68] And during the autumn of 1937, marches were prohibited after sunset in Hendon, Battersea, East Ham and Peckham. For the most part, however, the police exercised the greatest discretion. Section 3 was applied to regulate and control the routes of processions or to ban particular marches rather than to place wholesale bans on marches outside East London. Nor was the Public Order Act used to halt B.U.F. activities. Hence, in 1938, when the Fascists planned their National Socialist Day march to Bermondsey, it was permitted, although when they proposed to disband after the meeting and walk out of formation through the Rotherhithe tunnel to Limehouse for a second meeting, permission was refused.[69] They did, however, hold a meeting in Limehouse on the following day.

The third dispute between the B.U.F. and the police arose over the interpretation of Section 5 of the Public Order Act dealing with insulting words and behaviour. It was not unlawful to attack or criticize the Jews. It was even possible to make some quite outrageous statements. But the movement's Jew-baiting was likely to lead to disorder and abuse as it had in the past, except that now, the police armed with the Public Order Act could enforce the law more strictly. One of the chief offenders was E. G. 'Mick' Clarke, the District Leader of the B.U.F. in Bethnal Green and the author of *The British Union and the Jews*. In the summer of 1937, he was bound over for twelve months under the Public Order Act for using insulting language.

According to the police short-hand notes, he referred to the Jews as 'filthy and licentious', and stated that, 'Sir Philip Game has not got the guts of a louse, the damn old fool'.[70]

The magistrate, in his handling of the case, showed no patience towards Clarke and demonstrated the utmost antipathy. This prompted another B.U.F. attack on the police on the grounds of prejudice. Mosley initiated an exchange of correspondence with the Home Office challenging the police on three issues. He complained that the police arrested his speakers if they said anything that was regarded as provocative, while members of the audience could say what they pleased. Mosley complained of prejudice on the part of provincial police and maintained that the Public Order Act deprived the British Fascist Movement of the means to defend itself. He cited a B.U.F. meeting at Southampton in June. According to the Fascist Leader, there was only a very small detail of police to handle a very large crowd. Missiles were thrown at the platform but police did not act until requested to do so in the case of a specific person. B.U.F. supporters who moved to stop the stone-throwers were restrained by the police. Yet the Fascists suffered heavier penalties than their opponents. Mosley quoted from a letter, supposedly received from an Englishman resident abroad, asking what would have happened if the speaker had been the Chief Rabbi and his assailants Fascists. Finally, he complained that certain journals were openly inciting violence and transporting men long distances and at great expense to create disorder. He reminded the Home Secretary of his statement in the House of Commons that the police were responsible for restraining the organized opposition to a procession or a meeting.[71] Mosley implied that if the Fascists incited violence in their papers and transported men long distances to wreck Conservative or Socialist meetings the police attitude would be different.[72]

The Home Office reply denied the allegation of lack of impartiality. Definite instructions had been issued to the Metropolitan police that Section 5 of the Public Order Act should be used whether the offender be the speaker or a member of the audience. The Home Office noted that in the Metropolitan area between 1 January and 31 July 1937, there had been twenty-seven persons at Fascist meetings charged with insulting words and behaviour. Of those arrested, four were speakers, two were Fascists in the audience and six were of unknown political views. Fifteen were anti-Fascists. Mosley was reminded that twenty arrests had been made on the occasion of the Kentish Town march, and that it was not the job of the police to secure a hearing for speakers.[73] Mosley in his reply stated that he had the evidence of eye-witnesses as to the partiality of the police. He strongly objected to the statement that it was not the duty of the police to secure a hearing for speakers. He argued that it was the duty of the stewards at indoor meetings, and since stewards could not be used at outdoor meetings it was up to the police. If it was not their duty he wanted to know whether the B.U.F. could use stewards.[74]

The continuation of Fascist activities and the application of the Public Order Act affected the anti-Fascists as well and they had their complaints. The first occasion after the passage of the Public Order Act was, in fact, Mosley's first public meeting of 1937, when he appeared in the undressed black shirt at the Hornsey Town Hall. Incidents occurred at the meeting. Two members of the audience, independent of each other, sought out police officers so as to identify their assailants. The police ignored their approaches and refused to take action.[75] According to Ronald Kidd, the N.C.C.L., acting through Members of Parliament, approached the Home Secretary to hold a public inquiry into the conduct of the police. This was refused, but Sir John Simon did undertake a private inquiry, and he expressed his satisfaction with police behaviour. However, in a letter to an M.P., the Home Secretary stated that his officers had been reminded of their duty when undue violence was used by stewards at a meeting. The Secretary of the N.C.C.L. was able to write that there were no reports to the Council of serious cases where the police failed to intervene at indoor meetings after that date.[76]

Most of the alleged incidents of police prejudice and indifference occurred in East London. Mass provocation had been halted but intentional, although unorganized, violence continued. James Hall, the Labour M.P. for Whitechapel, stated during the debate on the Public Order Bill, 'In the East End of London the Jewish people have been constantly insulted and the speakers who have been responsible for it have had the protection of the police while doing so'.[77] Eighteen months later the Labour M.P. for Stratford East made a similar charge. Four onlookers had been arrested at a meeting where one of the speakers referred to the audience as 'scum' and to an individual as 'a hook-nosed unmentionable'.[78]

In July 1937, the B.U.F. and the Jewish Ex-Servicemen's Association were holding meetings in close proximity to each other in Stepney Green when the meetings were forcibly dispersed by the police. Nine anti-Fascists were arrested. Five were charged with insulting words and behaviour, three of whom were subsequently dismissed. One was charged with obstructing the police and bound over. Two were bound over in the juvenile court, and one was convicted on two charges of assaulting the police.[79] The N.C.C.L. undertook an inquiry but exaggerated the innocence of those concerned, for a number of the accused were not just innocent or outraged by-standers, but anti-Fascists with political associations. At the same time, one was arrested for blowing his nose and another for whistling. They were later discharged by the court. Moreover, the crowd was not unruly. According to the N.C.C.L., there was no need to disperse them, forcibly or otherwise. Finally, it was claimed that those arrested were treated unnecessarily roughly by the police.[80]

A little later in the month, Dan Chater, the Labour M.P. for Bethnal Green North-East, and others addressed a trade-union demonstration in Victoria Park. They were interrupted by Fascists and the police told them to close the meeting. Chater wrote to the Home Secretary asking him to receive a deputation.[81] Meanwhile, in the House of Commons, Dan Frankel, Labour M.P. for Mile End, directed a question to the Under-Secretary of State for the Home Office on the Stepney Green meeting.[82] The

N.C.C.L. held a meeting at the House of Commons presided over by Frankel, supported by Chater, D. N. Pritt and J. H. Hall. Sir Samuel Hoare received a deputation and announced that he and the Commissioner of Police were determined that the police should be impartial and that the matter would be investigated.[83]

In June 1938, officials of the Board of Deputies of British Jews interviewed Sir Philip Game. The Commissioner reassured the deputation that his information showed that the B.U.F. was a dying organization. He cited complaints from all quarters as to the manner in which he controlled their meetings in the East End. He thought this was ample proof of the impartiality of the police. Sir Philip felt that the most effective way of preventing trouble was to persuade the Jews to stay away from meetings. He assured them of police impartiality, but stated that there was 'naturally' some resentment on the part of the police at having to give up their free time in order to cope with disturbances to which the Jews had contributed by their presence. The deputation reported that there was no doubt that Sir Philip Game was doing all in his power to deal with the situation.[84]

Despite these reassurances the incidents continued. The following year, two members of the executive of the N.C.C.L. witnessed an 'unprovoked' assault by a police inspector on a Jew at a time when there was no disturbance.[85] An N.C.C.L. observer saw a mounted policeman strike a woman in the face with his stick at a Fascist meeting in South London. She was not causing any disturbance and after negotiations with the police she was awarded £100.[86] It was reported that as late as the end of 1939, an order had been issued to East London police that they were not to laugh at the witticisms of speakers or at adverse criticism of Jews while on duty.[87]

It was easy enough to attack the police, but it was more important to account for their behaviour and evaluate the criticism levelled against them. Despite left-wing anti-Fascist charges, there was no evidence of police Fascism. Given the circumstances, there was much to commend them. The belligerents were convinced of the righteousness of their causes. Others were intimidated, and hence, understandably sensitive. Still others were looking for trouble. Criticism of the police was also a convenient method of excusing the shortcomings of the adversaries and had a certain publicity value. The left-wing anti-Fascists were prone to indulge in this sort of propaganda and to accuse the police of favouritism at every opportunity. By their very nature they tended to be against the authority symbolized by the police. Anti-Fascists, in general, were uneasy about the police as a result of the latter's attitude towards the organized unemployed and their demonstrations, and as a result of their behaviour at Olympia and Thurloe Square.

The Blackshirts had a psychological advantage, although difficult to measure. Until 1937, like the police, they wore uniforms and claimed to stand for law and order. The Blackshirts were further able to identify with the police in that they claimed to be on guard protecting the right of free speech. In addition, they were a disciplined body of men. They marched in order, they dispersed when ordered and, for the most part, they stayed away from their opponents' meetings. When in uniform they were under strict orders not to attack the police, while the anti-Fascists, who were a more amorphous group, were more difficult to control. Once the uniforms were taken away, the psychological bond, as well as the discipline of identification, was broken. Consequently, more Fascists were arrested, and there were more Fascist criticisms of the police. Yet, the volume of arrests did not increase sharply for the Fascists remained a disciplined body who carried the Union Jack and claimed to be on the side of authority.

On the other side, the Communists and those labelled Communist were deemed to be opposed to the law and order that the police and Blackshirts were seen as protecting. In addition, the Jewish community was subjected to constant intimidation and violence. Many of the Jews, given the existing world situation, were left in a state of distress and hypertension, which occasionally would find need for an outlet. For the younger Jews, probably more politically conscious and aware of the sufferings of their parents and fellow-Jews, this meant the need for political action or even occasional violence. Perhaps, as a consequence, anti-Fascists were sometimes falsely arrested or dealt with unfairly by the police.

The police, in turn, could not always turn up at the right moment and would naturally resent criticism of their attempts to perform impossible feats. In addition, the Public Order Act and the police could not put a halt to the prejudice that already existed in that it was largely practised by women and was being picked up by small children.[88] According to the Warden of an East London Jewish Settlement, 'Christian' children refused to sit at the same desks with Jewish children. Some were even asking for transfers to schools where they would not be taught by Jewish masters.[89] William Joyce was known to have expressed great satisfaction when he heard that East London children were playing a version of 'cops and robbers' called 'Blackshirts and Jews'.[90] Moreover, to the ordinary constable the Jewish community may have seemed alien. There was every chance that he had been brought up with a stereotype notion of the Jew. In East London, he would have encountered Jews directly and would possibly have been unable to understand the habits, language and solidarity which often differentiated them. It would not have been unusual for the police to resent the Jews for being 'un-English'. It would not be difficult to imagine a policeman in such circumstances attributing the misdeeds of a few to the whole community.

Add to this the fact, as stated by Sir Philip Game, that the police were overworked. It was reported that 'special memoranda by Scotland Yard had been issued on the subject'. The police were lucky if they got one Sunday off during the whole of the summer. For many months, police in Stepney Green and Bethnal Green had to attend as many as fifteen meetings in a night.[91] The police were taken away from their regular duties and the resources of the Force were drained.[92] The Blackshirts had effective speakers and the mere process of repetition may have had an impact. The policeman on duty, listening to the speakers at meeting after meeting, night after night, was apt to be persuaded, if he was not bored first. In any case, he was more likely to be sympathetic towards a lone speaker and his small band of lieutenants than to a boisterous crowd determined that the speaker should not be heard. With these considerations in mind, it must be remembered that the police and the courts were often as strict with the Fascists as they were with the anti-Fascists. If more anti-Fascists and Jews were arrested than Blackshirts, it was, in part, because there were many more of them.

To prohibit or limit meetings further would probably have created more problems in that it would have placed more discretion in the hands of the police.* But the police could have been encouraged to take more notice of what the speaker was saying as well as to protect his right to say it. Efforts could have been made within the police force to create some sort of understanding with the people of East London and to win their confidence. Supervision could have been such that distinctions between political creeds, regardless of their source, were minimized so far as it might affect the discharge of a policeman's duty. There may have been some validity in the proposal of a contemporary critic who wrote, 'The most important single problem of civil liberty in England is to secure the control by democracy of the police'.[93] British Fascism did not create the problem of police behaviour nor did the Public Order Act resolve it.

NOTES

1. *The Manchester Guardian*, 17 July 1936.
2. 317 *H. C. Deb. 5s.* (16 November 1936), col. 1351.
3. The Labour Party, *Report of the Thirty-Sixth Annual Conference* (1936), p. 164.
4. Lord Morrison, *Interview*, 14 July 1959.
5. *The Times*, 8 October 1936.
6. *The Daily Telegraph*, 10 October 1936.

* Nor was it much of a help to tell the police that the Public Order Act, among others, was passed 'owing to various subversive activities'. J. Griffith Morgan, 'The Law of Public Meetings', *The Police Journal* (October 1937), p. 470.

7. *The Times*, 15 October 1936.
8. See *The Times*, 14 October 1936; *The Daily Herald*, 13 October 1936; *The News Chronicle*, 14 October 1936.
9. *The Times*, 17 October 1936.
10. *The Manchester Guardian*, 22 October 1936.
11. *The Times*, 3 November 1936; the Board of Deputies remained aloof from the activities of the Jewish People's Council because of the latter's obvious political motives. Board of Deputies of British Jews, *Minutes of the Co-ordinating Committee*, 12 November 1936.
12. 317 *H. C. Deb. 5s.* (3 November 1936), col. 12.
13. 103 *H. L. Deb. 5s.* (3 November 1936), col. 33.
14. 317 *H. C. Deb. 5s.* (16 November 1936), col. 1367.
15. For example, see *The Manchester Guardian*, 12 November 1936; *The Daily Telegraph*, 11 November 1936.
16. *The Times*, 17 November 1936.
17. See William Gallacher (Communist M.P. for Fife) speech 317 *H. C. Deb. 5s.* (16 November 1936), col. 1419; *The Daily Worker*, 8 October 1936; see James Maxton's speech, 318 *H. C. Deb. 5s.* (7 December 1936), col. 1764.
18. National Council of Civil Liberties and Haldane Society, *Notes for the International Conference of the International Juridicial Association* (1937), p. 7; Ronald Kidd, letter to the *New Statesman and Nation*, 12 December 1936, pp. 974–5; D. N. Pritt in the *New Statesman and Nation*, 14 November 1936, pp. 761–3, 757.
19. *The Evening Standard*, 12 November 1936; *The Morning Post*, 13 November 1936.
20. *Parliamentary Papers*, 1936–7 (30 v. 189, 1 Edw. 8).
21. Joseph Baker, *The Law of Political Uniforms, Public Meetings and Private Armies* (1937), p. 27.
22. 317 *H. C. Deb. 5s.* (16 November 1936), col. 1358.
23. *ibid.*, cols. 1376, 1408–9, 1428–9, 1449, 1470.
24. 318 *H. C. Deb. 5s.* (23 November 1936), cols. 121–38; (7 December 1936), cols. 1666–70; see also (23 November 1936), cols. 102–4.
25. 317 *H. C. Deb. 5s.* (16 November 1936), col. 1350.
26. *ibid.*, col. 1352.
27. *The Morning Post*, 21 October 1936.
28. For a comparative review of similar legislation see Karl Loewenstein, 'Militant Democracy and Fundamental Rights I and II', *American Political Science Review* (June 1937), pp. 417–32; (August 1937), pp. 638–58.
29. 317 *H. C. Deb. 5s.* (16 November 1936), col. 1356.
30. *ibid.*, col. 1357.
31. *ibid.*, col. 1358.
32. *ibid.*, col. 1359.
33. *Metropolitan Police Act, 1839*, (2 & 3 Vict. C.47), Section 52; *Town Police Clauses Act, 1837*, (10 & 11 Vict. C.89), Section 21.
34. Baker, *op. cit.*, p. 11.

35. 317 *H. C. Deb. 5s.* (16 November 1936), col. 1359.
36. *ibid.,* col. 1360.
37. *ibid.,* col. 1362.
38. *ibid.,* cols. 1364–5; the Public Order Act of 1963 has increased the maximum penalties under Section 5 and 6 of the 1936 Act.
39. *The Times,* 31 December 1936.
40. *The Daily Herald,* 31 December 1936.
41. *The Times,* 4 January 1937; *Action,* 9 January 1937.
42. *Action,* 30 January 1937.
43. *The Yorkshire Post,* 28 January 1937.
44. *The Times,* 30 January 1937.
45. *ibid.,* 3 June 1937.
46. *ibid.,* 17 June 1937.
47. *The Daily Telegraph,* 3 June 1937.
48. *The Times,* 11 June 1937; *Blackshirt,* 5 June 1937.
49. *The Daily Telegraph,* 3 June 1937.
50. 983 *H. C. Deb. 5s.* (21 June 1937), cols. 847–8.
51. *The Manchester Guardian,* 22 June 1937.
52. *The Daily Worker,* 19 June 1936.
53. *Action,* 26 June 1937.
54. *The Times,* 22 June 1937.
55. *ibid.,* 1 July 1937.
56. *ibid.,* 29 June 1937.
57. *Action,* 3 July 1937.
58. 326 *H. C. Deb. 5s.* (15 July 1937), col. 1456; *Report of the Commissioner of Police of the Metropolis for the Year, 1937* (Cmd 5761), p. 12.
59. *The Daily Herald,* 3 August 1937.
60. *The News Chronicle,* 6 August 1937.
61. *The Manchester Guardian,* 14 September 1937.
62. *The Times,* 21–3 September 1937.
63. *ibid.,* 4 October 1937; N.C.C.L., observer's report.
64. *The Manchester Guardian,* 4 October 1937.
65. *South London Press,* 5 October 1937.
66. *The Times,* 6 October 1937.
67. *Action,* 9 October 1937.
68. *Report of the Commissioner of Police of the Metropolis for the Year 1937, op. cit.,* p. 13.
69. *Action,* 16 April 1938.
70. *Blackshirt,* 17 July 1937; he was arrested on at least two other occasions. *Action,* 30 July 1937; *East End News,* 5 August 1938.
71. See 325 *H. C. Deb. 5s.* (21 June 1937), col. 848.
72. *Action,* 11 September 1937 (letter dated 5 August 1937).
73. *ibid.* (letter dated 18 August 1937).
74. *ibid.* (letter undated).
75. N.C.C.L., *Statements of Persons assaulted by Fascists and Eye-Witnesses of Fascist Violence at Fascist Meeting Hornsey Town Hall* (mimeographed), 25 January 1937.

76. Ronald Kidd, *British Liberty in Danger* (1940), p. 133.
77. 318 *H. C. Deb. 5s.* (23 November 1936), col. 645.
78. 332 *H. C. Deb. 5s.* (3 March 1938), cols. 1273-4.
79. *East London Advertiser*, 31 July 1937.
80. *Civil Liberty* (autumn 1937), pp. 13-14.
81. *The News Chronicle*, 20 July 1937.
82. 326 *H. C. Deb. 5s.* (19 July 1937), cols. 1794-805.
83. *The Daily Herald*, 30 July 1937.
84. Board of Deputies of British Jews, *Minutes of the Co-ordinating Committee*, 31 June 1938.
85. N.C.C.L., *Annual Report*, 1938-9, p. 9.
86. *ibid.*
87. *The Daily Telegraph*, 23 December 1939.
88. Board of Deputies of British Jews, *Memorandum on Jew-Baiting*, June 1937.
89. Basil Henriques, *The Indiscretions of a Warden* (1937), p. 98.
90. John Beckett, *Interview*, 14 December 1960.
91. *The Daily Herald*, 23 July 1937.
92. *Report of the Commissioner of Police of the Metropolis for the Year 1937*, *op. cit.*, pp. 12-13.
93. G. H. C. Bing, 'Civil Liberty', *Labour Monthly* (May 1937), p. 300.

# 12. The Decline of British Fascism

From 1936 to the outbreak of the Second World War, much of the interest of the politically conscious in Great Britain was focused on foreign affairs. Events moved swiftly. The Soviet Union was still purging its 'enemies' in January 1937. Although the British left may have been having some doubts about the Republican cause in Spain, the bombing of Guernica confirmed their allegiances. Neville Chamberlain replaced Baldwin as Prime Minister in the spring of 1937. That summer the Sino-Japanese war broke out. The militarist powers, Germany, Italy and Japan, were linked together in the autumn. The policy of appeasement led to Anthony Eden's resignation as Foreign Secretary in February 1938. Germany invaded Austria in March, and the '*Anschluss*' was proclaimed the following month. This left Czechoslovakia vulnerable. On 19 May, there were reports of troop movements and an incident on the Czechoslovakian border. The crisis had begun. The Munich settlement occurred that autumn and in March 1939 the Nazis marched into Prague. During the same month Madrid fell after Franco, with the aid of German and Italian troops, had turned the tide against the Republicans. Re-armament in Great Britain accelerated after Munich and pledges were given and alliances formed. The most bewildering alliance for the British Fascists and anti-Fascists was the Hitler–Stalin Pact of August 1939. But on 1 September

1939 Hitler entered Poland and Britain's Fascists and anti-Fascists turned to more immediate problems.

At the beginning of 1937, the B.U.F. was still very much a discredited movement. Moreover, the Government now had the power to control paramilitary organizations and to restrict the opportunities for organized violence. In the circumstances it was remarkable that Mosley did not disband his movement. It is useful to speculate briefly on why he persisted. If he had abandoned Fascism his political career would have been at an end. To have deserted the Fascist cause would have been an admission of failure out of the question for a man of such pride and egotism. The B.U.F. had also acquired its own institutional goals. The basic one, of course, was its own survival, which perhaps could be sustained by Jew-baiting and violence. As a result of the increase in international tensions, Mosley was able to find a new crisis and a new, if remote, prospect of coming to power, either to prevent a war or in the event of a Fascist victory.

The B.U.F. continued to concentrate on those areas in large urban centres that were poor and had a substantial Jewish community. Jew-baiting combined with violence, not only offered an explanation, but a type of action. The Fascists encouraged protest in the form of acts of intimidation and violence. This was supplemented by collective demonstrations, when and where the authorities permitted. The Mosleyites even tested their strength at the ballot box. At the same time, the Public Order Act and other legal devices were used to check them, and, for that matter, the anti-Fascists. This was the setting for the British Union in decline.

The Public Order Act, according to Sir John Simon, worked like a 'charm', and Herbert Morrison when Home Secretary in 1943 claimed 'It smashed the private army and I believe commenced the undermining of Fascism in this country'.[1] In a limited sense they were right for the Act deprived the B.U.F. of an advertisement in terms of its uniform and paramilitary displays and it restricted political violence. The Commissioner of Police reported that there had been an improvement in the conduct of meetings and demonstrations during 1937, although by the end of the year there were signs of organized disorder by a small number of militant extremists.[2] However, by 1937 the Government had other means at its disposal for controlling political violence and public order. The importance of the decision in Thomas *v.* Sawkins, which permitted the police to enter a meeting, if they had good reason to apprehend a breach of the peace, has already been pointed out.[3] A further decision was handed down in October 1936, in the case of Duncan *v.* Jones which granted greater powers to the police than were contained in Section 5 of the Public Order Act. It was decided, in effect, that if the police reasonably apprehended that a breach of the peace might occur if a meeting was held in a public place, they could exercise their common law duty by prohibiting the meeting. If an attempt was then made to hold a meeting, it would amount to a statutory offence of wilfully obstructing a police officer in the execution of his duties.[4]

In addition to the Public Order Act and the decisions of the courts, local authorities throughout the country had taken steps to curb the activities of the Fascists and other street-corner movements. Many towns began in 1935 to forbid the use of town or public halls by the Fascists, on the grounds that disturbances might take place causing damage to property. In some cases, the ban was only for particular meetings, but in many cases it was a blanket prohibition. Halls were banned in Bournemouth, Birmingham, Carlisle, Leyton, Grimsby, Norwich, Barnsley, Mitcham, Birkenhead, Shipley, Edmonton, Horsham, Wigan, Hull, Oxford and Cambridge. Other towns imposed conditions on the meetings. In Newcastle, under the rules of the hall, police had to be present at meetings.[5]

After the 'Battle of Cable Street', spurred on by the likelihood of legislation, Cardiff, Pontefract, Manchester, and Leeds permitted the B.U.F. to hire halls, but on the condition that uniforms were not worn. Moreover, in certain areas the use of private halls was refused to the Fascists.[6] One legal expert pointed out that the local police had only to make their disapproval known and the proprietor would refuse the hall to the promoter.[7] In a few places, outdoor meetings were banned. In Leicester, the market place was refused as a meeting place to the B.U.F. The Communists, however, were permitted to hold meetings there as long as they were not marked by disorder.[8] In Plymouth, the police imposed a ban on all street meetings.[9] In other areas, conditions were imposed upon outdoor meetings. Manchester, for example, prohibited uniforms on marches. After Mosley's meetings in Victoria Park and Finsbury Park in June 1936, the L.C.C. brought in a by-law prohibiting the use of loud-speakers in the parks under its authority, and several boroughs followed its example.[10]

Even after the enactment of the Public Order Act, meeting places were refused to or restrictions imposed upon the B.U.F. In Edinburgh in the autumn of 1937 permission was granted for Mosley to speak, but the use of amplifiers and a proposed march were banned.[11] As a result, the Fascists postponed their meeting. In the autumn of 1938, the Fascist movement found itself in a position where it could not rent a large hall or theatre in London.[12]

At the beginning of 1939, the B.U.F. claimed that main halls were banned in twenty-five centres outside the London area.[13] At the end of the year, *Action* declared that the movement was unable to hire a large hall anywhere in England for a meeting.[14] The ban, however, had been broken in part for mass meetings had been held at Earl's Court in July 1939, and in January 1940. Mosley was also permitted to speak in Manchester.

The B.U.F. also experienced a series of set-backs through the libel law.* Critics of the British law have claimed that its severity

* Libel actions were also brought against Arnold Leese (see Chapter 2) and Lieutenant-Colonel Graham Seton Hutchison whose National Workers' Party was virtually a one-man show. Hutchison described Attlee as a Jew and suggested that he contributed to the engineering of a world war, supported the white slave traffic and that he was grinding the poor. After Hutchinson had given an understanding to withdraw and had publicly apologized, Attlee withdrew the case. *The Times*, 22 December 1936; see also *The Daily Telegraph*, 5 November 1936, for a second libel action and see libel action brought by Captain A. H. M. Ramsay against *The New York Times*, *The Manchester Guardian*, 1 August 1941.

favours the maintenance of the *status quo* in that it acts as a deterrent to legitimate criticisms of the Establishment and of traditional institutions.[15] Regardless of the merits of this argument, and of the suggestion that this very severity may be an aspect of the high esteem placed on 'privacy, decency and reputation' by the British public, the law served as a check in Great Britain on a technique that was being exploited with success by Fascist movements in other countries.[16]

In fact the B.U.F. had only one major success.* It will be remembered that Mosley was awarded £5,000 damages in a libel action brought against the Daily News, Ltd. *The Star* had published a leading article on a report of a public debate in which Mosley was alleged to have stated that he would take over the Government by the use of force. Lord Chief Justice Hewart in his summing up asked the jury whether Mosley did not seem like a 'public man of no little courage, no little candour and no little ability'.[17]

Thereafter British Fascism did not fair nearly so well. Mosley brought charges of alleged slander against John Marchbanks, the General Secretary of the National Union of Railwaymen, for remarks made in a speech at Newcastle upon Tyne on 15 July 1934. The inconclusive nature of the verdict was probably more a defeat for the Fascists than an award against the defendants. At Newcastle Marchbanks had held up a document which was alleged to 'represent' secret instructions. These included a 'black list' of trade-union and Socialist leaders and prominent anti-Fascists as well as a plan to infiltrate the trade unions. There was also a scheme to find officers in the armed forces who would join the B.U.F. on the promise of jobs. Finally, it recommended weapons to be used by the Blackshirts.[18] Marchbanks declared, 'We have no objections to people expressing their views with regard to the political and industrial conditions and to show how social evils can be remedied, but we strongly object to any particular party assembling in the guise of a military machine

* John Beckett was awarded £1,000 in a slander suit against an anti-Fascist group which dissolved before he could collect. Colin Cross, *The Fascists in Britain* (1961), p. 144.

with the object of overthrowing by force the constitutional Government of the Country'.[19]

The case did not come before the court until 1936. As it turned out, the statements were based on information supplied by a Charles Dolan, who later published a pamphlet entitled *Mosley Exposed*.[20] Dolan was a Methodist pastor who had been a member of the Communist Party from 1921 to 1927 and had been to prison for political offences. He claimed to have been a paid speaker for the B.U.F. After being sacked, he admitted that he wrote to Mosley announcing his continued loyalty. Dolan also stated that he was trying to get back into the Communist Party. He claimed that he based his information about the weapons on a letter sent out before a meeting at Finsbury Park, and on what he had observed. Sir Patrick Hastings, representing Mosley, suggested that the Finsbury Park document was a forgery. The defence claimed that Dolan approached Marchbanks with information in April 1934, and that Marchbanks took notes and later dictated a statement which became the document. Marchbanks claimed that he said he had held a document which 'represented' secret instructions. The defence then took the position that they had attacked a political party not its leader.

Mr Justice Finlay, in summing up, stated that with the excitement of an audience a speaker may say things that, if he had time to think, he would not say, or that he would modify or qualify. In speaking of damages, he remarked that in political life one had to be prepared for hard knocks. The jury found in favour of Mosley, and awarded him one farthing damages, and directed that each should pay costs. Mr Justice Finlay felt that Marchbanks's words constituted a slander, but not a slander for which an action should be brought, and that the words were so near the truth or so near fair comment, as not to matter. He agreed that each should pay his own costs.[21]

Most of the libel suits were brought against the B.U.F., however. In the autumn of 1936, John C. Little, the chairman, and seven other members of the executive council of the Amalgamated Engineering Union brought action against John

Beckett, as editor of *Action*, B.U.F. Publications Ltd, Jeffcoats Ltd, and Blackfriars Press Ltd, for an alleged libel in the issue of the *Fascist Quarterly* for July 1935, and in a pamphlet, *Fascism and Trade Unionism*, by Beckett. The latter said that the officers of the A.E.U. were able to live in high comfort and to incur unlimited expenses because of their high salaries and so long as they scratched each others' backs. He complained about the lack of democracy in the union. While the workers were struggling at their jobs, the union officers could use their time and money to campaign for re-election. Finally, the author contended that the executive was carrying through proposals to increase annual subscriptions, while at the same time benefits were to be reduced. He concluded that under these officials the wages and salaries of the members had decreased while the wages and salaries of the staff had increased.[22]

Blackfriars Press maintained that they printed the words innocently and that they had apologized. The other defendants denied that the words were defamatory and argued that they were true in substance and fact and pleaded fair comment. Mr Justice Singleton found for the plaintiffs, but his judgment was qualified. For example, he did not find the passage about scratching each others' backs an attack on the honesty of the union officials. Beckett may have been wrong in what he said about elections, but he did not think it defamatory. However, the article and the pamphlet did contain defamatory matter. In awarding damages, however, he did not think that the union officials suffered great injury in view of the fact that the readers would know where the attack was coming from. The officials were awarded a total of £600 and costs.[23]

A more sensational case resulted from an article also written by John Beckett soon after he took over the editorship of *Action* in 1936. Beckett set out to demonstrate that the sources of public communication were subservient to and controlled by the great financial houses in the City. *The Daily Telegraph* was 'almost' the most glaring example. He then tried to prove that Lord Camrose was of Jewish extraction, and that he and the Berry family were associated by business interests and marriage with prominent Jewish businessmen.[24] By the time the case came to court, Beckett had left the B.U.F. and was associated with William Joyce in the National Socialist League.

The plaintiffs alleged that the article had conveyed that Lord Camrose was an unscrupulous, unpatriotic Jewish financier bound to other Jewish financiers and running *The Daily Telegraph* with that interest above all. They claimed that Beckett's allegations were inaccurate, and that there had been no special instructions to the staff of *The Daily Telegraph* to suppress or exaggerate news about the Fascists. Roland Oliver, K.C., in opening the case, stated that Action Press Ltd was a dummy company and that those behind it knew that if they lost the case they had no means to pay any damages. He maintained that Sir Oswald had seen the article before publication and approved it. The defence denied that the words were defamatory – 'there was nothing derogatory in being a Jew or to call a man a Jew' – and also pleaded fair comment and justification.

Not so Beckett who delivered a vitriolic address to the special jury and went on to denounce the B.U.F. He disagreed with the line of defence. When he wrote the article, he believed it was true because of his reliance on those who had given him the information. He never meant it to be the inoffensive article that defence counsel suggested. Unfortunately, he discovered that the two cardinal facts of the article were wrong. He stated, that 'to his mind two of the deadliest insults to address a man were to tell him that he was a Jew and that his financial interests were far greater outside this country than in it'.[25] When he discovered that these facts about Lord Camrose supplied by his 'titled friend' were inaccurate, he wanted to apologize. But he would not apologize for his attack on *The Daily Telegraph* and he attacked the 'Press Lord' system. He chided Mosley for hiding behind an attack of influenza in order to opt out of responsibility for approving the article and for sending his secretary and typist to testify to that effect. He described the 'one share clerks', who were the directors of Action Press Ltd, as those who fought to open the door for Sir Oswald. He concluded by congratulating Lord Camrose for being man enough not to hide behind a £100 company and an attack of influenza. He felt the damages should be small because the article had appeared, 'in a paper of no importance, representing a movement of no importance and with a circulation of no importance'.[26]

The court's dilemma was how to avoid a Fascist trap. If the words were declared defamatory, the Fascists' cause would gain its own peculiar justification, and if not, there might be no limit to their charges. The jury responded by awarding Lord Camrose £12,500 damages and £7,500 to *The Daily Telegraph*. The severity of the verdict, however, created other problems. First, in the majority of cases the printer was by common assent the least guilty party but might be the only defendant of any substance.[27] Action Press was worthless as a company, and Argus Press was left liable for the whole £20,000. The only recourse for Argus Press, a reputable firm that also printed *The Financial News* and *The Observer*, was a second trial against *Action* and Beckett to claim proportional shares of the damages under the Law Reform Act of 1935. Second, there was a danger that, if the jury's award of large-scale damages became a rule, radical and *avant-garde* papers would have difficulty finding printers. Finally, as Roland Oliver pointed out during the proceedings, organizations, in this instance Action Press, could vilify anyone they liked, and if taken to court they could not lose.

Subsequently, B.U.F. publications were more carefully edited, although the tone of the papers was not significantly modified. The difficulty in securing printers was offset by the fact that those who felt libelled knew that they had to contend with worthless companies, a fact that may have deterred others in the past. Hence, when *Action* in 1938 called Tom Driberg, who was then writing under the name of William Hickey in *The Daily Express*, a Jew, Driberg did not go to court. Instead he wrote to *Action* and requested them to publish his denial prominently in two issues, which they did in one issue, and to refrain from repeating the libel.[28] One year later *Blackshirt* printed an article which imputed that Horatio Meyer & Co., Ltd, a furniture firm, was controlled by alien Jews and imposed unfair working conditions. The company started litigation but settled out of court requesting Sanctuary Press, W. &. J. Hosted (publishers), W. E. Luckin (printers) and Michael Goulding to apologize publicly in *Blackshirt* and to contribute £10 each to St Thomas's Hospital.[29]

The B.U.F. was further crippled by financial difficulties, and the measures taken to retain its solvency contributed to the alteration in the nature of the movement. The B.U.F. concentrated its resources in East London for the L.C.C. elections in March 1937. A fortnight after the poll, Mosley held a meeting of his salaried staff and announced that he was reducing their number from 143 to thirty. In a public statement the Leader admitted that the drastic reduction was necessary as a result of the precarious state of finances. He emphasized that no one was expelled and that they were free to give voluntary service.[30] Most of those dismissed, despite their titles, composed the clerical and custodial staff, but two of the movement's inner circle, William Joyce and John Beckett, were also victims. John McNab, the editor of the *Fascist Quarterly* and a close personal friend of Joyce, and Captain Vincent Collier, one of the leading National Propaganda Officers, also left the B.U.F.[31] They joined Beckett and Joyce in founding the National Socialist League.

It soon became evident that more than economies were involved and Alex Scrimgeour, from whom Joyce had solicited funds for the B.U.F., now turned his support to the National Socialist League.[32] In a statement to the Press on the formation of the League, Beckett declared that Mosley was surrounded by flatterers who shielded him from the truth. Mosley was under the impression that the rank and file were contented and that all was well in the districts. On the contrary, according to Beckett, the selection of Parliamentary candidates had caused seething discontent because the districts were not consulted.[33] Joyce denounced Mosley for imitating the Continental Fascists, which was rather surprising considering his own predisposition towards Nazi Germany.[34]

The decision to fire Joyce and Beckett was the result of a long-standing power struggle that had been taking place within the organization and reflected the ascendancy of a paramilitary faction. That this was the case was made clear in a letter published in the provincial Press by a former National Propaganda Officer after he had resigned from the movement. He maintained that the B.U.F. was 'bureaucracy run mad'. The B.U.F. could not be made into a political organization for such attempts were met at every turn by a paramilitary bureaucracy. He found that the political side had been completely subordinated to the Blackshirt organization which controlled the whole movement.[35]

The internal rivalry dates back to the spring of 1934 when, as a result of organizational difficulties, the bureaucratic control of National Headquarters was extended. At the same time, those who were responsible for this extension of control, F. M. Box, John Beckett and Bill Risdon, attempted to re-shape the B.U.F. along the lines of a political party. A military faction led by Neil Francis-Hawkins resisted this effort to re-structure the B.U.F. At first the political faction had the upper hand since they were the more prominent members of the movement. As the likelihood of the B.U.F.'s becoming a political force grew more remote and the interests of the inner circle gained precedent over goals of the movement, the military faction gained favour.

Mosley's eventual response was to formularize the split. At the beginning of 1935 he announced that the B.U.F. would henceforth be divided into a political and a Blackshirt organization. He would retain the leadership of both, but would appoint a different officer to conduct each one. This division, according to the Leader, would preserve the purity of Blackshirt membership and provide an organization for those unable to wear the uniform.[36] The plan never really got off the ground for Mosley announced a further reorganization in March which he spelled out in May 1935.[37] Structurally the emphasis of the movement was to be placed on the single entity. The military faction came out the winner for Francis-Hawkins retained his post as Director of Blackshirt Organization and was made responsible for the organization of the entire movement. The Political Department, as it was now named, remained in existence, but with the restricted function of providing technical instruction for 'Blackshirt officers in political work'. Meanwhile Box was not only relieved of responsibility but, as far as can be ascertained, left the B.U.F. Risdon was appointed Chief Agent but was responsible to Francis-Hawkins.

The consolidation of internal power did not end there, however. In 1936, the Political Department was incorporated into the Department of Organization and Francis-Hawkins was elevated to the newly created post of Director-General of Organization with the responsibility for both the administrative and political machinery of the B.U.F.[38] This was given formal recognition in the movement's first constitution published later that same year.[39] According to former B.U.F. officials and members of the political faction, however, Francis-Hawkins on assuming his new post wanted to demonstrate a superior organizing ability over his predecessor. By stressing the political or electoral role of the B.U.F., a possible way was found to keep the branches functioning and even expanding. The selection of prospective Parliamentary candidates was also a method of rewarding local officers and granting them recognition throughout the movement. The creation of an election fund was a way of soliciting money. As late as July 1939, *Action* was telling members to prepare for a General Election and was boosting the election fund.[40] Finally, with events turning against the B.U.F., the selection of candidates and the contesting of local elections was needed to demonstrate to the public that the B.U.F. was more than a movement for the promotion of violence. This attempt to legitimate the B.U.F. was formalized in a further reorganization in 1938 and by the publication of a new constitution.[41] Meanwhile further resignations had taken place mainly from the political side of the movement.

Hence in 1937, Kingsley Martin was able to write, 'One thing, at any rate, is clear: that Sir Oswald's form of Fascism is making less than no progress in England at the moment'.[42] Events in Huddersfield and Berwick were typical. In Huddersfield three open-air meetings were scheduled for 7 October but audiences failed to gather.[43] In Berwick a meeting of farmers and agricultural employees to be addressed by R. A. Plathen, who was the movement's leader in Scotland, was a fiasco. The meeting was attended by Plathen, the local B.U.F. representative and two reporters. It was closed after half an hour.[44] In addition to the absence of an audience for these meetings, there were no stewards or Fascists present. The situation was hardly better a year later when the B.U.F. staged a propaganda march headed by the Birmingham Drum Corps in Walsall. There were not more than twenty marchers.[45]

The most impressive evidence for the decline of British Fascism was supplied by the Vigilance Committees of the Board of Deputies of British Jews. During the first year of the existence of what was to become the Defence Committee, the Board established groups of observers in various sections of the country which made confidential reports of B.U.F. activities to the London centre. From these reports it is possible to gauge the extent of Mosley's support in the provinces from 1936 to 1939. In Birmingham, there was a smouldering of B.U.F. activity, but on the whole it was insignificant. The reports in *Blackshirt* were exaggerated. Bradford reported that the Fascists had no strength at all. In Manchester, there continued to be a small amount of activity. This included the holding of public meetings, an anti-Semitic campaign mostly carried out by chalking-up and sticky-backs, and private organizational functions such as policy and speaking classes. But the Blackshirts were not considered significant. In Sheffield, the little activity reported was badly supported. Similar reports were filed from other centres in Yorkshire. In Bristol, where during the early days of the movement there had been considerable activity accompanied by disorder, political activity had returned to normal.

The Blackshirts were always rumoured to have a good deal of support in the coastal towns and seaside resorts, but these reports were contradicted by the Board's observers.[46] In Brighton, for example, meetings were still being held and clashes occurred, but the B.U.F. had shut down its local headquarters. However, some centres, like Worthing, continued to thrive despite the general decline in B.U.F. support in other areas. Fascist activity in Scotland and Wales was also negligible.

In Cardiff, the B.U.F. abandoned its usual premises and opened a small shop in a slum street, where Julius Streicher's *Der Stürmer* was displayed. For the most part, however, even anti-Semitic activities were non-existent.[47] In the spring of 1939, the Secretary of the Defence Committee admitted that there was a problem of anti-Semitic pro-Nazi propaganda, but that the B.U.F. had taken a back seat. The principle offender was alleged to be the Militant Christian Patriots, an anti-Zionist organization formed in 1939 which became pro-Hitler and distributed propaganda from Nazi sources until it became disenchanted with that form of Fascism because of the Hitler–Stalin pact.[48]

Reports in Fascist papers and from anti-Fascist observers of Fascist progress in certain areas prompted special investigations by the Board of Deputies. The first was undertaken in October 1937, in Norfolk and Lincolnshire. The B.U.F. had made extravagant claims of progress in Norfolk, and there were three prospective Parliamentary candidates there. It also claimed a favourable reception in Lincoln, where a candidate had been put forward. The Norwich and district agent of the Labour Party denied the B.U.F. claim, as did a prominent Conservative J.P. and former managing editor of the *Eastern Daily Press*. The Labour agent argued that trade-unionism and the Free Church were strong counter-influences in the area. In the countryside, the Fascists had the support of a few farmers, but it was doubted whether in an election these men would abandon their former political leanings. The Conservative stated that B.U.F. policy in the area made no references to the Jews. He could not understand the Dowager Lady Downe's candidature for the B.U.F. She was a lady who had great charm and was well-liked, but he doubted that even her personal popularity would gain many votes. A young woman employed in the estate office of Lord Walsingham, who had no sympathy whatever with the British Fascists, was the candidate for South-West Norfolk. The investigator's own survey of the countryside revealed few, if any, traces of B.U.F. penetration.[49]

The investigator interviewed the editor and chief reporter of the *Lincolnshire Echo* and concluded that there was even less cause for apprehension there. The maximum number of adherents in Lincoln or the area was about 200. Mosley, personally, was the only Fascist who had aroused any interest. His meetings were well-attended, but largely out of curiosity. The investigator also talked with a prominent member of the aristocracy who resided in the area and whose circle was described as 'influential'. She stated that Mosley was not trusted by her circle because of his past record. He was also a man of such erratic nature as to lead one to believe that he had developed megalomania.[50]

A second investigation was undertaken during the spring of 1939, as a result of anti-Fascist reports about the activities of Lady Pearson in Sandwich, Canterbury, Dover, Deal and Wolmer. Interviews with a number of working-class people elicited the remark from one man, that he'd 'sooner give tuppence to a Jew-boy any day than buy a copy of the *Blackshirt*'. The sentiment was endorsed by others. The investigator interviewed one Blackshirt who was a labourer, seventy-five years old, of Scots ancestry, and who had lived in Sandwich for thirty-five years. He wore the B.U.F. badge, but seemed more anxious to hide it than to display it. He claimed that he joined to 'give the rising generation a chance'. On further investigation, it was discovered that he was Lady Pearson's gardener. Despite Lady Pearson's efforts, Fascism was reported as making little headway in Sandwich. The Blackshirts would hold an occasional meeting in the market place, where once they had held many. At the date of the report there had not been a meeting for some time. The membership of the local branch was about half a dozen and it was necessary to import speakers from Canterbury. Young men and the working class in general opposed Mosley because he stood for dictatorship. The investigator interviewed guests at a very 'county teashop' owned by Lady Pearson. The clientele was drawn from the local well-to-do residents. They regarded Mosley as a turn-coat, and as someone who was not to be trusted. His matrimonial adventures also seem to have told against him.[51]

In Canterbury, the Blackshirts had a relatively prosperous-looking bookshop close to Kings School. It was stocked not only with British Union publications, but with the propaganda of the Imperial Fascist League, Britons Publishing Company and the Militant Christian Patriots. In the window, there was a centrepiece of a hammer and sickle interlaced with a Star of David. The investigator was unable to estimate the membership, but concluded that the Fascists were fairly active and more numerous than in Sandwich. In Deal and Wolmer, the Fascists based in Canterbury were active in the summer months in an attempt to capture the holiday-makers. They had no effect on the local population. There was no Fascist headquarters and seemingly no Fascist activity in Dover.[52]

Although the Fascists steadily lost ground, much of the tension in East London remained. This was true despite the Public Order Act, the all-night patrols of police and the large reinforcements of police drafted into the area when there was a probability of disorder.[53] In part, this was accounted for by the B.U.F.'s election campaigns, as well as its peace campaigns. In 1937 the Metropolitan police had to supervise 11,804 meetings and processions of which over 7,000 were Fascist or anti-Fascist.[54] Not only was this an increase over 1936, but the total rose by over 700 to 12,483 in 1938.[55]

Equally ominous were the provocations and anti-Semitic incidents which were becoming a part of the daily routine of East End life. In streets that were solely or mostly occupied by Jewish shopkeepers, it was the practice of Fascist gangs to break windows. Jews walking in the streets would be greeted with offensive remarks, and if they showed their resentment they would be physically attacked. In January 1937, a Jewish coster and a woman were pushing barrows along one street when they were attacked by some forty Mosleyites, who tipped the barrows over. The police arrested three people, two of whom were discharged and one fined.

A Fascist passing down a street in Limehouse on 5 March shouted, 'Heil Mosley', and was greeted by his comrades on the pavement who shouted, 'Perish Judah'. Two weeks later the Secretary of the Hackney Citizens' Council, while driving a van down Mile End Road, was attacked by a large party of Black-shirts shouting anti-Jewish slogans. They clambered onto the van and struck him in the face. The following month a number of Fascists assembled at a street corner in Limehouse and threw rotten oranges at passing Jews. It was reported that on that same night a gang of men using an axe and stones had smashed several stained glass windows at a synagogue in Leytonstone. The gang, numbering six, were dressed in black jackets and flannel trousers.[56]

This period was also distinguished by the movement's electoral activity. This was not only an attempt to circumscribe the limitations imposed by the Public Order Act. Nor was it only an excuse to provoke violence, although it has been interpreted as being utilized for that purpose. It has already been shown that the initial decision was based on other factors. As early as December 1933, reports circulated that the B.U.F. would run 500 candidates at the next General Election.[57] Again in the spring of 1934, it was reported that the B.U.F. planned to oppose Lord Winterton at the next General Election.[58] At the same time members of the inner circle had become convinced that the movement would not be taken seriously unless it was prepared to present an alternative government.[59] In the autumn, it was announced that the energies of the movement would be devoted to parliamentary and not municipal elections.[60] But the Blackshirts did not contest the General Election of 1935, although they campaigned throughout the country.

In the spring of 1936, months before the enactment of the Public Order Act, Mosley announced that the B.U.F. would contest the next General Election and that candidates would be selected shortly. In November, the first 100 constituencies were announced and the first of nine lists of candidates was published soon after.[61]

The B.U.F. reversed its decision not to contest municipal elections in July 1936 and the entire resources of the movement were devoted to the L.C.C. elections in March 1937.[62] In January it was announced that six candidates would stand in Bethnal Green South-West, Shoreditch, and Limehouse. Alexander Raven Thomson and E. G. 'Mick' Clarke were selected for Bethnal Green South-West. Thomson held the position of Director of Policy and was the Parliamentary candidate for Hackney South. He did not have a reputation as a particularly good speaker. Clarke, on the other hand, was described by one ex-B.U.F. official as a 'terrific mob-orator'. A furniture worker, in his twenties, Clarke was also a B.U.F. Parliamentary candidate in Bethnal Green. He became a Propaganda Officer and was known as the 'Julius Streicher of the B.U.F.', a label that was probably due to his parading about in a full-length black leather great-coat and to his rabid anti-Semitism.

Anne Brock Griggs and Charles Wegg-Prosser were the candidates for Limehouse. Mrs Griggs who was in her early twenties, was the wife of an architect and the mother of two children. Like Raven Thomson, she was a professional Fascist, holding the position of Chief Women's organizer and being one of the two leading women speakers. She was the prospective B.U.F. Parliamentary candidate for Poplar South and was later interned under the Defence Regulations. Wegg-Prosser, a young man from a prominent English Catholic family, had evidently been a Blackshirt for some years in Hertfordshire.[63] His background was a political asset in East London in playing the Irish off against the Jews. He had a short career as a rising Blackshirt orator before he broke with the movement four months after the L.C.C. elections. He wrote a denunciation of Mosley and the B.U.F., which was subsequently published as a pamphlet by the Jewish People's Council.[64] Mosley selected J. A. Bailey and William Joyce to stand in Shoreditch. Bailey was a forty-one-year-old East London woodworker, who had collected a personal following. A veteran of the First World War, Bailey was also the prospective B.U.F. Parliamentary candidate for Shoreditch. He broke with Mosley some months after the election. Mosley was unwilling to risk his own reputation by standing as a candidate. But he put forward the movement's number-two speaker, Joyce, a formidable platform orator by any standards.

The official campaign opened early in February. The groundwork, of course, had been prepared for several months. The

Public Order Act had placed severe restrictions on B.U.F. activities but the Mosleyites altered rather than discarded their previous political style. Individual acts of intimidation were prevalent, and although uniforms and processions were banned street-corner meetings were permitted. In the autumn, a number of official branch headquarters, renamed Black Halls, were opened and efforts were made to contact the locals and stir up dissension.[65]

According to Mosley, the Fascists chose to contest the L.C.C. elections in the East End because 'the enemy' should be attacked where his 'corrupt power' was the strongest.[66] Wegg-Prosser, after leaving the B.U.F., wrote that Mosley had written the election addresses for all six candidates.[67] These were provocative documents. Bailey and Joyce, for example, were pledged, 'to fight to the end for the people's cause against the tyranny of Jewish power'. Their election address was divided into sections in the following order: 'Our Challenge to Jewry', 'Mind Britain's Business' and 'Let East London Lead'.[68] There was no mention of Fascism or the corporate state.

Mosley backed his candidates with the resources of the National Headquarters. In Shoreditch alone, fifty-seven meetings were scheduled with as many as five a night. Fascist speakers were imported into the area, including Mosley, Beckett and Tommy Moran. The campaign was abusive. George Dunlop, a twenty-seven-year-old clerk, who had two previous convictions for his activities as a Fascist speaker, referred to the Jews at an election meeting as 'scum' and the 'sweepings of the ghetto'. The police ordered him to close the meeting, but he refused. After several requests he was arrested.[69]

The results as announced on 6 March 1937 were as follows:

*Bethnal Green (South-West)*

| | |
|---|---|
| T. Dawson (Labour) | 7,777 |
| Mrs R. S. Keeling (Labour) | 7,756 |
| A. Raven Thomson (B.U.F.) | 3,028 |
| E. G. Clarke (B.U.F.) | 3,022 |

| | |
|---|---|
| A. J. Irvine (Liberal) | 2,298 |
| H. K. Sadler (Liberal) | 2,228 |

*Stepney (Limehouse)*

| | |
|---|---|
| R. Coppock (Labour) | 8,272 |
| Miss H. M. Whately (Labour) | 8,042 |
| V. G. Weeple (Municipal Reform) | 2,542 |
| G. E. Abrahams (Municipal Reform) | 2,431 |
| Mrs A. Brock Griggs (B.U.F.) | 2,086 |
| C. Wegg-Prosser (B.U.F.) | 2,086 |

*Shoreditch*

| | |
|---|---|
| Mrs H. Girling (Labour) | 11,098 |
| S. W. Jeger (Labour) | 11,069 |
| S. L. Price (Municipal Progressive) | 3,303 |
| R. S. Falk (Municipal Progressive) | 3,217 |
| William Joyce (B.U.F.) | 2,564 |
| J. A. Bailey (B.U.F.) | 2,492 |
| C. E. Taylor (Independent Labour) | 385 |

There was no change in the three constituencies. Taking into account that there were two seats to fill in each constituency, so that each elector had two votes, and that an elector may have cast only one ballot or may have split his vote between two parties, the Fascists polled 17·8 per cent of the total votes cast. At least 7,678 people voted for B.U.F. candidates. They made their best showing in Bethnal Green where Raven Thomson and Clarke received 23·17 per cent of the votes and finished ahead of the Liberals. In Limehouse Mrs Brock Griggs and Wegg-Prosser finished at the bottom of the poll with 16·3 per cent of the vote. Joyce and Bailey were the least successful, polling only 14·8 per cent of the vote in Shoreditch.

Mosley would never acknowledge or believe in defeat. When he saw the results of the polls, he sat down with pencil and paper and shortly announced in triumph that the B.U.F. had won a greater victory than Hitler in his first election contest.[70] In a public statement, Mosley argued that the Nazis in 1928 had polled only 2·7 per cent of the vote, but that they were able to return twelve members to the Reichstag. In 1930, he continued, eighteen per cent of the poll gave the Nazis 107 members of the Reichstag. As far as the British Union was concerned, there were factors adverse to any new movement. Since the B.U.F. was a youth movement, very few of the members had the right to vote. Mosley then attacked the electoral system. He concluded that the Blackshirts in their first election obtained the best result recorded by a Fascist or National Socialist movement in any great country.[71]

Despite the fact that nearly 8,000 people voted for Fascist candidates, their showing was quite poor. The B.U.F. had concentrated its resources and energies in the area where they expected the most support. The result was an increased, but primarily anti-Fascist, poll. If the B.U.F.'s strength was in youth, it was in youth under the voting age and probably the more susceptible or bored teenager. Mosley, in his comparisons, neglected to mention that Hitler and the other Fascists had been contesting national elections.

The B.U.F. electoral activities did not end with the L.C.C. elections. Fascist candidates stood in the municipal elections of 1937 and 1938. National headquarters, however, reverted to its 1934 ruling and the candidates fought the elections on their own initiative and out of their own pockets, relying on local resources and personnel.[72] Moreover, the candidates nominated were local small-fry. The only ones with some prominence in the movement were Mick Clarke in Bethnal Green, J. A. Bailey in Shoreditch, Richard Plathen, who stood in Edinburgh, and a prospective Parliamentary candidate in Sheffield.

In 1937, sixty-six candidates stood in twenty-nine boroughs with a total of eighty-six seats. Forty of them contested seats in Bethnal Green, Shoreditch and Stepney. Outside London, seventeen candidates stood in sixteen wards. Again no B.U.F. candidate was successful. Their most impressive results were in Bethnal Green East where nine Fascist candidates polled between 1,805 and 1,434 votes, or 21·4 per cent of the total vote cast. But even here, the B.U.F. candidate who came highest among the unsuccessful candidates was 247 votes below the lowest Labour Party vote. The Fascists finished at the top of the poll of unsuccessful candidates in four other East London wards. They were, however, well below the lowest Socialist vote. In the provinces, the highest Fascist vote was recorded in Castle ward in Bridgnorth, Suffolk, where the candidate polled 183 votes in a straight fight against a Conservative who received 496 votes.[73] In eight of the provincial contests, the B.U.F. polled less than 100 votes. The lowest vote was that of a Fascist candidate in a Northampton ward, who polled twenty-seven votes compared to the winning Labour candidate's 1,191 votes.[74] Counting the votes cast for the highest B.U.F. candidates in the poll in their constituencies, at least 8,412 people voted Fascist with 8,190 of this vote in London.*

The Mosley publications followed the example of the Press in general and gave the elections little publicity. After the results, however, the *Blackshirt* announced that the vote was extremely heartening. The results were viewed, with one or two exceptions, as being better than those of any other new movement at its first attempt.[75]

Despite the poor showing, the B.U.F. encouraged its district organizations to fight the municipal elections in November 1938.[76] This campaign, however, was even less ambitious than the previous year's. The difference was that the Blackshirts did not contest borough elections in East London with the result that twenty-three candidates contested twenty-seven seats in twenty-two constituencies.† They received over 200 votes in four wards and less than 100 votes in ten wards. The highest vote was 242 in Manchester, Colleyhurst, while in two contests Fascists received only twenty-three votes each.[77] They did, however, gain one success in Eye, Suffolk, the area of the earlier tithe disputes. Five candidates contested four seats and the Fascist with 179 votes was fourth behind three Conservatives and thirteen votes ahead of the Liberal.[78] Counting votes

---

* These figures can only be taken as a rough indicator, for in constituencies where there were multiple seats it was possible for an elector to cast his vote(s) for Fascists other than the most successful one.

† The municipal elections in Chingford in April 1938 are included in the November results.

for the highest B.U.F. candidate in each ward, 2,401 people voted Fascist.[79]

These local elections were fought on local issues with the B.U.F. exploiting anti-Semitism where possible. The three Parliamentary by-elections that the B.U.F. was to contest were fought mainly on an anti-war platform which differed little from earlier peace campaigns at the time of the Abyssinian and Rhineland crises. In March 1938, Mosley launched a 'Stop the War' campaign in response to the reaction to Hitler's take-over of Austria.[80] In July, a 'British First' campaign was opened with four marches and nineteen meetings in London.[81] The Board of Deputies recorded that the campaign was a flop. They looked forward to further defections from the Fascist ranks arguing that the purpose of the campaign had been to arouse the drooping faith of Mosley's followers.[82]

British Union activities did indeed decline over the following twelve months. The ban on processions continued in East London and further limitations were placed on processions held in other parts of London. Moreover, the Fascists were refused the use of halls for meetings. Nevertheless, Mosley made it clear where he stood. Chamberlain's negotiations with Hitler were described as an act of courage. According to the Leader, the Labour Party and the 'jackals of Jewish Finance' were trying to rob Britain and Europe of peace.[83] The pre-war peace drive culminated at a meeting at Earl's Court in July 1939. The meeting had added significance for the B.U.F. since it was the first large hall that it had been able to hire in London over the past year. According to *Action*, now edited by Raven Thomson, 'The conspiracy of Left and Right had, however, overlooked the largest hall of all – at Earl's Court – presumably because it was never thought that the British Union would dare the attempt.'[84]

For a few hours, the B.U.F. was able to resume its old tactics of publicity and propaganda. The meeting displayed the standard histrionics minus the uniforms. The Blackshirts claimed an audience of 30,000 and maintained that it was the largest ever to attend an indoor meeting. The Press reported an attendance of 20,000 people.[85] It was, however, the largest indoor meeting that the Fascists had ever organized and the size of the audience was impressive by any standards. According to *The Manchester Guardian*, the most significant part of the meeting, apart from its size and enthusiasm, were the jeers which spontaneously followed the reference to Churchill and the even greater support of the audience for Mosley in his attack on Baldwin.[86] The Jews were attacked, but mainly by implication. Mosley, however, warned that Britons would not die in a 'Jews' quarrel'.[87]

The second phase of the peace campaign began with Britain's entry into the war. Mosley issued a statement that the British Union stood for peace, but requested members not to hinder the war effort and to cooperate as the law demanded.[88] Blackshirt meetings were now peace meetings and the slogan was 'Join the British Union and work for Peace'.[89] Mosley employed a new gimmick at his public meetings by asking his audience to vote for or against the war. At the Stoll Theatre in London, Mosley spoke to an estimated 2,400 people. He argued that the British people had not been consulted on whether they wanted war and he demanded a referendum.[90]

The Emergency Powers Regulations placed further restrictions on propaganda activities. Processions were banned in London after the start of the war. The police were more diligent at Fascist meetings. In October 1939, for example, Anne Brock Griggs was arrested and bound over. She was charged under the Public Order Act and under Section 39B of the Defence Regulations for, 'Endeavouring to influence public opinion in a manner likely to be prejudicial to the defence of the realm.' Two more Fascists were fined for resisting the police by going to her aid.[91] In May 1940, prior to the internment of leading Mosleyites, the police embarked on what appeared to be a concentrated campaign against the B.U.F. This included numerous arrests, the closing of meetings and the refusal to grant permission to hold meetings.[92]

The B.U.F., however, was not the only organization advocating selective pacifism. Nor did the Public Order Act and various other restrictions solely affect its activities. Included among the B.U.F.'s competitors were the National Socialist League, the British Council Against European Commitments, the British Peace Party, the ventures associated with Captain A. H. M. Ramsay, Conservative M.P. for Peebles, and the Link. Following the purge of the National Headquarters staff of the B.U.F. in the spring of 1937, Joyce, Beckett and a few close associates founded the National Socialist League. Joyce with his great store of energy and pathological hatred of the Jews spent almost every evening on the platform. On two occasions he was charged with assault but both cases were dismissed. Beckett and John MacNab published the League's organ, the *Helmsman*. They had to make a living by other means, however, and the organization was left in Joyce's hands. There were never more than two or three hundred members, about a hundred of whom were in London.[93]

British National Socialism as conceived by Joyce was intensely nationalistic and the League was 'openly and unashamedly imperialistic'. Political and economic reform was based on Fascist and Guild Socialist principles and differed little from those set forth by Arnold Leese's Imperial Fascist League. In foreign affairs, Joyce prescribed an alliance between Britain and Germany so that with the assistance of Italy a bulwark against the twin Jewish manifestations, Bolshevism and International Finance, could be formed.[94]

In September 1938, Joyce joined forces with Viscount Lymington to form the British Council Against European Commitments. The Council was essentially a coordinating body and the National Socialist League retained its former identity as did Lymington's English Array, a secret society which stressed racial purity in its programme.[95] A third affiliate was a group called the League of Loyalists.[96] Beckett and Viscount Lymington published a monthly, *New Pioneer*, which championed non-involvement and was Fascist and anti-Semitic in sympathy. The venture, however, amounted to little for Lymington and Beckett joined forces with the Marquis of Tavistock, later the Duke of Bedford, in the British Peace Party. Beckett and presumably Lymington had by now broken with Joyce on the grounds that greater moderation was necessary especially over the Jewish question.[97] Joyce had told Beckett that if war broke out he would fight for Hitler because the war would be against Jewry.[98]

The British Peace Party incorporated many of the proposals for monetary and parliamentary reform of the Social Credit Movement in which the Marquis of Tavistock had been active.[99] Although the Party counted sincere pacifists among its members, it also included, according to Tavistock, those who would not fight to defend Russia or Poland.[100] The Party's organ, *The People's Post*, proclaimed: 'We have no right to say that Hitler is hopeless before a fair test has been made of him and a fair test has never yet been made.'[101] The Party's activities were confined to holding occasional meetings, publishing and the contesting of one by-election. Therefore, it did not need an extensive organization. Tavistock was chairman, Beckett secretary and Ben Greene, whose pacifism led him to the radical right, was treasurer.* These three along with Viscount Lymington and John Scanlon formed an executive committee. Scanlon was a journalist and author of several books on the Labour Party. He had been associated with the B.U.F. and wrote weekly articles on labour matters for its publications under the name of John Emery. The eccentric explorer and Arabist, H. St John B. Philby, stood as the Party's candidate at a by-election in Hythe in 1939. The campaign was conducted on an anti-war platform stressing the need for negotiations and warning against an arms race.[102] Among his supporters at the by-election were Lady Domville, wife of Admiral Sir Barry Domville – the leader of the Link, and Captain Vincient Collier, the former B.U.F. and National Socialist League Officer. Philby forfeited his deposit. He returned to the Middle East and was on his way to the United States in 1940 when he was detained under the Defence

---

* Greene was interned in 1940 and released in 1941. He filed suit against the Home Secretary on the grounds that he had been falsely detained and libelled but the case fell through when the chief witness for the prosecution turned out to be a Government agent. *The Manchester Guardian*, 6 April 1943.

Regulations – an order that was later unconditionally revoked.[103]

Captain A. H. M. Ramsay participated in three ventures in order to propagate his beliefs. According to Lord Vansittart his meetings were imbued with rabid Nazism and anti-Semitism.[104] The Coordinating Committee was formed by a number of right-wing groups including the British Empire Union, the National Citizens' Union, the British Democratic Party and the Militant Christian Patriots to present a united front against Communism.[105] But the organizations fell out in the autumn of 1938 and the Committee was abandoned early in 1939. Both the Right Club and the Nordic League were private organizations with no public activities. The Right Club had a membership of 350 including the American, Tyler Kent, and Anna Wolkoff.[106] It was widely known that the Duke of Wellington, who was President of the anti-Communist Liberty Restoration League and President of the pro-Franco Spanish Children's Repatriation, presided at several of their meetings. A meeting of the Nordic League addressed by Ramsay in April 1939 was chaired by a member of the B.U.F. supported by Brigadier-General R. B. D. Blakeney and E. H. Cole of the Imperial Fascist League.[107]

Two groups that ostensibly promoted Anglo-German relations but in doing so preached selected pacifism were the Anglo-German Fellowship and the Link. Despite their close association it is important to distinguish between them. The Fellowship was founded as the Anglo-German Association after the First World War to improve relationships between the two countries. The original president, Lord Reading, resigned over the Nazi persecution of the Jews and the society fell into abeyance until reconstituted in October 1935. In 1937, included in its 700 subscribers were sixty members of both Houses of Parliament and three directors of the Bank of England.[108] In 1938, it had nearly 1,000 members. Many of them were reactionaries who saw Nazism as a crusade against Bolshevism or who favoured the Munich agreement. For example, Lord Mount Temple was Chairman of the Anti-Socialist and Anti-Communist Union and was also Chairman of the Fellowship.

He stated in the House of Lords in 1937 that, 'It will not be Germany's fault if there is war, but the fault of other powers who have not treated her as she should be treated.'[109] In November 1938, he resigned his office, but not his membership, in protest to the retaliation of the Germans against the Jews as a result of the murder of a German attaché in Paris.[110] Yet Lord Mount Temple, along with other members of the Fellowship, signed a letter to *The Times* defending the Munich agreement. The letter, which incidentally was sent from the headquarters of the Link, was also signed by Lord Londonderry, Lord Redesdale, Captain Ramsay and Admiral Sir Barry Domville, the founder and Chairman of the Link.[111]

The Link was organized to propagandize against war with Germany.[112] The Home Secretary stated in 1939 that it was being used as an instrument of the German Propaganda Service and that one of its active organizers had received money from Germany.[113] This was denied by the Link which admitted at the time that a weekly bulletin printed in Germany had been distributed.[114]

The Link was founded in September 1937, by Domville and E. C. Carroll, a former editor of the British Legion paper, who had been editing the Anglo-German Review which was thereafter utilized by the Link.[115] Domville was already on the Council of the Fellowship but felt that there was a need to coordinate those Anglo-German friendship organizations already in existence and to provide an organization to enlist popular support.[116] He had an impressive career behind him having served as Director of Naval Intelligence, President of the Royal Naval College at Greenwich and Vice-Admiral Commanding the War College. His autobiography was suitably titled, *From Admiral to Cabin Boy*, for he was interned under Defence Regulation 18B, which he interpreted to have been a part of the Jewish plot for world domination as outlined in the *Protocols of the Learned Elders of Zion*.[117]

With the exception of the British Peace Party, however, the B.U.F. was the only organization to test their case at the polls. Two Parliamentary by-elections were contested in the winter of

1940 at which the Fascists attempted to make peace or non-involvement the issue. Tommy Moran was nominated to stand in the Silvertown Division of West Ham and Sydney Allen in North-East Leeds. Moran was a National Headquarters organizer and speaker, who had been selected as the prospective Parliamentary candidate for Merthyr. Moran, an ex-miner, was an engineer by trade and a former light-heavyweight boxing champion in the Royal Navy.[118] He resigned as secretary of his local Labour party in 1933 and on joining the B.U.F. he founded the Derby branch. Allen was a poultry dealer, a First World War veteran and an early member of the B.U.F. As for their constituencies, Silvertown was a working-class area with a strong Labour bias and North-East Leeds was predominantly lower middle class in an urban centre with the third largest Jewish population in England. Silvertown had given the Labour candidate a majority of just under 14,000 votes in 1935. Harry Pollitt, who was now the leader of the British Communist Party, was also contesting the seat. The Conservatives had held North-East Leeds for over twenty years and they had had a majority of just under 12,000 in 1935.

Mosley, speaking in support of Moran at Silvertown, called for an immediate peace and championed the establishment of 'British Socialism through the British Revolution'. This meant the establishment of National Socialism as opposed to International Socialism.[119] In Leeds, Mosley again advocated immediate peace. According to the Leader, the B.U.F. was only interested in fighting where the Empire and Britain were menaced and in leaving each great nation to its natural sphere of influence.[120] In his election address Allen declared himself a 'peace candidate'. Allen stated that Mosley and every member of the B.U.F. who was old enough fought in the First World War, that this was no quarrel of the British people but one of Jewish Finance. The Conservatives tricked the British people into war by promising that Russia would be on their side. Instead, there was the 'biggest double cross of history'. He concluded that Britain should spend its money on rebuilding rather than on war.[121]

The campaigns passed without incident and Moran and Allen were soundly defeated. In Silvertown, both Pollitt and Moran lost their deposits. Labour retained the seat with 14,343 votes, while Pollitt and Moran polled 966 and 151 votes respectively.[122] Allen had a straight fight in Leeds and received 722 votes to the Conservative's 23,882 votes. After the result was declared, Allen refused to shake hands with the victor. He announced that this was a fight not a sham battle and that the 'British Union does not shake hands with its enemies'.[123]

Commenting on the Silvertown election, *Action* admitted that Moran had received a very poor vote. The paper declared that the B.U.F. had no excuses, but argued that the election had been fought in a Labour stronghold, that no attempt had been made to answer the British Union case and that the 'defenders of patriotism' had suffered at the hands of Jewish power turning the truth upside down.[124] In analysing the Leeds by-election, *Action* saw a considerable advance over Silvertown, but admitted that the vote remained small. *Action* went on to claim that the Conservative candidate never had an audience of over 200, while there were nearly 1,000 at Mosley's meeting. *Action* thereby concluded that seventy-two per cent of those who had heard Blackshirt speakers had voted for the British Union.[125]

The B.U.F. contested its third Parliamentary by-election at Middleton and Prestwich just prior to the detention of the movement's leaders in May 1940. The Fascist candidate was Frederick Haslam, a forty-three-year-old engineering designer and First World War veteran who had been a B.U.F. member for four years. Middleton and Prestwich was a safe Conservative seat and Haslam had a straight fight with the National Government candidate when the I.L.P. withdrew. His programme was based on the standard B.U.F. case, that Great Britain should stop fighting because the interests involved were largely those of International Jewish Finance. Mosley spoke at two meetings. The second one had to be closed after half an hour when the crowd wrecked the platform and loud-speakers.[126] The poll took place on the day of Mosley's detention. Haslam received 418 votes, the Conservative 32,036.[127]

Although all three B.U.F. candidates had lost their deposits, the Fascists planned to contest still another by-election. It was announced that Mick Clarke would stand in the by-election in Bow and Bromley caused by the death of George Lansbury. Clarke, however, was detained under Defence Regulation 18B before the election took place.[128]

Why then did the B.U.F. contest the elections? Whatever the results it was likely to receive some publicity. There was an electoral truce among the established parties so that in all probability the poll would be low and the B.U.F. percentage higher than in ordinary circumstances. There was also a remote possibility of catching the voters napping and the B.U.F. would have the opportunity of picking up protest votes from several sources. They were standing against a Communist in Silvertown and there had been the likelihood of an I.L.P. candidate in Middleton and Prestwich. A victory over either candidate would have been of some value. The particular constituencies were possible pockets of B.U.F. support. Although Silvertown was a solid Labour stronghold, it was in reasonable proximity to the centre of B.U.F. activities in East London. The same would have been true for Bow and Bromley and, in addition, the B.U.F. had been active there. Moreover, Mick Clarke would have been a known candidate. North-East Leeds was predominantly lower middle class and the B.U.F. had been campaigning to enlist support from that sector of the population. Leeds itself had a large Jewish population. Middleton and Prestwich was in Lancashire, which the B.U.F. considered to be a provincial stronghold. Electoral activity also had an organizational value. It assured the faithful that the movement would remain active as long as it was permitted to do so. Mosley, on the eve of his detention, stated that he did not cease political activity because he wanted to provide people with an alternative to the present Government, if and when they desired to make peace. He also declared that if Britain was invaded he would fight for Britain.[129] Finally, and despite Mosley's above statement, his continued political activity assured the Continental Fascists of his support. Mosley's greatest display of patriotism would have been to cease political activity for the duration of the war.

The Government permitted the B.U.F. to function for eight months after the war began before detaining those 'active as organizers in furthering the objects under the Union', which was deemed under Emergency Powers Defence Regulation 18B to be prejudicial to the public safety or defence of the realm. Among those detained in the first round-up were Mosley, Raven Thomson, Francis-Hawkins, George Sutton, Bill Risdon, B. D. E. Donovan, the head of the London Command, his assistant, Captain U. A. Hick, Mick Clarke, Olive Hawks, Hector McKechnie, who was Director of Meetings, and seven prospective Parliamentary candidates.[130]

A further order, early in July, under Defence Regulation 18A, suspended the activities of the B.U.F. as an active political movement. The Mosleyites issued a final circular telling their members that Britain was now threatened by invasion and they should do everything that they could do to help the nation. National Headquarters was declared closed except for the maintenance of records, and national and district activities were suspended.[131]

Why were some 700 members of the B.U.F. detained?[132] It was not a crime against the state to be a Fascist. Nor, as *Action* suggested, was Defence Regulation 18B aimed specifically at Mosley or the B.U.F. because it was alleged that they were under foreign influence.[133] Hugh Ross Williamson, a prospective Labour Party candidate who appeared on B.U.F. platforms and wrote for *Action* in 1939, later reported a feeling in Labour Party circles that Mosley's detention was made a condition of Labour's participation in the Government, an explanation partly subscribed to by Williamson himself.[134] This was unlikely, for both the Government and the Labour Party were too busy to quarrel over a discredited politician and a negligible political force.[135]

Before the Defence Regulation 18B Advisory Committee, Mosley stated that there appeared to be two grounds for detaining the B.U.F. officers. First, there was the suggestion that they were traitors, and second that their propaganda was undermining civilian morale. The Chairman, Norman Birkett, replied, 'speaking for myself, you can entirely dismiss the first suggestion'.[136] Those detained under 18B were not detained because they were traitors. Mosley's second reason comes nearer to the spirit of the Defence Regulation. They were detained because their views and activities had become prejudicial to the public safety or the defence of the realm. They were preaching anti-war propaganda and anti-Semitism at a time when Great Britain was nearing a crisis, and this could have had a detrimental effect on the morale of the nation.

## NOTES

1. Viscount Simon, *Retrospect* (1948), p. 216; 395 *H. C. Deb. ss.* (1 December 1943), col. 471.
2. *Report of the Commissioner of Police of the Metropolis for the Year 1937* (Cmd 5761), pp. 12–13.
3. See Chapter 8.
4. 1936 1 K. B. Duncan *v.* Jones (16 October 1936); see 444 *H. C. Deb. ss.* (24 November 1947), col. 1755.
5. *Blackshirt*, 31 May 1935.
6. *ibid.*, 28 February 1936.
7. Professor R. S. T. Chorley, *The Threat to Civil Liberties* (1938), p. 7.
8. *Blackshirt*, 9 August 1935.
9. *ibid.*, 30 August 1935.
10. *Action*, 25 February 1939.
11. *The Bulletin and Scots Pictorial*, 15 September 1937; *Edinburgh Evening Dispatch*, 16 September 1937.
12. *Action*, 17 December 1938.
13. *ibid.*, 25 February 1939.
14. *ibid.*, 14 December 1939.
15. See, for example, Peter Hood, *Ourselves and the Press, A Social Study of News, Advertising and Propaganda* (1939), pp. 45–6; Kingsley Martin, *Fascism, Democracy and the Press* (1938), p. 14.
16. David Riesman, 'Democracy and Defamation: Fair Game and Fair Comment I', *Columbia Law Review* (September 1942), pp. 1120–21, 1090, 1092–111; see also Herman Rausching, *The Redemption of Democracy* (1941), p. 67; Edmond Taylor, *The Strategy of Terror* (1940), p. 40.
17. See Chapter 7.
18. *The Daily Telegraph*, 16 July 1934; *Newcastle Journal*, 16 July 1934.
19. *The Times*, 4 February 1936.

20. C. Dolan, *Mosley Exposed* (n.d.).
21. 'Mosley *v.* Marchbanks', *The Times* (*Law Reports*), 4–8 February 1936; *The Manchester Guardian*, 4–8 February 1936.
22. John Beckett, 'Fascism and Trade Unions', *Fascist Quarterly* (July 1935), p. 332.
23. *The Times* (*Law Reports*), 4–6, 10 November 1936.
24. *Action*, 2 April 1936.
25. *The Times* (*Law Reports*), 16 October 1937.
26. *ibid.*
27. *World Press News*, 2 December 1937.
28. *Action*, 5 March 1938; 16 April 1938.
29. *Blackshirt*, March 1939; *East London Blackshirt*, May 1939.
30. *Blackshirt*, 20 March 1937.
31. For the relationship between Joyce and McNab see J. A. Cole, *Lord Haw-Haw* (1964), especially pp. 55–92.
32. *ibid.*, p. 76.
33. *The Morning Post*, 13 April 1937.
34. *ibid.*
35. S. Probyn, *Birmingham Evening Dispatch*, 9 July 1937.
36. *Blackshirt*, 18 January 1935; there was a model for the B.U.F. in the Nazi Party with its carefully organized political structure and its storm troops division.
37. *ibid.*, 24 May 1935.
38. *ibid.*, 10 January 1936.
39. B.U.F., *Constitution and Regulations* (1936).
40. *Action*, 15 July 1935.
41. *Blackshirt*, 22 January 1936; British Union, *Constitution and Rules* (1938).
42. *New Statesman and Nation*, 10 April 1937, p. 585.
43. *Huddersfield Daily Express*, 8 October 1937.
44. *Berwick Journal*, 18 February 1937.
45. *Walsall Observer*, 9 July 1938.
46. See Chapter 6.
47. Board of Deputies of British Jews, *Reports of the Vigilance Committees for 1937–1939*.
48. Board of Deputies of British Jews, *Secretary's Report*, March 1939; *The Free Press*, October 1939; see also Militant Christian Patriots, *Zionism* (1936); *Zionism and the Christian Church* (1936); *The Cuckoo in the Socialist Nest* (1938); *Do You Know That* (1938), leaflet; *What We Are Asked to Fight About* (1938), leaflet; 'Virgil', *The World's Enemies* (1938); 'Pro Patria', *Refugees Before Britain* (1939), leaflet.
49. Board of Deputies of British Jews, *Memorandum on Fascist Activities in Norfolk and Lincoln*, October 1937.
50. *ibid.*
51. Board of Deputies of British Jews, *Report of Investigations into BUF Activities in Sandwich and Surrounding Districts*, spring 1939.
52. *ibid.*

53. *The Daily Herald*, 21 July 1937; *Report of the Commissioner of Police of the Metropolis for the Year 1937, loc. cit.*
54. *Report of the Commissioner of Police of the Metropolis for the Year 1937, loc. cit.*
55. *ibid., 1938* (Cmd 6073), pp. 8–9.
56. Board of Deputies of British Jews, *Memorandum on Jew-Baiting*, June 1937.
57. *The News Chronicle*, 18 December 1933.
58. *The Times*, 25 May 1934.
59. A. K. Chesterton, *Interview*, 22 December 1960; John Beckett, *Interview*, 14 December 1960.
60. *Blackshirt*, 5 October 1934.
61. *Action*, 7 November 1936.
62. *ibid.*, 16 July 1936.
63. *ibid.*, 9 January 1937.
64. C. Wegg-Prosser, *Fascism Exposed* (1938).
65. *The Morning Post*, 21 October 1936.
66. *Action*, 13 March 1937.
67. Wegg-Prosser, *loc. cit.*
68. British Union, *Election Manifesto* (East London) 1937.
69. *East London Advertiser*, 27 February 1937.
70. John Beckett, *Interview*, 14 December 1960.
71. *Action*, 13 March 1937.
72. *Blackshirt*, 6 November 1937.
73. *Bridgnorth News*, 5 November 1937.
74. *Mercury and Herald* (Northampton), 5 November 1937.
75. *Blackshirt*, 6 November 1937.
76. *ibid.*, August 1938.
77. *The Manchester Guardian*, 2 November 1938.
78. *Suffolk Chronicle and Mercury*, November 1938.
79. See footnote p. 284; the B.U.F. also contested local by-elections in Liverpool Wavertree, Islington and St Pancras with similar results. See *Liverpool Daily Post*, 12 January 1937; *Islington Gazette*, 28 January 1938; *St Pancras Gazette*, 26 March 1938.
80. *Action*, 19 March 1938.
81. *Blackshirt*, July 1938.
82. Board of Deputies of British Jews, *Report of the London Area Committee*, July 1938.
83. *Action*, 24 September 1938.
84. *ibid.*, 3 June 1938.
85. *The News Chronicle*, 17 July 1938.
86. *The Manchester Guardian*, 17 July 1939.
87. *Action, loc. cit.*
88. Oswald Mosley, *Mosley's Message to British Union Members and Supporters*, 1 September 1939, leaflet.
89. *Action*, 23 September 1939.
90. *The Manchester Guardian*, 16 October 1939.

91. *Action*, 6 November 1939.
92. *ibid.*, 23 May 1940.
93. John Beckett, *Interview*, 14 December 1960.
94. William Joyce, *National Socialism Now* (1937), p. 83.
95. *The Star*, 26 February 1937.
96. *News Review*, 15 September 1938.
97. *The Jewish Chronicle*, 21 October 1937.
98. John Beckett, *Interview*, 14 December 1960.
99. See *The Manchester Guardian*, 25 January 1936.
100. *Tribune*, 30 June 1939.
101. *The People's Post*, October 1939.
102. See Philby's letter in *The Manchester Guardian*, 27 June 1939.
103. *The Times*, 30 October 1960.
104. 140 *H. L. Deb. 5s.* (12 March 1946), col. 39.
105. British Empire Union, *Empire Record*, 11 June 1940.
106. *The Manchester Guardian*, 1 August 1941.
107. *Report of Branch Meeting of the Nordic League*, 27 April 1939, (mimeographed), courtesy of the Fabian Society.
108. G. Ward Price, *I Know These Dictators* (1937), p. 155.
109. 104 *H. L. Deb. 5s.* (27 February 1937), cols. 309–12.
110. *The Evening Standard*, 19 November 1938; twenty others resigned their membership, *ibid.*, 13 January 1939.
111. *The Times*, 10 December 1938.
112. See speech by Domville quoted by John Parker, M.P., 330 *H. C. Deb. 5s.* (21 December 1937), col. 1863.
113. 350 *H. C. Deb. 5s.* (3 August 1939), col. 2049. Professor A. P. Laurie, a former principal of the Heriot Watt school and a member of council of the Link admitted that he had received £150 from a German publisher for a book defending the German case, *The Daily Telegraph*, 8 August 1938.
114. *New Statesman and Nation*, 20 August 1938.
115. Admiral Sir Barry Domville, *From Admiral to Cabin Boy* (1947), p. 78; Carroll claimed the Review was independent of the Fellowship, *New Statesman and Nation*, 19 December 1936.
116. *The Observer*, 28 November 1937.
117. Domville, *op. cit.*, p. 84.
118. *Action*, 3 April 1937.
119. *ibid.*, 22 February 1940.
120. *The Yorkshire Post*, 13 March 1940.
121. Sydney Allen, *Election Address* (North-East Leeds), March 1939.
122. *East End News*, 27 February 1940.
123. *The Yorkshire Post*, 13 March 1940.
124. *Action*, 29 February 1940.
125. *ibid.*, 21 March 1940.
126. *The Daily Telegraph*, 20 May 1940.
127. *The Manchester Guardian*, 24 May 1940.
128. *Action*, 23 May 1940.

129. *ibid.*
130. *ibid.*, 30 May 1940.
131. *The Daily Herald*, 11 July 1940.
132. 365 *H. C. Deb. 5s.* (7 November 1940), col. 1424.
133. *Action*, 30 May 1940.
134. *Catholic Herald*, July 1942; see also *Action*, 22 February 1940.
135. Lord Morrison, *Interview*, 14 July 1959.
136. 367 *H. C. Deb. 5s.* (10 December 1940), col. 839.

# 13. A Civil Society

An attempt has been made to describe the course of a Fascist movement in a stable democracy. The value of the undertaking is made clear when British political development is contrasted with pre-war Germany, Italy and France. As suggested at the outset, the underlying causes of success and failure are deeply rooted in a nation's history and in its values and beliefs in that they influence the response to crisis and social change. The difficulty in this argument, however, is that the response may not always be appropriate to a particular set of social, economic and political conditions. It is therefore important to account for the immediate causes of success and failure.

Britain was not immune from Fascist doctrines. Thousands of people were attracted in a positive sense for one reason or another and thousands in a negative sense in that they were willing to reject the recognized parties and established institutions. Although a distinct group, there were also the appeasers who composed a closed but more influential circle. That Fascism, no matter how dreary the form, should attract adherents is sufficient cause for a democracy to reflect. An apparent economic crisis, mounting unemployment, a proportion of the population living in conditions of poverty and distress and governments perceived as lethargic or at best orthodox created a climate of opinion receptive to radical criticism. The growth of Fascism in Europe, the Soviet model, demands for economic reform and experimentation elsewhere and easy solutions suggested by anti-Communism and anti-Semitism created a climate of opinion susceptible to radical solutions. A talented and attractive leader was available whose courage and sincerity had been tested. He seemingly possessed the resources to mobilize opinion and to make a serious political impact.

Yet Sir Oswald Mosley's British Union of Fascists, unlike its Continental models, challenged but never seriously threatened the stability of the political system. That this was the case can be credited to a number of factors.

To begin with radical opinion does not necessarily imply a coherent whole. There were various descriptions and prescriptions for Britain's difficulties. Moreover, where there was agreement in terms of a critique it did not necessarily follow that unity on a common course of action could be reached. Most important of all Mosley mistook this climate of opinion for the prevailing one. Although there was criticism, and this very fact can be a source of strength in itself, there was little evidence that the basic political and economic structure was deteriorating beyond repair. Where there were weaknesses, the basic structure was sustained by the beliefs and values upon which it ultimately rested.

The crisis that Mosley predicted never materialized and the signs of economic recovery appeared in Great Britain without a drastic restructuring of the economic order on the part of the government. It has been shown that because Britain did not experience the boom of the 1920s, the crash was not as severe as elsewhere. The nature of distress and deprivation was also uneven so that an illusion of national well-being, especially in the South, worked against a crisis movement. In any event, although there may be a propensity for Fascism or dictatorship to emerge from crisis, it is not predetermined. Again it admits to an inadequate understanding of British political development.

Furthermore, British Fascism as an ideology was never clearly presented. The merits of Mosley's early proposals which were incorporated in the movement's doctrine were submerged by the more dramatic aspects of Fascism. Mosley's immediate and constructive proposals as set forth in *The Greater Britain* suffered from the bad publicity of his earlier failures. At the same time, Fascism was not successfully adapted to the British political culture. It was also not clear what values the Fascists were trying to preserve or exploit. Consequently, as the possibility of attaining power grew more remote, Mosley and his colleagues grew more desperate and their pronouncements more hysterical. The attempt to re-shape policy increased active hostility towards the movement. Anti-Communism, anti-Socialism and nationalism had more respectable and responsible outlets. Anti-Semitism alienated support from extreme nationalists and anti-Communists and at the same time failed to provide a mass following, although it sustained those who remained loyal to the B.U.F. Selective pacifism did not resolve the conflict between the movement's militant nationalism and its support of Continental Fascism.

The B.U.F. by a show of discipline and strength hoped to gain support for the introduction of a new political and economic order. This was accompanied by organized violence which came to characterize the movement. Violence had by no means been absent, yet one of the significant features of modern British politics has been the degree to which violence as a political weapon has been minimized. Its use or the likelihood of its use aroused the politically conscious into active and occasionally organized opposition and alerted the authorities and established political parties. Official restraint and tolerance was exercised until the 'Battle of Cable Street' when articulate opinion was outraged and the Government took action. The Public Order Act was another blow to British Fascism. Sir Oswald Mosley on being shown the relevant passages which Sir Harold Nicolson intended to publish in his Diaries commented, 'It seemed to me that we had the clear choice of organizing to overcome the violence or of closing down; our only effective means of spreading our ideas was public meetings. . . . I do not think it is fair therefore to accuse me of loving violence, as some have done.'[1] No attempt has been made here to accuse Sir Oswald Mosley of 'loving violence'. At the same time his 'clear choice' is unequivocally rejected.

The practice of Fascism on the Continent did not recommend the local brand, especially since the latter was based, in part, on a foreign political programme. The rise of Nazism in Germany with its purges and oppressions brought further discredit to a movement criticized for its political style. Anti-Semitism was identified with Nazism which was not only foreign but possibly antipathetic to British interests.

Mosley was a leader of many qualities, but he also possessed certain negative characteristics which were harmful to the movement. He was a discredited politician and many were unwilling to take him seriously. His radicalism was rather tempered by his ambition and arrogance. He was impatient, which led to miscalculations, and he tended to overestimate his strength. His mystique of leadership made him impatient of advice and susceptible to flattery; he therefore favoured sycophants rather than competent lieutenants. He failed to understand the strength of institutions and resistance to change. He was a desperate man clinging to a mythology in order to rationalize his failure and justify his political existence.

The internal politics of the B.U.F. was a disrupting force. Difficulties in the selection and control of personnel resulted in a high rate of turn-over among the membership. Hence, the absence of continuity in policy and in political style was matched by an unstable membership. This had an adverse effect on morale and added to intolerable tensions that had arisen from factional disputes. The intense struggle for the power that Mosley was willing to share within the movement meant that organizational goals and life gained priority.

Finally, there was the viability of British political and social institutions. There had been no significant breakdown or alteration in the rules of the game making it necessary for those with frustrations or resentments to seek satisfactions outside the established system. Short of this there was little that the B.U.F. could promise that was not already promised by another party. Hence Fascism as an alternative to parliamentary democracy failed to stimulate the imagination of the British public. The political parties were successful in maintaining their membership. The failure of the Labour Government to undertake far-reaching reforms was reassuring to the right-wing elements of the middle class. Socialism was no longer a threat. The formation of a National Government followed the Labour Government. The very term 'National Government' was reassuring. As far as the more conservative elements of the electorate were concerned, the Socialists were out of power, while the more 'sensible' elements of the Labour Party had been cleverly harnessed and incorporated into a government. A National Government also implied a patriotic government determined to solve Britain's problems in a British manner. This was believed to be an ingenious British way of facing up to a crisis. By this method, the nation was united in order to seek a solution for the benefit of all. As for the left, Labour Party supporters, after recovering from the initial repercussions of the formation of the National Government, were able to rationalize Labour's failure by the betrayal of its leaders. The Labour Party could now proceed in a 'truly' Socialist and radical direction according to this thinking. For those still unconvinced about the probability of a social renaissance led by the Labour Party, there was the I.L.P. For others there was the Communist Party and other left-wing fringe groups.

It emerged that there was not a large reservoir of socially isolated, economically depressed and politically frustrated people from whom the Fascists could recruit. The established political parties were able to organize and hold the discontented, for the accepted channels for economic and political action were still open and accessible. The state was neither omnipotent nor remote, for the institutional pluralism of British society provided a buffer as well as a link between the state and the individual. There was also a pluralism of loyalties which meant that interests were represented and loyalties engaged elsewhere. A worker who was a member of a trade union might not have been an active member but he was loyal in that he looked to the trade union to protect his interests. It was also possible that the British class structure militated against the Fascist movement. It provided a focal point for loyalty and identification and had thrown up its own organizations to protect its interests. Mosley made little headway on class lines because he could not break class ties and because the B.U.F. was of little use in that class interests were already effectively represented. He seemed to have sensed that his only chance was that a particular class might have felt itself to be unduly threatened. Fascism's ultimate dilemma in Britain was the presence of a sense of community which at one and the same time contained and was nurtured by competing interests and loyalties.

It is therefore possible to conclude on a cheerful note for the effect of Fascism on British institutions and beliefs was negligible. Paramilitary politics failed to gain legitimacy and indeed was outlawed. The possibilities for organized political violence were also restricted. A price of course had to be paid. The Government's reluctance to bring in legislation because of its justifiable caution for the further suppression of civil liberties meant that the residents of East London, Jew and Gentile, were subjected to a campaign approaching a siege of terror. Once legislation had been enacted more power was placed in the hands of the authorities at the expense of civil liberties.[2] More power was placed in the hands of the police, who in the execution of their difficult tasks had not always performed their duties in an impartial manner.

Fascism – updated – and allied movements have re-appeared in Britain but there is little likelihood of their emerging from the political fringe. Yet it has already been demonstrated that Commonwealth immigration and racial prejudice are exploitable issues. The legacy of British Fascism, however, is not racialism but the principle established that it is just and proper to legislate for the protection of a particular segment of the community.

NOTES

1. Nigel Nicolson (ed.), *Harold Nicolson, Diaries and Letters, 1930–39* (1966), p. 115 *n.*
2. For post-war problems and subsequent legislation see the excellent study by David Williams, *Keeping the Peace* (1967).

# Bibliography

## GENERAL WORKS

Almond, G. and S. Verba, *The Political Culture*, Boston: Little, Brown, 1965

Bagehot, W., *The English Constitution*, London: Collins, 1963 edn.

Beer, S. H., 'The Analysis of Political Systems', S. H. Beer and A. B. Ulam, eds, *Patterns of Government*, New York: Random House, 1962

—— *Modern British Politics*, London: Faber & Faber, 1965

Bell, D., ed., *The Radical Right*, New York: Doubleday, 1964

Bendix, R., *Nation-Building and Citizenship*, London: Wiley, 1964

—— 'Social Stratification and Political Power', *American Political Science Review*, June 1952

Birch, A. H., *Representative and Responsible Government*, London: Allen & Unwin, 1964

Crick, B., 'On Method and Matter', *Government and Opposition*, May 1966

Eckstein, H., 'The British Political System', S. H. Beer and A. B. Ulam, eds, *Patterns of Government*, New York: Random House, 1962 edn.

—— *Pressure Group Politics*, London: Allen & Unwin, 1960

Finer, S. E., *Anonymous Empire*, London: Pall Mall Press, 1958

—— 'The Political Power of Private Capital, Part II', *Sociological Review*, July 1956

Gorer, G., *Exploring English Character*, New York: Criterion Books, 1955

Guttsman, W. L., *The British Political Elite*, London: Mac-
Gibbon & Kee, 1964

Kornhauser, W., *Politics of Mass Society*, London: Routledge &
Kegan Paul, 1960

Lipsett, S. M., *Political Man*, London: Heinemann Educational
Books, 1960

McKenzie, R. T. and A. Silver, 'Industrialism and the Working-
Class Tory', R. Rose, ed., *Studies in British Politics*, 1966

Moore, Barrington, Jr, *Social Origins of Dictatorship and Democracy*, London: Allen Lane The Penguin Press, 1967

Neumann, F., *The Democratic and Authoritarian State*, London:
Collier-Macmillan, 1957, 1964

Nordlinger, E., *The Working-Class Tories*, London: MacGibbon
& Kee, 1967

Pollock, James K., *et al.*, *British Election Studies*, Wahr, 1950,
1951

Pye, L. and S. Verba, eds, *Political Culture and Political Development*, Princeton University Press, 1965

Rothman, S., 'Modernity and Tradition in Britain', *Social Research*, Autumn 1961

Shils, E., 'Ideology and Civility: On the Politics of the Intellectual', *Sewanee Review*, Summer 1958

—— *The Torment of Secrecy*, London: Heinemann, 1956

## HISTORICAL

Amery, L. S., *My Political Life: The Unforgiving Years, 1929–
1940*, London: Hutchinson, 1955

Ashworth, W., *An Economic History of England 1870–1939*,
London: Methuen, 1960

Bassett, R., *1931, Political Crisis*, London: Macmillan, 1958

Beloff, M., 'The Sixth of February', James Joll, ed., *The Decline
of the Third Republic*, London: Chatto & Windus, 1959

Blaxland, G., *J. H. Thomas: A Life for Unity*, London: Muller,
1964

Boothby, R., *I Fight to Live*, London: Gollancz, 1947

Boyle, A., *Trenchard*, London: Collins, 1962

British Association for the Advancement of Science, *Britain in Recovery*, London: Pitman, 1938

Brockway, A. F., *Inside the Left*, London: Allen & Unwin, 1942

—— *Socialism Over Sixty Years*, London: Allen & Unwin, 1947

Brown, W. J., *So Far . . .*, London: Allen & Unwin, 1943

Bullock, A., *The Life and Times of Ernest Bevin*, vol. I, London: Heinemann, 1960

Childs, Sir Wyndham, *Episodes and Reflections*, London: Cassell, 1930

Clynes, J., *Memoirs*, London: Hutchinson, 1937

Cole, G. D. H., *A History of the Labour Party from 1914*, London: Routledge & Kegan Paul, 1948

—— 'Socialist Control of Industry', C. Addison, *et al.*, *Problems of a Socialist Government*, London: Gollancz, 1933

Cole, G. D. H. and M. I. Cole, *Condition of Britain*, London: Gollancz, 1937

Cole, M. I., ed., *Beatrice Webb's Diaries, 1924–1932*, London: Longmans, Green, 1956

Crook, W. H., *The General Strike*, University of North Carolina Press, 1931

Cross, C., *Philip Snowden*, London: Barrie & Rockliff, 1966

Dalton, H., *Call Back Yesterday: Memoirs, 1887–1931*, London: Muller, 1953

—— *The Fateful Years: Memoirs, 1931–1945*, London: Muller, 1957

Dowse, R. E., *Left in the Centre*, London: Longmans, Green, 1966

Foot, M., *Aneurin Bevan, Vol. One: 1897–1945*, London: MacGibbon & Kee, 1962

Gottlieb, H. B., *England and the Nazi Regime – Great Britain Opinion, 1933–1938*, Unpublished D.Phil. thesis, Oxford, 1958

Granzow, B., *A Mirror of Nazism: British Opinion and the Emergence of Hitler, 1929–1933*, London: Gollancz, 1964

Graves, R. and A. Hodge, *The Long Weekend*, London: Faber & Faber, 1940

Gunther, J., *Inside Europe*, London: Hamish Hamilton, 1936 edn.

Halifax, E. W. L. Wood, Earl of, *Fulness of Days*, London: Collins, 1957

Hamilton, M. A., *Arthur Henderson*, London: Heinemann, 1938

Hanson, A. H., 'The Purpose of Parliament', *Parliamentary Affairs*, Summer 1964

Harrison, J., *The Reactionaries: Yeats, Lewis, Pound, Eliot, Lawrence: A Study of the Anti-Democratic Intelligentsia*, London: Gollancz, 1967

Haxey, S., *Tory, M.P.*, London: Gollancz, 1939

Henriques, B. L. Q., *The Indiscretions of a Warden*, London: Methuen, 1937

Hood, P., *Ourselves and the Press, A Social Study of News, Advertising and Propaganda*, London: John Lane, 1939

Hyde, D., *I Believed*, London: Heinemann, 1951

Johnson, T., *Memories*, London: Collins, 1952

Jupp, J., *The Left in Britain: 1931–1941*, Unpublished M.Sc. (Econ.) thesis, London, 1956

Lambeth, Lord Morrison of, *Herbert Morrison: An Autobiography*, London: Odhams Press, 1960

Lansbury, G., *My England*, London: Selwyn & Blount, 1934

Lee, J., *To-morrow Is A New Day*, London: Cresset Press, 1939

Lenin, V. I., 'The British Liberals and Ireland' and 'Constitutional Crisis in Britain', *On Britain*, Moscow: Foreign Language Publishing House, 1959 edn.

Londonderry, C. S. H. Vane-Tempest-Stewart, Marquis of, *Ourselves and Germany*, Harmondsworth: Penguin Books, 1938

McCarthy, M., *Generation in Revolt*, London: Heinemann, 1953

McHenry, D. E., *The Labour Party in Transition, 1931–1938*, London: Routledge & Kegan Paul, 1938

Macmillan, H., *The Middle Way*, London: Macmillan, 1938

—— *Winds of Change 1914–1939*, London: Macmillan, 1966

McNeill, R., *Ulster's Stand for Union*, Murry, 1922

Marjoribanks, E. and I. Colvin, *The Life of Lord Carson*, 3 vols, London: Gollancz, 1932–6

Martin, K., *Harold Laski*, London: Gollancz, 1953

Mitford, J., *Hons. and Rebels*, London: Gollancz, 1960

Mosley, L., *Curzon, The End of an Epoch*, London: Longmans, Green, 1960

Mowat, C. L., *Britain Between the Wars, 1918–1940*, London: Methuen, 1956 edn.

Muggeridge, M., *The Thirties, 1930–1940 in Great Britain*, London: Hamish Hamilton, 1940

Nichols, B., *News from England*, London: Jonathan Cape, 1938

Orwell, G., *The Lion and the Unicorn*, London: Secker & Warburg, 1941, 1962

Pakenham, Frank, Earl of Longford, *Born to Believe*, London: Jonathan Cape, 1953

Paton, J., *Left Turn!*, London: Secker & Warburg, 1936

Pelling, H., *The British Communist Party*, London: Black, 1958

Piratin, P., *Our Flag Stays Red*, London: Thames Publications, 1948

Political and Economic Planning, *Report on the British Press*, 1938

Pollitt, H., *Serving My Time*, London: Lawrence & Wishart, 1940

Postgate, R., *The Life of George Lansbury*, London: Longmans, Green, 1951

Price, G. W., *I Know These Dictators*, London: Harrap, 1937

Priestley, J. B., *English Journey*, London: Heinemann, 1934

Pritt, D. N., *The Autobiography of D. N. Pritt*, Part One, London: Lawrence & Wishart, 1965

Ravensdale, M. I. Curzon, Baroness, *In Many Rhythms*, London: Weidenfeld & Nicolson, 1953

Raymond, J., *The Baldwin Age*, London: Eyre & Spottiswoode, 1960

Rentoul, Sir Gervais, *This is My Case*, London: Hutchinson, 1944

Richardson, H. W., *Economic Recovery in Britain 1932–1939*, London: Weidenfeld & Nicolson, 1967

Rothermere, H. S. Harmsworth, Viscount, *My Fight to Rearm Britain*, London: Eyre & Spottiswoode, 1939

—— *Warnings and Predictions*, London: Eyre & Spottiswoode, 1939

Sampson, A., *Macmillan: A Study in Ambiguity*, London: Allen Lane The Penguin Press, 1967

Scanlon, J., *The Decline and Fall of the Labour Party*, London: Peter Davies, 1932

Sharf, A., *The British Press and Jews Under Nazi Rule*, Oxford University Press, 1964

Shinwell, E., *Conflict Without Malice*, London: Odhams Press, 1955

Sillitoe, Sir Percy, *Cloak Without Dagger*, London: Cassell, 1955

Simon, J. A. Simon, Viscount, *Retrospect*, London: Hutchinson, 1952

Skidelsky, R., *Politicians and the Slump*, London: Macmillan, 1967

Snowden, P., *Autobiography*, 2 vols, London: Nicolson & Watson, 1934

Somervell, D. C., *The Reign of King George the Fifth*, London: Faber & Faber, 1935

Stewart, A. T. Q., *The Ulster Crisis*, London: Faber & Faber, 1967

Strachey, J., *The Coming Struggle for Power*, London: Gollancz, 1932

—— *The Menace of Fascism*, London: Gollancz, 1933

Strauss, P., *Cripps – Advocate and Rebel*, London: Gollancz, 1943

Symons, J., *The Thirties*, London: Cresset Press, 1960

Taylor, A. J. P., *English History 1914–1945*, Oxford University Press, 1965

Templewood, S. J. G. Hoare, Viscount, *Nine Troubled Years*, London: Collins, 1954

Thomas, J. H., *My Story*, London: Hutchinson, 1937

Thurtle, E., *Time's Winged Chariot*, Chaterton, 1945

Tint, H., *The Decline of French Patriotism*, London: Weidenfeld & Nicolson, 1964

Toynbee, P., *Friends Apart*, London: MacGibbon & Kee, 1954

Vansittart, R. G., Baron, *The Mist Procession: Autobiography*, London: Hutchinson, 1958

Weir, L. M., *The Tragedy of Ramsay MacDonald*, London: Secker & Warburg, 1938

Wertheimer, E., *Portrait of the Labour Party*, London: Putnam, 1930

Williamson, H. R., *Who is for Liberty?*, London: Michael Joseph, 1939

Winterton, C. T. Winterton, Earl, *Orders of the Day*, London: Cassell, 1953

Wood, N., *Communism and British Intellectuals*, London: Gollancz, 1959


## FASCISM (GENERAL)

Arendt, H., *The Origins of Totalitarianism*, London: Allen & Unwin, 1958

von Beckerath, E., 'Fascism', *Encyclopedia of Social Sciences*, 1937

Borgese, G. A., *Goliath: The March of Fascism*, London: Gollancz, 1938

Brady, R., *The Spirit and Structure of German Fascism*, London: Gollancz, 1937

Bramsted, E. K., *Goebbels and National Socialist Propaganda, 1925–1945*, London: Cresset Press, 1965

Bullock, A., *Hitler, A Study in Tyranny*, London: Odhams Press, 1964

Finer, H., *Mussolini's Italy*, London: Cass, 1964

Fromm, E., *The Fear of Freedom*, London: Routledge & Kegan Paul, 1942

Gentile, G., 'The Philosophic Basis of Fascism', *Foreign Affairs*, January 1928

Germino, D. L., *The Italian Fascist Party in Power*, Oxford University Press, 1959

Gerth, H., 'The Nazi Party: Its Leadership and Composition', R. K. Merton, *et al.*, *Reader in Bureaucracy*, Free Press of Glencoe, Ill., 1952

Harris, H. S., *The Social Philosophy of Giovanni Gentile*, University of Illinois Press, 1966

Heiden, K., *Der Führer*, Boston: Houghton Mifflin, 1944

Hibbert, C., *Benito Mussolini*, London: Longmans, Green, 1962

Jarman, T. L., *The Rise and Fall of Nazi Germany*, London: Cresset Press, 1956

Kirkpatrick, Sir Ivone, *Mussolini, Study of a Demagogue*, London: Odhams Press, 1964

Lang, S. and E. von Schenck, *Memoirs of Alfred Rosenberg*, Chicago: Ziff-Dares, 1949

Lasswell, H. D., 'The Garrison State', *American Journal of Sociology*, January 1941

—— 'The Psychology of Hitlerism', *The Political Quarterly*, July 1933

Lipsett, S. M., 'Social Stratification and Right-Wing Extremism', *British Journal of Sociology*, December 1959

Mosse, G. L., *Nazi Culture*, New York: Grosset & Dunlop, 1966

Mowrer, E. A., *Germany Puts the Clock Back*, Harmondsworth: Penguin Books, 1937

Mussolini, B., 'The Political and Social Doctrine of Fascism', *The Political Quarterly*, July 1933

Neumann, F., *Behemoth: The Structure and Practice of National Socialism*, London: Gollancz, 1942

Neumann, S., *Permanent Revolution*, London: Praeger, 1965 edn.

Nolte, E., *Three Faces of Fascism*, London: Weidenfeld & Nicolson, 1965

Parsons, T., *Essays in Sociological Theory*, London: Collier-Macmillan, 1954 edn, Chs. VI, VII

Pulzer, P. G. J., *The Rise of Political Anti-Semitism in Germany and Austria*, London: Wiley, 1964

Rausching, H., *The Redemption of Democracy*, New York: Alliance Book Corp., 1941

Reisman, D., 'The Politics of Persecution', *Public Opinion Quarterly*, Spring 1942

Rocco, A., *The Political Doctrine of Fascism*, New York: International Conciliation Pamphlet, 1926

Rogger, H. and E. Weber, eds, *The European Right*, University of California Press, 1966 edn

Rossi, A., *The Rise of Italian Fascism*, London: Methuen, 1938

Rügdiger, E., *Between Hitler and Mussolini – Memoirs*, London: Hodder & Stoughton, 1942

Salvemini, G., *Under the Axe of Fascism*, London: Gollancz, 1936

Schneider, H. W., *Making the Fascist State*, Oxford University Press, 1928

Schuman, F., *The Nazi Dictatorship*, New York: Knopf, 1935

Spitz, D., *Patterns of Anti-Democratic Thought*, London: Collier-Macmillan, 1965 edn

Tannenbaum, E. R., *The Action Française*, London: Wiley, 1962

Taylor, E., *Strategy of Terror*, Boston: Houghton Mifflin, 1940

Weber, E., *Varieties of Fascism*, London: van Nostrand, 1964

Weiss, J., *The Fascist Tradition*, London: Harper & Row, 1967

Welk, W. G., *Fascist Economic Policy*, Oxford University Press, 1938

## FASCISM IN GREAT BRITAIN

Bechhofer-Roberts, C. E., ed., *The Trial of William Joyce*, Old Bailey Trial Series, 1946

—— 'The Blackshirts', *Round Table*, September 1934

Benewick, R. J. (unsigned), 'Mosley's Anti-Semitism, 1933–1939', *Wiener Library Bulletin*, Nos 3–4, 1959

Board of Deputies of British Jews, Documents: *Minutes of the Co-ordinating Committee, July 1936–March 1939; Secretary's Reports 1936–1939; Vigilance Committees Reports 1936–1939; Special Investigations; Observers' Reports; Special Memoranda*

Bondy, L. W., *Racketeers of Hatred*, London: Newman Wolsey, 1946

Catlin, G. E. G., 'Fascist Stirrings in Britain', *Current History*, February 1934

Cross, C., *The Fascists in Britain*, London: Barrie & Rockliff, 1961

Huxley, A., *Point Counter Point*, London: Chatto & Windus, 1928

Mallon, J. J., 'Fascist Provocation in East London', *Daily Telegraph*, 28 October 1938

POLITICAL VIOLENCE AND PUBLIC ORDER

Mandle, W. F., *Anti-Semitism and the British Union of Fascists*, London: Longmans, Green, 1968
—— 'The Leadership of the British Union of Fascists', *The Australian Journal of Politics and History*, December 1966
Martin, K., *Fascism, Democracy and the Press*, New Statesman and Nation publication, 1938
—— 'Fascism and the Daily Mail', *The Political Quarterly*, April 1934
Mitford, N., *Wigs on the Green*, London: Thornton Butterworth, 1935
Mullally, F., *Fascism Inside England*, London: Claude Morris Books, 1946
Rosten, Leo G., 'The Rise of Oswald Mosley', *Harpers Magazine*, September 1934
Rudlin, W. A., *The Growth of Fascism in Great Britain*, 1935
Skidelsky, R., 'Great Britain', S. J. Woolf, ed., *European Fascism*, London: Weidenfeld & Nicolson, 1968
West, R., *The Meaning of Treason*, Harmondsworth: Penguin Books, 1965 edn
Wilkinson, E. C. and E. Conze, *Why Fascism?*, London: Selwyn & Blount, 1934


ANTI-SEMITISM AND RACIALISM

Adler, H., 'Jewish Life and Labour in East London', Sir H. Llewellyn Smith, ed., *The New Survey of London Life and Labour*, London: King, 1934, vol. VI, pp. 268–98
Allport, G. W., *The Nature of Prejudice*, London: Addison-Wesley, 1954
Brotz, H., 'The Position of the Jews in English Society', *Jewish Journal of Sociology*, April 1959
Deakin, N., ed., *Colour and the British Electorate*, London: Pall Mall Press, 1964
Eysenck, H. J., *Sense and Nonsense in Psychology*, Harmondsworth: Penguin Books, 1957, 1958, Ch. 7
Fineberg, S. A., 'Can Anti-Semitism be Outlawed?', *Contemporary Jewish Record*, No. 6, 1943

316

Fox, M., 'Three Approaches to the Jewish Problem', *Antioch Review*, March 1946

Freedman, M., 'The Jewish Population of Great Britain', *Jewish Journal of Sociology*, June 1962

Freedman, M., ed., *A Minority in Britain*, London: Vallentine, Mitchell, 1955

Fyvel, T. R. ('R. J. Feiwel'), *The Insecure Offenders*, London: Chatto & Windus, 1961

Gartner, L. P., *The Jewish Immigrant in England, 1870–1914*, London: Allen & Unwin, 1960

Golding, L., *The Jewish Problem*, Harmondsworth: Penguin Books, 1938

Goldman, W., *East End My Cradle*, London: Art and Educational Publishers, 1940

Gould, J. and S. Esh, eds, *Jewish Life in Modern Britain*, London: Routledge & Kegan Paul, 1964

Kantorowitsch, M., 'Estimate of the Jewish Population of London, 1929–33', *Journal of the Royal Statistical Society*, Part II, 1936

Kullmann, M., 'Notting Hill Hustings', *New Left Review*, January–February 1960

Kyle, K., 'North Kensington', D. E. Butler and R. Rose, *The British General Election of 1959*, 1960

Lowenthal, L. and N. Guterman, *Prophets of Deceit*, New York: Harper & Row, 1949

Parkes, J., *An Enemy of the People: Anti-Semitism*, Harmondsworth: Penguin Books, 1945

Potter, B., 'The Jewish Community', C. Booth, ed., *Life and Labour of the People in London*, London: Macmillan, 1892, vol. III, pp. 185–92

Robb, J. H., *Working-Class Anti-Semite*, London: Tavistock Publications, 1954

Tumin, M., *An Inventory and Appraisal of Research on American Anti-Semitism*, New York: Anti-Defamation League of B'nai B'nith, 1961

## MOSLEY PRIOR TO THE B.U.F.

*Action*, 8 October 1931–13 December 1931

Axon, E., ed., *The Mosley Family: Memoranda of Oswald and Nicholas Mosley of Ancoats*, Manchester: Chatham Society, 1902

Diston, M., *The Sleeping Sickness of the Labour Party*, New Party, 1931

Diston, M. and R. Forgan, *The New Party and the ILP*, New Party, 1931

Joad, C. E. M., *The Case for the New Party*, New Party, 1931

—— 'Prolegomena to Fascism', *Political Quarterly*, January 1931

Letts, Rev. E. F., *The Family of Mosley and their Brasses in Manchester Cathedral*, Lancashire and Cheshire Antiquarian Society, 1893

MacDougal, J., *Disillusionment*, New Party, 1931

Mandle, W. F., 'The New Party', *Historical Studies*, October 1966

—— 'Sir Oswald Mosley's Resignation from the Labour Government', *Historical Studies*, 1961

Melville, C. F., *The Truth About the New Party*, London: Wishart, 1931

Mosley, Sir Oswald, *Family Memoirs*, (printed for private circulation), 1849

—— *Industrial Problems and the Socialist*, Independent Labour Party, 1929

—— 'Lost Lib-Lab Opportunity in 1929 Parliament', *New Outlook*, May 1966

—— *Revolution By Reason*, Birmingham Labour Party, 1925

—— *Why We Left the Old Parties*, New Party, 1931

—— 'Will an Ape and Tiger Never Die', *Yea and Nea*, Brentans, 1923

New Party, *The New Ashton*, April 1931

—— 'Sir Oswald Mosley, Bart., John Bull', *Vanity Fair*, 1 September 1898

Strachey, J., 'The Mosley Manifesto: Why We Have Issued It', in *The Spectator*, 13 December 1930

—— *Revolution by Reason*, Leonard Parsons, 1925

Strachey, J. and C. E. M. Joad, 'Parliamentary Reform: The New Party's Proposals', *Political Quarterly*, July 1931

Young, A., *et al.*, *A National Policy*, London: Macmillan, 1931

## PUBLICATIONS OF THE B.U.F. AND ITS MEMBERS

*Action*, 21 February 1936–6 June 1940

*Action News Letter*, 30 April–7 May 1940

*Blackshirt*, February 1933–May 1939

British Union (B.U.F.), *Britain and Jewry*, London: Abbey Supplies, n.d.

—— *British Union News*, June 1939

—— *British Union Quarterly*, 1937–40

—— *Constitution and Rules*, 1938

—— *Election Address*, East London, 1937

—— *The Empire and the British Union*, 1937

—— *Fascism and Agriculture*, 1936(?)

—— *Lancashire Betrayed*, 1938(?)

—— *Manifesto and Application*, 1932

—— *Medical Policy*, 1936(?)

—— *The Miners' Only Hope*, n.d.

—— Miscellaneous Pamphlets and Leaflets, in the Wiener Library and through the courtesy of the Board of Deputies of British Jews.

—— *Pictorial Record, 1932–1937*, 1937

—— *Red Violence and Blue Lies*, 1934

—— *Strength, Through Health*, n.d.

—— *Yorkshire Betrayed*, 1938(?)

B.U.F. and National Socialists, *Constitution and Regulations*, London: Abbey Supplies, 1936

Allen, S., *Election Address*, (North-East Leeds), March 1939

Allen, W. E. D., 'The Fascist Idea in Britain', *Quarterly Review*, October 1933

Beckett, J., 'Fascism and Trade Unionism', *Fascist Quarterly*, July 1936

Beckett, J. and A. Raven Thomson, 'Problems of the Distributive Trade', *Fascist Quarterly*, 1 January 1936

Chambers-Hunter, W. K. A. J., *British Union and Social Credit*, London: Greater Britain Publications, n.d.

Chesterton, A. K., *The Apotheosis of the Jew*, London: Abbey Supplies, n.d.

—— *Creed of a Fascist Revolutionary*, n.d.

—— *Fascism and the Press*, London: B.U.F. Publications, n.d.

—— *Oswald Mosley: Portrait of a Leader*, London: Action Press, 1937

Clarke, E. G., *The British Union and the Jews*, London: Abbey Supplies, n.d.

Drennan, J. (W. E. D. Allen), *BUF, Oswald Mosley and British Fascism*, London: Murray, 1934

*Fascist Week*, November 1933–May 1934

*The Fascist Quarterly*, January 1935–October 1936

Fuller, J. F. C., 'The War in Spain: Its Character and Form', *British Union Quarterly*, April–June 1937

—— *What the British Union Has to Offer Britain*, London: Greater Britain Publications, n.d.

Gordon-Canning, R., *Arab or Jew?*, London: Greater Britain Publications, n.d.

—— *The Inward Strength of a National Socialist*, London: Greater Britain Publications, n.d.

—— *Mind Britain's Business*, London: Greater Britain Publications, 1938

Goulding, M., *Peace Betrayed*, London: Greater Britain Publications, n.d.

Heyward, P., *Menace of the Chain Stores*, London: Greater Britain Publications, n.d.

Hill, F. D., *'Gainst Trust and Monopoly*, London: Abbey Supplies, n.d.

Jenks, J., *The Land and the People*, London: Greater Britain Publications, n.d.

Joyce, W., *Dictatorship*, 1933

—— *Fascism and India*, London: B.U.F. Publications, 1933

—— *Fascism and Jewry*, London: B.U.F. Publications, 1936

—— *Fascist Educational Policy*, London: B.U.F. Publications, 1933(?)

—— 'Obituary of Edward Carson', *Fascist Quarterly*, January 1936

'Lucifer' (W. Joyce), *The Letters of Lucifer*, London: B.U.F. Publications, 1933

Miles, A. C., *Fascism and Shipping*, 1934(?)

Mosley, Sir Oswald, *Blackshirt Policy*, London: B.U.F. Publications, 1935

—— *The British Peace – How to Get It*, Greater Britain Publications, n.d.

—— 'The Case for Fascism', *The Listener*, 23 March 1933

—— *The Facts*, London: Euphorion Distribution, 1957

—— *Fascism*, London: B.U.F. Publications, 1936

—— *Fascism Explained: Ten Points of Fascist Policy*, 1933

—— *Fascism in Britain*, 1933(?)

—— 'Fascism – It's Here to Stay', *Sunday Chronicle*, 23 July 1933

—— *The Greater Britain*, London: B.U.F. Publications, 1932, 1934, 1939 edns

—— *Mosley's Message to British Union Members and Supporters*, (leaflet), London: British Union, 1939

—— *My Answer*, London: Mosley Publications, 1946

—— *My Life*, London: Nelson, 1968

—— *Taxation and the People*, London: Abbey Supplies, 1937(?)

—— *Tomorrow We Live*, London: Greater Britain Publications, 1936, 1938 edns

—— 'Why We Wear the Blackshirts', *Sunday Dispatch*, 12 January 1934

—— 'The World Alternative', *Fascist Quarterly*, July 1936

Raven Thomson, A., *Civilization as Divine Superman*, London: Williams & Morgate, 1932

—— *The Coming Corporate State*, London: Greater Britain Publications, 1937

—— *The Economics of British Fascism*, London: Bonner, 1933(?)

—— 'Finance, Democracy and the Shopkeeper', *Action*, 6 March 1936

—— *Our Financial Masters*, London: Abbey Supplies, n.d.

Risdon, W., *A Guide to Constituency Organization*, 1935

—— *A. R. P.*, n.d.

—— *Strike Action or Power Action*, London: Abbey Supplies, 1938(?)

Roe, G. Mandeville, *The Corporate State*, 1934

Wegg-Prosser, C. F., 'The Worker and the State', *Fascist Quarterly*, April 1936

Wilson, J. R., *et al.*, *Pharmacy and British Union*, London: Abbey Supplies, n.d.

## OTHER FASCIST, ANTI-SEMITIC OR RIGHT-WING ORGANIZATIONS

Allen, W., *Lady Houston, One of the Few, a Memoir*, London: Constable, 1947

Anti-Socialist and Anti-Communist Union, *Handbook*, n.d.

—— Miscellaneous Pamphlets and Leaflets at the British Museum

—— *Socialism in the Schools*, 1927

Bedford, H. W. S. Russell, Duke of, Miscellaneous Pamphlets at the Wiener Library

Bedford, J. R. R. Russell, Duke of, *A Silver-Plated Spoon*, London: Cassell, 1959

Belloc, H., *The Servile State*, T. N. Foulis, 1911

Belloc, H. and C. E. Chesterton, *The Party System*, S. Sioift, 1911

Blakeney, R. B. D., 'British Fascism', *The Nineteenth Century*, January 1925

British Empire Union, *The British Empire Fascisti*, n.d.

—— *Danger – An Important Warning to the Free and Independent People of Great Britain*, (broadsheet), 1920

—— *The Edge of the Precipice – Educating for Bolshevism* (broadsheet), 1920

—— *Empire Record*, (periodical)

—— *Industrial Unrest*, 1920

—— *Our Campaigns of 1921*, 1921

British Fascists, *British Fascism*, June 1930–June 1934

—— *British Fascisti Bulletin*, June 1924–January 1925

—— *British Lion*, June 1926–June 1929

—— *The Bulletin*, February–May 1925

—— *Fascist Bulletin*, June 1925–June 1926

—— *Memorandum of Association*, 1924

British People's Party, *People's Post*, July 1939–February 1940

The Britons and Britons Publishing Society, *The Britons*, 1952

—— *Kol Nidre*, n.d.

—— Miscellaneous Pamphlets and Leaflets

Brittain, Sir Harry, M.P., *Hands Off Britain*, Anti-Socialist and Anti-Communist Union, 1927

Central Council of Economic Leagues, *National Campaign to Combat Socialism*, (circular), 1924

Chesterton, C. E., *Party and People*, London: Alson Rivers, 1910

Chesterton, G. K., 'The Patriotic Idea', Lucien Oldershaw, ed., *England: A Nation*, London: R. Brimley Johnson, 1904

Day, J. W., *Lady Houston*, London: Allen Wingate, 1958

Domville, Sir Barry, *From Admiral to Cabin Boy*, London: Boswell, 1947

Douglas, C. H., *Social Credit*, London: Cecil Palmer, 1924

Evans-Gordon, W., *The Alien Immigrant*, London: Heinemann, 1903

—— 'The Stranger Within Our Gates', *The Nineteenth Century and After*, (*Twentieth Century*), February 1911

Fry, L., *An Analysis of Zionism*, Militant Christian Patriots, 1936

Hargrave, J. G., *The Confession of the Kibbo Kift*, London: Duckworth, 1927

Howard, A., *The Beast Marks Russia*, Britons Publishing Society, 1938

Hutchison, G. S., *Meteor*, London: Hutchinson, 1933

—— *Truth*, London: National Workers Party of Great Britain, 1936

—— *Your Verdict*, 1934

Imperial Fascist League, *Agriculture Comes First*, n.d.

—— *The Fascist* (periodical), 1929–39

—— *Freemasonry*, 1935

—— *The Government of the Future-Fascism* (broadsheet), n.d.

—— *Jewish Press-Control*, 1936
—— *Kosher Fascism in Britain*, n.d.
—— Miscellaneous Pamphlets and Leaflets in the Wiener Library
—— *P.E.P. or Sovietism by Stealth*, 1935
—— *Race and Politics*, n.d.
'Inquire Within', *Light Bearers of Darkness*, London: Boswell, n.d.
Joyce, W., *National Socialism Now*, London: National Socialist League, 1937
Lane, A. H., *The Alien Menace*, London: Boswell, 1934 edn
Leese, A., *Devilry in the Holy Land*, London: Imperial Fascist League, 1938(?)
—— *Disraeli the Destroyer*, London: Imperial Fascist League, n.d.
—— *Fascism*, n.d.
—— *Jewish Ritual Murder*, 1938
—— *The Mass Madness of September, 1938 and Its Jewish Cause*, London: Imperial Fascist League, 1938
—— *Out of Step*, 1947
Marsden, V. (translator), *Protocols of the Learned Elders of Zion*, Britons Publishing Society, n.d.
Militant Christian Patriots, *The Cuckoo in the Socialist Nest*, 1938
—— *Zionism*, 1936
—— *Zionism and the Christian Church*, 1936
Murchin, M. G., *Britain's Jewish Problem*, London: Hurst & Blackett, 1939
National Fascisti (publisher), *The Fascist*, 1925–6
—— *Manifesto*, 1926
—— *The Tribune*, 1926
National Political League, *National Campaign*, 1920(?)
—— *Our Dangerous Intellectuals* (leaflet), 1921
National Socialist League, *Five Policy Points*, n.d.
—— *The Patriot*, February 1922–March 1930
'Pro Patria', *Refugees Before Britain!*, Militant Christian Patriots, 1939
Samuel, A. M., M.P., *How to Raise the Standard of Living*, Anti-Socialist and Anti-Communist Union, 1926

*Saturday Review*, 1932–6

Skelton, N., M.P., *The Cause and Cure of Socialism*, Anti-Socialist and Anti-Communist Union, 1926

Social Credit Secretariat, *Social Creditor*, Liverpool, 1938–9

'Virgil', *The Invisible War Makers*, Militant Christian Patriots, 1938

—— *The World's Enemies*, Militant Christian Patriots, 1938

Webster, Mrs N. H., *Germany and England*, Boswell Publishing Co., 1938

—— *The Need for Fascism in Great Britain*, British Fascists, 1926

—— *Secret Societies and Subversive Movements*, Boswell Publishing Co., 1924

—— *Spacious Days*, London: Hutchinson, 1951

Williams, H. G., *The National Income*, Anti-Socialist and Anti-Communist Union, 1926


## ANTI-FASCIST PUBLICATIONS

All British Anti-Fascist Committee, *All About Sir Oswald Mosley*, Sheffield, 1937

Birch, J. E. L., *Why They Join the Fascists*, People's Press, 1937

Co-ordinating Committee Against Fascism, *Jews and Fascism*, n.d.

Dolan, C. M., *Mosley Exposed*, n.d.

Douglas, J. L., *Spotlight on Fascism*, Communist Party of Great Britain, 1935(?)

Ex-Servicemen's National Movement, *The BUF by the BUF*, London: Anchor Press, 1938(?)

Graves, R., *East End Crisis*, Socialist League, London Area Committee, n.d.

Hannington, W., *Fascist Danger and the Unemployed*, National Unemployed Workers' Movement, 1939

Independent Labour Party, *They Did Not Pass*, 1936

Jewish Labour Council Workers' Circle, *Sir Oswald Mosley and the Jews*, 1935(?)

Kidd, R., 'Anti-Semitism in East London', *Left Book News*, November 1936

Labour Defence Council, *Development of Fascism in Great Britain*, 1924

Labour Research Department, *Mosley Fascism: The Man, His Policy and Methods*, 1935

—— *Who Backs Mosley?*, 1934

Louis, M., 'What I Saw Inside Olympia', *New Leader*, 15 June 1934

Miles, A. C., *Mosley in Motley*, Ex-Servicemen's National Movement, 1937

National Constitution Defence Movement, *Vigilance Pamphlets*, 1937–8

National Council of Labour, *Fascism: The Enemy of the People*, 1934

—— *What Is This Fascism?*, 1934

National Council of Labour and the Co-operative Union, *Statement on Fascism at Home and Abroad*, 1934

Printing and Allied Trades Anti-Fascist Movement, *Printers and the Fascist Menace*, 1934

Rust, W., 'Mosley and Lancashire', *Labour Monthly*, May 1935

Strachey, J., 'Fascism – It Leads to Terror', *Sunday Dispatch*, 23 July 1933

Strawbridge, W. A., *Trade Unionism and the Menace of Fascism*, National Council of Labour Colleges, n.d.

Trades Union Congress, General Council, *United Against Fascism*, 1934

Trades Union Congress and the Labour Party, *Speakers Notes – Fascism in Great Britain*, 1934

Union of Democratic Control, *Eye-Witnesses at Olympia*, 1934

'Vindicator', *Fascists at Olympia*, London: Gollancz, 1934

Wall, A. M. and H. Morrison, *The Labour Movement and Fascism*, London Trades Council and London Labour Party, 1934

Wegg-Prosser, C. F., *Fascism Exposed*, Jewish People's Council Against Fascism and Anti-Semitism, 1938

Young Communist League, *Ten Points Against Fascism*, n.d.

Youth Anti-Fascist Committee, *British Fascism Explained*, Union of Democratic Control, 1935(?)

## PUBLIC ORDER

Baker, J., *The Law of Political Uniforms, Public Meetings and Private Armies*, London: H. A. Just, 1937

'Barrister', *Justice in England*, London: Gollancz, 1938

Bing, G. H. C., 'Civil Liberty', *Labour Monthly*, May 1937

Brownlie, I., *The Law Relating to Public Order*, London: Butterworth, 1968

Chorley, Professor R. S. T., *The Threat to Civil Liberty*, Haldane Society, 1938

'Complete Statutes of England' in Halsbury's *Laws of England*

Crew, A., *The Conduct of and Procedure at Public, Company and Local Government Meetings*, London: Jordan, 1950 edn

Crew, A., assisted by E. Miles, *The Law Relating to Public Meetings and Procedure*, London: Pitman, 1937

'Curtis, J.', 'A Guide to British Liberties', *Fact*, No. 6, 1937

Goodhart, A. L., 'Public Meetings and Processions', *Cambridge Law Journal*, 1937

—— 'Thomas *v.* Sawkins: A Constitutional Innovation', *Cambridge Law Journal*, 1936

Jennings, W. I., 'Public Order', *The Political Quarterly*, January 1937

Kidd, R., *British Liberty in Danger*, London: Lawrence & Wishart, 1940

Loewenstein, K., 'Legislative Control of Political Extremism in European Democracies', I and II, *Columbia Law Review*, April, May 1938

—— 'Militant Democracy and Fundamental Rights', I and II, *American Political Science Review*, June, August 1937

Marshall, G., *Police and Government*, 1965

Morgan, J. G., 'The Law of Public Meetings', *The Police Journal*, October 1937

—— *Meetings, Uniforms and Public Order*, London: Jordan, 1936

—— 'Public Order and the Right of Assembly in England and the United States: A Comparative Study', *The Yale Law Journal*, January 1938

National Council for Civil Liberties, *Civil Liberty*, April 1937–
March 1942

—— *Disturbances in East London*, (mimeographed), 1937

—— Miscellaneous Publications at the British Museum and
through the courtesy of the N.C.C.L.

—— *Report of a Commission of Inquiry into Certain Disturbances
at Thurloe Square, South Kensington, on March 22nd, 1936*, 1936

—— *Sir Oswald Mosley's Albert Hall Meeting, March 22nd, 1936*

—— *Extracts from Eye-Witnesses* (mimeographed), 1936

—— *Statements of Persons Assaulted by Fascists and of Eye-
Witness Accounts of Fascist Violence, Fascist Meeting Hornsey
Town Hall, 28th January, 1937* (mimeographed), 1937

National Council for Civil Liberties and the Haldane Society,
*Notes for the International Conference of the International Juri-
dicial Association*, 1937

Reisman, D., 'Democracy and Defamation: Control of Group
Libel', *Columbia Law Review*, May 1942

—— 'Democracy and Defamation: Fair Game and Fair Comment I', *Columbia Law Review*, September 1942

Street, H., *Freedom, the Individual and the Law*, Harmondsworth:
Penguin Books, 1963

Thompson, W. H., *Civil Liberties*, London: Gollancz, 1938

Wade, E. G. S., 'The Law of Public Meetings', *Modern Law
Review*, December 1938

—— 'Police Powers and Public Meetings', *Cambridge Law Journal*, 1937

Williams, D., *Keeping the Peace*, London: Hutchinson, 1967

## ANNUAL REPORTS, ETC.

*Annual Register*, 1920–40

Independent Labour Party, *Report of Annual Conference*, 1924–9

Labour Party, *Report of Annual Conference*, 1929–39

National Council for Civil Liberties, *Annual Report*, 1937–9

Trades Union Congress, *Report of Annual Trades Union Congress*,
1934–9

## GOVERNMENT PUBLICATIONS

*Census of England and Wales*, 1932, 1935, 1950
City of Manchester, *Minutes of the Watch Committee*
House of Commons Debates. 5th Series, Vol. 112–445, 1919–47
House of Lords Debates. 5th Series, Vol. 86–116, 1934–40
Ministry of Labour, *Reports*, 1930–39
*Royal Commission on Alien Immigration*, 1903
*Royal Commission on Police Powers and Procedure*, 1928–9
*Report of the Commissioner of Police of the Metropolis for the Year*, 1932–40
*Report of the Departmental Committee on the Duties of the Police with Respect to the Preservation of Order at Public Meetings*, 1909
*Report of the Unemployment Assistance Boards*, 1935–9
*Special Report from the Select Committee on Procedure on Public Business*, 1931
*Twenty-Second Abstract of Labour Statistics of the United Kingdom*, 1922–36

## GOVERNMENT DOCUMENTS (FOREIGN)

Germany. Foreign Ministry, *Politik 29, England, Band 1*, December 1925–February 1936, Serial 7602H.
Italy. *Fascism in England, 1934*. Part of the Confidential Report of the Ministry for Foreign Affairs on Fascist Movements Abroad, 1934 (Job 35 – 017749 – 59).

# Index

Morris, Lord (1st Baron of St Johns) 40

Morris, Sir William (later Lord Nuffield) 68, 79, 197, 198

Morrison, Herbert (later Lord Morrison of Lambeth) 187, 222, 224, 235–6, 237, 264

Mortimer, Raymond 75

Mosley, Lady Cynthia (née Curzon) 54, 151
  Labour M.P. for Stoke-on-Trent 54
  resigns from Labour Party 73
  New Party 74, 77, 78, 81

Mosley, Diana (Lady Mosley, née Mitford) 126

Mosley, Lady Maud (née Edwards-Heathcote) 52, 188

Mosley, Sir Oswald (4th Baronet) 52

Mosley, Sir Oswald (5th Baronet) 52–3, 56

Mosley, Sir Oswald (6th Baronet)
  personal qualities 19, 51–2, 68n, 81–2, 264, 301, 303
  education 52
  family background 52–3
  Conservative M.P. for Harrow (1918–20) 53
  marriage to Cynthia Curzon 54
  Independent Conservative M.P. for Harrow (1920–23) 54
  Independent M.P. for Harrow (1923–4) 53
  career in Labour Movement 52, 54, 56–68, 73
  develops policy on unemployment 57–8
  appointed Chancellor of Duchy of Lancaster 59
  resignation from Labour Government 63
  Speech at Labour Conference, Llandudno (1930) 64, 65
  New Party 73–84, 133
  contests Stoke-on-Trent for New Party 81
  testifies to Select Committee on Procedure of Public Business 76–7
  visits Rome 82, 88
  forms B.U.F. 51, 52

Mosley, Sir Oswald–cont.
  alliance with Rothermere 98–104, 108
  Albert Hall (1934) 91–2
  libel action against the Daily News Ltd 141–2, 267
  anti-Semitism 151–8
  Olympia (1934) 170–82
  Worthing (1934) 184–6
  Hyde Park (1934) 186–9
  financial contributions to B.U.F. 195, 196, 197
  arrives at East London March 228
  libel action against Marchbanks 267–8
  detention 294
  candidate for North Kensington, General Election (1959) 16

Mosley Manifesto 66, 67–8, 75

Mosley Memorandum 60–62, 64, 65, 66, 67

Mulchay, Major-General Sir Francis 33

Mullins, Bernard 184

Munich Agreement 163, 263

Murray, Basil 209

Mussolini, Benito 22n, 32, 44, 51, 57, 78, 82, 88, 99, 100, 102, 132, 148, 153, 154, 159, 160, 161, 194, 200, 201

*My Life*, (Mosley) 10, 63n, 70n, 72n, 83n, 84n, 96n, 102n, 106n, 131n, 137n, 143n, 151n, 153n, 168n, 215n

Nathan, Major H. L. 95

National Citizens' Union 22, 28, 40–42, 289

National Council for Civil Liberties 204, 205, 206, 207–9, 232, 238, 252, 254–5, 256

National Council of Labour 174, 175, 187

National Fascisti 22, 31, 35, 36–9, 49n

National Government (1931–5) 14, 32, 193, 304

National Labour Party 67

National Minority Movement 34

*National Policy, A* 66, 68, 76, 81, 147, 149, 160